Ralph Edwards
of
Lonesome Lake

D0770687

DEDICATION

This book is dedicated to conservationists everywhere and particularly to the younger generation in whose hands lies the future of all our endangered species. Don't waste what isn't yours; don't keep what is only on loan; give back a little for others.

Ralph Edwards

Ralph Edwards Conservation Fund

c/o Canadian Nature Federation
75 Albert Street
Ottawa, Ontario, Canada
K1P 6G1

Will gladly issue tax deductible receipt for all donations. See Foreword for details.

Ralph Edwards
of
Lonesome Lake

Ed Gould

hancock

house

ISBN 0-919654-74-6 (Hard cover)
ISBN 0-88839-100-5 (Soft cover)
Copyright © 1979 Ed Gould

Second hard cover printing 1981
First soft cover printing 1981
Second soft cover printing 1983
Third soft cover printing 1986
Fourth soft cover printing 1989
Fifth soft cover printing 1999

Cataloging in Publication Data

Ralph Edwards of Lonesome Lake

ISBN 0-919654-74-6 (hard cover)
ISBN 0-88839-100-5

1. Edwards, Ralph A., d. 1977
2. Frontier and pioneer life - British
   Columbia. I. Gould, Ed. 1936-

FC3827.1.E39A3 971.1'04'0924 C78-002076-6
F1088.E39

Published simultaneously in Canada and the United States by

HANCOCK HOUSE PUBLISHERS LTD.
19313 Zero Avenue, Surrey, B.C. V4P 1M7
(604) 538-1114 Fax (604) 538-2262

HANCOCK HOUSE PUBLISHERS
1431 Harrison Avenue, Blaine, WA 98230-5005
(604) 538-1114 Fax (604) 538-2262
Web Site: www.hancockhouse.com *email:* sales@hancockhouse.com

Table of Contents

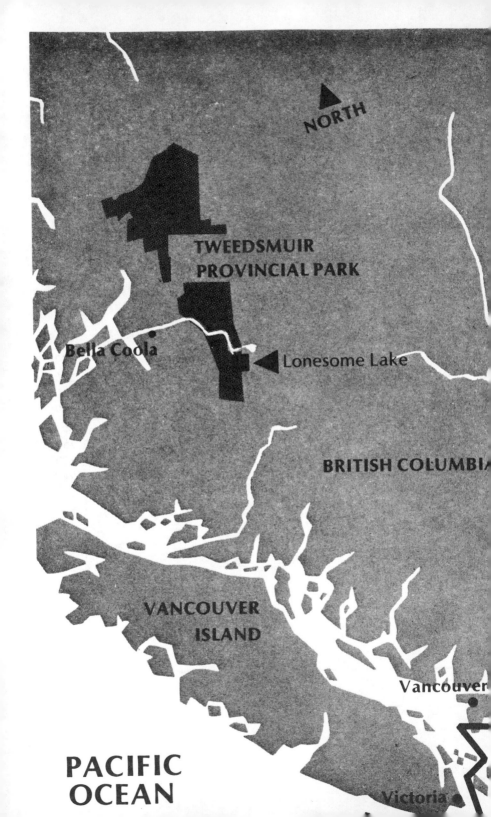

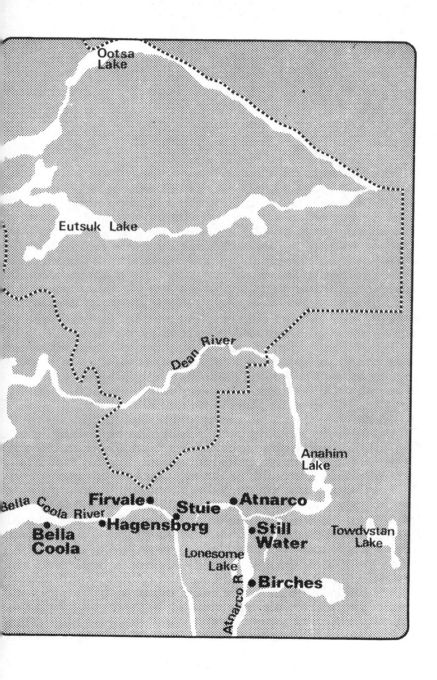

Ootsa
Lake

Eutsuk Lake

Dean River

Anahim
Lake

Bella Coola River

Firvale

Stuie ●Atnarco

●Hagensborg

Bella
Coola

●Still
Water

Towdystan
Lake

Lonesome
Lake

Atnarco R.

●Birches

FOREWORD

Ralph Edwards had a dream. It was a simple dream, but with far-reaching repercussions: to live in the wilderness surrounded by mountains and to be his own keeper. Initially his homestead was a seventy-five mile walk from the nearest post office. Yet this man's personal life, his family's unselfish toil to help save the vanishing trumpeter swans from near extinction, is a story that has touched millions. It is an exciting dramatic wilderness tale with a happy ending. Exciting and dramatic both because of the rugged wild setting among the majestic Coast Mountains of British Columbia and because Ralph and his cast of grizzly bears, cougars and incorrigible bulls never stopped their antics; and happy because the trumpeter swans have now reached safe numbers and are the only species to have crossed that bridge from endangered status to safe.

When Ralph first entered the Coast Mountain wilderness he regarded the environment as hostile—the trees crowded out his hard won vegetable plots, the deer ate what was left, and cougars and bears killed his livestock. He trapped and killed in order to survive—at times almost in revenge for the unfair obstacles nature placed in the way of his efforts.

But changes followed. He worked hard to clear and fence land so he was less dependent on killing game or needing to trap animals to buy food—trapping was his only source of dollars. Soon he experimented with the captive breeding of mink, marten and beaver so that they wouldn't die the terrible death in traps that he had witnessed so many times.

Every winter Ralph was touched by the majestic beauty of the great white trumpeter swans that wintered in his remote valley. He had heard of their rareness and near extinction. When a severe winter storm dammed the river, flooded the shallow feeding areas and the birds as a consequence were starving to death, he backpacked 100 pound sacks of grain over the seventy-five mile icy mountain trail to feed them. A further bond was developed.

The continuing plight of the swans became a focal point of the Edwards' life. Not only was there the winter ordeal of two or three mile daily hikes in minus-zero degree weather to feed them, but during summer and fall their grain, up to twelve tons annually, had to be carried and boated the seventy-five miles.

The wilderness was becoming a home of which he was truly a part. It was no longer a hostile environment to be conquered but was a place in which he could live in relative harmony. Ralph learned he must leave enough fish and deer not only for the otter and wolf but so he could have more himself the next year. Ralph was a practicing conservationist.

Ralph, his equally capable wife Ethel, and their daughter Trudy, who carried on the swan story to its most successful conclusion (see *FOGSWAMP* for her story of the swans' life), developed a purpose and direction in life that has brought joy to millions through books, magazines, TV and film.

During the preparation of the manuscript and before Ralph died, we had some long talks about the wilderness. It was Ralph's desire to donate 50% of his royalties to conservation, but to which society he asked. He wanted to make it easier for somebody else to help save some necessary land or aid an endangered species. Specifically he wanted the funds to be made available to non-professional individuals or groups with a conservation-oriented project. I suggested we set up a Ralph Edwards Conservation Fund, administered by a non-profit organization. He was a little embarrassed at the suggested name—but the twinkle in his eyes sparked a resounding 'yes'. Arrangements have been made for the Canadian Nature Federation to administer the Ralph Edwards Conservation Fund and tax deductible receipts will be issued for all donations over $10.00.

Ralph and his family, through saving the Lonesome Lake population of trumpeter swans, played the largest role in bringing the endangered species to respectable numbers. If this man and his family can do this, so too can others. If a helping hand is necessary, I hope the Ralph Edwards Conservation Fund will be there with some funding.

Send your inquiry or donations to:

Ralph Edwards Conservation Fund
c/o Canadian Nature Federation
75 Albert Street
Ottawa, Ontario, Canada
K1P 6G1

David Hancock

1

In The End
Was The Beginning

"If God had given me a choice, I probably would have chosen to have been born a bird." (Ralph Edwards)

The airplane bucked its way up the Bella Coola Valley on an uneven bank of air, each new rise and fall as unexpected as the next. Capricious winds, up-drafts and down-drafts present many surprises in this country. The Coastal Range, a parade of uneven teeth that jut from a rug of forest, rivers, lakes and streams, all the way up the British Columbia coast, provide a perfect breeding ground for wild weather.

Below me, the forest was a quiet room, furnished in the finest of woods, carpeted in velvet, where even on the windiest, coldest of days, I could travel silently and quickly, reasonably comfortable - if properly prepared. Up here, it was different. You are always prepared but never prepared at the same time.

This day, the weather was good. It could change suddenly, but I was not concerned about it nor about the capabilities of my tiny two-seater Taylorcraft. It had carried freight and passengers, human and otherwise, over this rocky obstacle course many times before. Why should today be different? Both plane and pilot had been given a clean bill of health. Still . . . there was this feeling.

I gently eased the throttle forward for the extra power required to lift the aircraft over 9000 foot Defiance Mountain,

9250 foot Stupendous Mountain, 7500 foot Mt. Marvin. We would then cruise over green, placid Turner Lake and sideslip past spectacular Hunlen Falls, 1300 feet of quicksilver that cascades into Lonesome Lake.

Lonesome Lake. My name for my home for more than fifty years. A tiny kingdom scratched foot by foot out of the Canadian wilderness. A site so remote, it is accessible only to pilots like myself foolish enough to want to fly over nearly perpendicular peaks or rugged enough to trudge in along a rocky trail too narrow in places for two grizzlies to pass at the same time.

As I approached the first of the increasingly high gray rock walls, studded here and there with stunted trees and patches of snow, the plane simultaneously lost power and fell into a windy chasm - a drop of at least forty or fifty feet. Such jolts have torn wings from airplanes. I glanced quickly at the instrument panel and was relieved to see I was still 1500 feet above sea level, but as my gaze steadied on the landscape below, I was astounded to find that the plane was virtually standing still.

A Taylorcraft is a wonderful machine - a little slow, but stable and easy to handle. Right then I counted heavily on that stability because the wind was so strong I couldn't tell whether I was going ahead or backwards. I could have sworn the mountain was moving in the opposite direction.

Instead of responding to my frantic verbal suggestions or regaining normal power when I checked the carburetor, heat and throttle settings, the plane continued losing altitude and refused to surge up and challenge those giants which stood between me and Lonesome Lake. The Taylorcraft began to lose altitude at a rapid rate. Thankfully, the engine had not completely quit. That was some consolation but engine power, not consolation, keeps planes aloft.

At the rate of descent it wouldn't be long before I would be part of that green rug beneath me or a bloodied mark on a rocky slab. Rather than risk total engine failure and a forced landing on God knows what sort of surface, I elected to use the remain-

11

ing power to set down on the river below. I leaned the Taylor-craft into a shaky, steep left turn and it began to glide determinedly toward the flood-swollen river I'd been following up the valley.

Seat belt secured, I braced myself for the confrontation between pontoons and the muddy water. Under decreased power the plane brushed the river's face gracefully but as it settled on the surface, the face turned ugly and a battle began for control of my little bird. Water splashed over the floats, sloshed up to the windscreen and after shuddering a few times like a distressed gull, a bumpy argument with wind, current and waves broke out.

Born of the Atnarko and Hotnarko Rivers farther east the Bella Coola River reaches its maturity before finally blending with other inlets running into the Pacific Ocean. It was in a savage mood. The twenty five mile an hour upsteam wind and rough water were allied against my navigating safely past rocks, islets, sweepers, uprooted trees and other debris set loose by flood and erosion.

This wasn't my first forced landing in this turbulent river. Other times the engine had conked out or bad weather had forced me to use the Bella Coola for a landing strip but it was never quite like this. "Sailing" the aircraft through this obstacle course was going to be quite an experience.

My goal was the Wilderness Airlines seaplane dock about twelve miles downstream. I felt confident I could poke my way through the floating impedimentia and deal with the winds and current changes, but another more dangerous factor now developed. When I had had the plane overhauled the mechanic assured me that he had repaired leaks in the front float compartments. Airplane pontoons have separate compartments so that if one or more are ruptured, others will, or should, keep the plane afloat. Regardless of the word of the mechanic, the compartments were rapidly filling up with water so that the nose of the plane was beginning to droop like a sad seagull.

Something however was in my favor. As I was hitting the river, a Wilderness Airlines pilot flying down the valley to his

12

dock saw my predicament and dipped his wing indicating he understood that I was on my way to the same destination. All I had to do now was to stay afloat long enough to get to that dock where a rescue crew would undoubtedly be awaiting my arrival.

Miraculously I escaped hitting any protrusions or floating wreckage but the faulty compartments were nearly full of water as I came abreast of the Wilderness dock. Several men were waving and directing me into a berthing area. The dock consisted of two long floats on the south side of the river. A ramp ran between them.

My problem now was to cross the river against current and wind and to avoid hitting two other aircraft parked in the dock positions easiest for me to attain. I managed to maneuver past the first plane but the current was so strong it was impossible to get in above the second plane so my only alternative was to turn into the main stream of the river and try a second time.

Lack of engine power and the droopy snout of the plane prevented me from turning back upstream and I was rapidly approaching a small island in the middle of the river. Once more I attempted to turn cross-wind and cross-stream but as soon as the nose was turned away from the wind it tipped forward almost into the water.

Anger and frustration were rising in me. I felt helpless and desperate in this trying situation. I could have cheerfully throttled the mechanic who had checked out the plane. Either his workmanship was shoddy or I had unknowingly damaged the floats on landing. And then I thought, what an unlucky break that they didn't realize my wounded little bird had lost much of of its power and did not clear the docking area to make it easier for me to tie up.

Meanwhile, the plane continued to float downstream, getting closer and closer to that island as I was unable to turn the plane around. There was little power left. As long as I traveled straight ahead the wind would hold the waterlogged front up but a sudden change of wind or current could alter the situation and I was in serious danger of tipping over.

What I could not understand was why Wilderness had not sent out a rescue boat or done something to help me get into the docking area. Surely they sensed my problem. I may have been a bit wild as a pilot. The locals, I know, joked about some of my exploits. But I had basic sense and judgment or I'd never have been able to survive in the wilderness for fifty years. Hell . . . I learned to fly when I was sixty two years old!

While I was cursing my dilemma, I felt a tug at the tail of the plane. There was limited vision from the cockpit but I could see a boat with two men in it had pulled in behind the plane. I couldn't make out what they were attempting to do and I had my hands full steering the plane to avoid hitting logs and rocks and to maintain an upright position by aiming into the wind.

The man holding the tail finally let go and the fellow in control of the boat circled around to the front to where I could see them. I couldn't figure out from his gestures whether he wanted to take me in tow or wanted me to try another cross-wind, cross-stream turn. He was a man I recognized, a pilot himself, so I decided he wanted me to try to turn about again. It was a foolish move.

I applied all the power the Taylorcraft had and placed the rudder at hard left. In an instant the plane swung left, a strong gust of wind caught and lifted the right wing forcing the left wing and the nose under the waves. I unbuckled my seat belt and stood up in the sloping cockpit. The boat came directly alongside and one of the men yelled at me: "Stay there, Ralph. I'll come and get you."

Cripes, I thought. You'll come and get **me**, will you? You'd better watch out for yourself. **I'm** all right.

Before I understood what was happening, he had jumped out of the boat and was up to his armpits in the swift current. He struggled to maintain his balance on the slippery rocks underfoot and finally did slip and fall.

"You stay where you are!" I yelled at him above the screaming wind. As he thrashed about in the icy waters of the river, I stepped off the pontoon and made my way toward him. As I was a much shorter man, the water was nearly up to my neck but I am proud of my sense of balance, gained from packing supplies over a twisted, rocky trail into Lonesome Lake for fifty years.

I soon had an arm around him and we both stood shivering while the boatman circled around the plane and headed back toward us. It was only then that I observed what was happening to the plane. A sudden violent rush of wind had caught the wing and flipped the plane upside down in the shallow water so it began to slide, dragging the propellor and tail over the rocks. It came to rest against rocks close to the islet I had been trying to avoid. In a short time it would be pounded to pieces.

The boatman helped me and my "rescuer" into the boat and we sat glum and silent on the short ride back to the sea-plane dock. Amid a chorus of explanations and queries from a dozen flapping tongues, I made my own decision for action. I hitched a ride into the town of Bella Coola, about two miles west, and borrowed some sturdy cables.

After securing the plane as best I could in its upside down position, I headed up river to my brother Earle's place at Hagensborg, a small community in the Bella Coola Valley, about eight miles east of the Wilderness dock. Earle and his wife Isabel were gratified to see that I was safe, but also a bit angry at the turn of events.

"Maybe you should give up flying, Ralph," Isabel said as I warmed up in the cozy kitchen of the spacious farm house. "You might kill yourself next time."

"I wasn't in any danger," I remonstrated. "If I had gotten some cooperation I would have been fine. But I couldn't seem to make those guys understand that I couldn't bring the plane across that current with those damn leaking floats pulling the nose under."

Isabel brought in some hot coffee and a plate of sandwiches. I wolfed a mouthful down and swallowed some scalding coffee. Isabel took up her lecture where she'd left off: "What would have happened if you'd been crippled in one or the other of those crashes you've had? I can just see you hobbling around on crutches. You, who's always been so independent all your life."

15

"I've been independent because I've never had anybody to depend on," I argued. That wasn't strictly true; dozens of times in my life I've been fortunate enough to have someone to count on. This is particularly the case with my dear wife Ethel - who would now be anxiously awaiting my return to the lake - and my daughter Trudy. "God helps them that helps themselves," I added defiantly.

"You don't have to quote me chapter and verse of that old philosophy, Ralph, " Earle said. Two years younger than me, Earle too had been schooled in the Seventh Day Adventist faith of hard work and enterprise. "But there's no sense in arguing with him, Isabel. You know as well as I do that Ralph will listen to all the advice in the world, then go out and do just what he wanted to do in the first place. But darn it, Ralph, Isabel's right. Everyone around here says you're getting too old to fly. Why don't you hang up your wings and take it easy for a change. You've always got to be up and doing."

"Old, hell!" I fumed. "I had a checkup two weeks ago and the doctor said that aside from eyestrain from too much reading I am in better shape than men half my age. I still put in a twelve hour day and I can work the pants off anybody I know."

It was all academic anyway. I probably wouldn't be flying anymore. It would cost more than I could afford to have the plane repaired and I wasn't going to go into debt. "I'm going out for a walk," I said. "I've got some thinking to do."

I stalked out into the cool, starry night. The wind had calmed considerably clearing the sky of its earlier cloud. At the little church adjacent to my brother's property I turned and walked slowly up the road that leads through the Bella Coola Valley. I had never felt so dejected in my life.

There had been times before when I had felt life was harsh and nature dealt me some blows that taught me a lesson or two. This latest setback seemed grossly unfair. What had happened that had caused that engine to act up? Had the mechanic properly fixed the pontoons? Had I hit something that made them leak like that? No rhyme or reason to it at all. If I had to give up flying it would be like losing my arms. If God had given me a

16

choice, I would have been a bird.

The next morning I learned the news about my airplane. The mechanics at Wilderness Airlines declared that it was beyond repair. After being pulled by a bulldozer through the river off the little island where I had secured it with the cables, it was reduced to a ragged heap of metal and fabric. Sick at heart, I took the low offer given for the salvageable parts and the engine. The plucky little Taylorcraft which was such an important part of my life was now history. What lay ahead for **me?**

2

Looking Backwards

"Ootsa Lake? That's a hell of a trip . . . and worse than hell when she snows." (Mark Marvin)

I was concentrating so intently I must have walked ten or twelve miles from the Hagensborg farmhouse without realizing how far I'd come. The sun was already starting to come up. A half a dozen cars and trucks stopped and their drivers offered me rides. I told them I preferred to walk; I had a lot of thinking to do.

I turned around and began to amble back to where Earle and Isabel were probably sitting up waiting for me to return. The road, widened and paved, was a far cry from the rough, narrow trail I had tramped and ridden over in 1912 as a young man seeking a challenge and a way of life that suited my independent spirit. Now, with the loss of the plane, I had to consider whether life would open up alternatives, more challenges - or stagnation.

It made my blood boil when people mentioned old age to me. I didn't feel old. I was in the prime of life. Like that doctor when he examined my sore knee. What did age have to do with that? "You have to remember this knee is seventy-five years old," he said. "So what?" I said. "So is this other knee. But it isn't **sore!**"

As I walked back I felt infused with a new spirit of confidence. I had been knocked down before. And I had fought

18

back. Sometimes it was a physical fight, such as when old man Tucker on the Wilson ranch in California tried to stab me with a pitchfork because I wouldn't do things his way. I picked up another pitchfork and we fenced around until I knocked his to the ground. When he complained to the foreman, **he** ended up getting fired.

Then there was the time when I worked for the railroad gang here in British Columbia and a big Irishman named Murphy tried to bully me because I was working too hard and making him look bad. He tried to twist my head off, and would have done, until I managed to hit him in the breadbasket with my knee. He complained. And he got fired too!

It had been a long time since I had found anything worth fighting over. I had once fought nature with that same ebullience. Then I had learned to love and respect her. I had given something back for all I had taken from her. I could never give enough back; I had been receiving her bounty for more than fifty years. But the world credited me with helping save one of her endangered species - the trumpeter swan - from extinction. That was something.

My wife Ethel and I had raised three children who were proving themselves to be useful individuals in their own ways. It had been a hard life for us all. But as fire tempers steel, we were sharper for the experience and our marks may even have been deeper then a lot of people's who stayed away from the flame.

My steps quickened. The gloom that had hung over me all evening and into the night and morning, dissipated like fog before the sun.   And like a drowning man, the thoughts of my past, problems I had solved, the challenges I had faced reeled through my mind.

Fifty four years, 1912 to 1966, is a long time to spend in one place, particularly a place as remote as Lonesome Lake. The commercial center, Bella Coola, sixty miles to the west, is difficult to reach even today. In a valley of incredible beauty, it lies at the head of a narrow inlet about seventy miles inland from the Pacific Ocean, roughly 300 miles north of Vancouver.

It is the second of three main outlets through the coast ranges to the ocean.

Alexander Mackenzie, a Scottish explorer, was the first white man to discover this valley when he made his historic trek across Canada on foot and descended into it from the interior plateau in July 1793.

As Mackenzie and his party of Canadian voyageurs approached the valley floor they could see smoke from fires of an Indian village on the river bank; later he estimated the distance to be about thirty two miles from tidewater. The greeting he got from the chief and his tribe led him to name the spot Friendly Village.

After a short visit and an exchange of gifts, Mackenzie and his men negotiated with the Indians for a canoe ride to another village near the mouth of the river. This later became the site of the Hudson's Bay trading post and is now the townsite of Bella Coola, a clean, modern community where whites and Indians live in relative harmony side by side.

The valley was settled in 1894 by a colony of Norwegians whose clearings and log cabins were scattered in the lower part of the valley along the single dirt track. At the time of my arrival this wagon road extended eastward up the valley about forty miles to a "stopping place" called Stuie. From there a narrow horse trail wound its way for another fifteen miles to the next stopping place, a clearing in the wilderness called Atnarko.

These stopping places were usually only a single homestead clearing in the woods, a day's pack horse trip from the stopping place on either side where travelers and their horses could spend the night and get a meal of some sort.

Roughly speaking, the Bella Coola River, fed by streams from both sides of the valley, flows swiftly for forty miles from Stuie to North Bentinck Arm inlet. The town itself had been my supply depot for more than fifty years and since acquiring the plane, it had also been our mail center.

It is a friendly community, one I liked from the day I first arrived. When I came up in the coastal steamer from Vancouver in 1912, all I had was a young man's hopes and dreams, a horse, a rifle, the clothes on my back and a few personal possessions. I was glad to leave the ship, even though it had been a pleasant trip. Not so the horse.

He preferred to stay in the hold and it took some encouragement to get him to come up from below and even more to force him down the gangplank. Three days at sea had reinforced his natural tendency to resist anything new, but a combination of promises of oats and a few well-directed kicks in the flanks by the tired crew, convinced him to join the rest of the passengers and onlookers on the muddy shore. Before leaving, as a farewell gesture of defiance and contempt, he kicked part of the wooden railing to pieces. The crew were glad to see the last of him.

I loaded the beast with my few provisions and led him up the narrow path to the village. Other passengers and residents who had come down to meet the ship - the highlight of the week - crowded along beside me.

"Any place to stay around here?" I asked a grizzled fisherman who was attempting to get around my horse without getting a hoof in his face. "You mean just for the night,or are you plannin' on a longer visit?" he asked, looking me over for identification. Country people can tell by looking at a stranger many things that escape the sophisticated eye of the urban dweller.

What he saw was a ruddy complexioned youth of smaller than average stature with a good pair of shoulders and - so I've been told many times - twinkling friendly eyes. I hastened to answer his question while his gaze continued to sum me up. "I don't rightly know how long I'm going to be here. I want to get some information about Ootsa Lake. I hear they've got homestead land up there. I thought I'd maybe get some and start a ranch - on a small scale, of course."

The oldtimer snorted. "Ootsa Lake? I should **think** you'd be wanting some information before you head off into that forsaken country." Surely he was mistaken? I had been told by a Canadian in California there was lush meadowland just waiting there to be settled on. I'd get a second opinion before changing my mind about its potential.

"There's the hotel over there," the fisherman told me. "The manager there will be able to put you and your horse up and maybe tell you a little about your Ootsa Lake. Good luck." He strode off, a slight chuckle echoing in his wake.

"What sorta place you lookin' for?" the hotel manager in the lobby asked after the details of stabling the horse and arranging for a room for myself had been attended to. "I hope to homestead, start a farm or ranch," I answered. "Barring that, I thought I'd take a look at what's available along the way."

"There's no land around here," he answered. "Leastways, what's available that's any good is already taken up long ago." "What about beyond those mountains?" I asked, pointing out the window along the valley toward some peaks that rose like saw teeth out of the early morning mist. "Snow, grizzly bears and trees big around as a house," the hotelman said.

Determined not to be discouraged, I asked again about Ootsa Lake. "Lord, man, that's more'n a hundred miles north of here on a horse trail that'll be covered in snow before you get over the mountains," he said. "Stick around town a few days. Don't take my word for it. When you see what you're up against you might decide to go back to wherever it was you came from."

I told the hotel manager I had very limited funds and offered to cut wood or do other chores in exchange for room and board. He agreed and for the next two days I washed dishes, chopped wood and mopped floors. I also asked residents questions about the area and obtained several maps. It was a discouraging task.

I was amazed to find how ignorant many people were of what lay beyond the mountains and a little discouraged by their negative comments. "You'll be lucky to find a piece of land worth a damn," was the general opinion. I found it almost unbelievable that more people hadn't traveled further inland. I suppose they had good reason: They were mostly fisherfolk and their main route to civilization was by ocean. Nevertheless, my curiosity about what lay to the east was uncontainable.

22

After the third day, the manager came to where I was chopping wood behind the hotel to inform me that a certain Mark Marvin was in town. Mark Marvin was a legendary character who was bound to know all about any subject I'd care to discuss. He lived at Atnarko, a "stopping place" between two other small settlements, Stuie and The Precipice, on the way to Anahim Lake, the first major supply town on the way into the Chilcotin country.

Mark Marvin looked me over from hat brim to boot tops. I could almost read what was going through his mind. What was a brash American, barely out of school, with nothing but a few nickels to rub together doing in this country? It was a look I was becoming accustomed to.

"You want to go to Ootsa Lake?" he asked. "That's a hell of a trip at the best of times and worse than hell when she snows. Why don't you try for some land around Atnarko?" "People I've been speaking to say there's no land available anywhere this side of the mountains," I told him. "Don't believe everything they tell you hereabouts," Mark said. "Folks don't take too kindly to strangers asking about free land. They might be thinkin' about takin' it up themselves at a later date. My advice to you is to scout around Atnarko first and then decide if you want to stay here at all."

"What's this Atnarko area like?" I asked. Mark Marvin described the Atnarko Valley as a canyon dammed at frequent places by side creeks which brought down great quantities of broken rock and other debris during freshets—a rush of flowing water. Certain parts of the lakes in the area are very deep and do not freeze readily, often remaining open into January.

"The canyon bottom is less than a quarter of a mile wide and at the foot of each lake there are rapids," he said. "Sounds pretty rugged," I admitted. "What's the timber like? Hard to clear? I've been told there's firs there big around as a house and 200 feet tall." "There's cottonwood, cedar, fir, spruce and some balsam." Mark said. "There's also the hardwoods: Birch, willow and alder. Quite a selection. And on the hillsides, where they can gain a hold, there's some really big fir and lots of pine. You can scratch out a garden plot."

I thanked Mark Marvin for his advice about Ootsa Lake. First things first, however. I bought a horse from a local Indian for five dollars, loaded my own horse with provisions, including my rifle, a second hand axe, cooking utensils and—with mounting excitement—headed up the valley.

As I have described, the rutted road extended only about forty miles where it petered out into a number of trails and paths worn there years ago by Indians and animals. The horse trail continued in a northeasterly direction to Anahim Lake over an incredibly high wall of mountains.

A surprising number of small farms had been established along the roadside and I stopped at each to enquire about available land. Although I was met with a certain wary friendliness, the answer was always the same: "There's no available land around here. Better try further east."

I kept pushing onward but there was no change in the message: No land. I finally arrived at Firvale, a tiny community about twenty miles east of Bella Coola. It was near the end of the day and I was tired and so were the horses. I knocked on the door of a farmhouse and was greeted by a pleasant-looking woman in a long cotton dress, flowered apron and long hair tied neatly in a bun. She wore no makeup but her complexion was rosy and her eyes sparkled with good humor and obvious health.

"What can I do for you, son?" she said. A faint accent indicated she was an American. "Do you mind if I water my horses and use your barn to sleep in tonight?" I asked. "I'll cut wood or do chores for the favor." She smiled. "Sure. There's a bucket at the well and if you want to make a fire to cook a meal, there's wood in the shed. Just don't set the place ablaze."

I watered the horses and tethered them near the road. After some difficulty I got a fire going and tried to boil some beans in the frying pan. I might just as well have tried to boil a rock and after it got soft, thrown the beans away and eaten the rock. The woman must have been watching my culinary efforts with amusement because she came out and invited me in for supper.

A few minutes later her husband, a big raw-boned chap with a red face, came in from doing chores. He shook hands with me without saying anything, washed his hands and face at a sink in a room behind the kitchen, then came in and sat down at the table. Two small children joined us and the man recited a prayer thanking the Good Lord for providing the meal and for other favors.

No one said anything during supper. Suddenly the man looked me over and asked: "Where was it you said you were from?" "Well..." I began, "I've just come up from California but I've been across the States, working at different jobs. I was born in Hot Springs, Georgia." There was a long silence. Embarrassed by it, I nervously added that I was looking for a piece of land where I might farm.

The man rose from the table, lit a coal oil lamp, and sat down again while his wife busied herself with the dishes. The children were hustled off to bed and darkness descended over the valley. "Why do you want to go lookin' for land and work your guts out every day when you can get a nice soft job back there in the States?" the man said.

I could have asked him the same thing. Certain unmistakable signs were present in the house which indicated that the couple were Seventh Day Adventists, the religion I was raised in. Others I had spoken to in the valley had told me how they had come to the Bella Coola area to escape persecution in the United States. They also sought independence and wanted to avoid the pressures of life in the big cities.

"I'm not much interested in big places and having to work for other people," I told the farmer. "I want to get a piece of land I can call my own and start a farm or ranch—just like you've done here."

The man looked me over, head cocked to one side, a half-smile on his face. "This is a tough country and you gotta fight hard and run fast just to stay in one place. Why...we been here for years and all we got scratched out is a little bitty piece of land hardly big enough for a few cows and a garden." He looked down for a moment at his gnarled hands.

"If it don't snow too early in the fall, if the winter's mild and the spring isn't too late or too wet, and the valley don't flood, you might get enough hay off to feed your stock." He looked me over again, even more critical than before. "What kinda background you got that makes you think you can stomach this way of life?"

While the lamp flickered on the wallpapered walls of the kitchen, I told the man and his wife, who had come back to sit down with us, a little about my past and why I had chosen British Columbia as a place to stake a claim on independence. I knew it couldn't have been dissimilar to theirs.

As a God-fearing Adventist, I had been told the way to Salvation lay through hard work, strict adherence to the literal truth of the Bible and the avoidance of tobacco, coffee, tea or any stimulants, liquor, drugs, blood transfusions and - of course - church attendance on Saturday, not Sunday. We were expected to practise what was preached, every hour of every day. Adventism was a way of life, not a compromise between religion and commercialism.

I told them how I had learned to do a man's work before I was twelve years old as I was shunted from relative's place to relative's place while growing up. My longest stay was at my uncle Will and aunt Annie Graham's farm in South Lancaster, Massachussets, where I was sent because the schools were better there than at Sylva, North Carolina, where my parents lived. They were both studying to be medical missionaries.

Each morning uncle Will would get me up at five o'clock to begin chores, throwing in a little advice to strengthen my beliefs, which were thinnest at that time of the day. "Hard work and honesty are the twin virtues of the farmer," he'd say. "Stick to them and you'll be independent from everybody except the Lord God Almighty." I longed for that independence some mornings as I struggled through prayers and hymns sung around the organ in the parlor before breakfast. Independence Day couldn't come quick enough for me.

26

After I'd helped uncle Will milk six cows, fed the bull calf they were fattening for winter beef, threw grain and hauled water for the chickens and ducks and cleaned out the barn, aunt Annie would call me in for breakfast. I then washed dishes, mopped the kitchen and pantry floors and peeled vegetables for the next meal. After lunch I bucksawed four-foot lengths of wood for the fireplace and stacked it in the shed behind the house. After dinner, milking and more chores.

That was summertime work, of course. In the winter there was approximately the same amount of physical labor to complete but school work had to be somehow crammed into the same time frame. Whether my farmer friends in Firvale, British Columbia, were impressed with my story as a youth or not was difficult to judge. They didn't say anything.

"Talk is cheap," uncle Will used to say. "Work is hard. Show you're a hard worker and you won't have to go around telling everybody about it." Despite their lack of reaction, I decided to continue with my description of life at uncle Will's.

I described the house. Two stories high, it had ancient hand-hewed oak beams supporting low ceilings and the whole building was permeated with the smell of well-aged wood. I vowed one day I would build such a house and locate it somewhere I could look out on water and mountains. Although hardly remote, the Graham farm house was in a picturesque setting, on a slight rise. Between it and the big red barn ran a pathway that was overhung with a grape arbor.

Fruit trees grew everywhere. The largest apple trees had bountiful arms that spread thirty feet or more over the ground. All apples and pears that were edible and had not been devoured on the scene by an ever-hungry schoolboy were utilized in some way. They wound up in a barrel in the cool cellar, were preserved in glass sealers or were fed to the animals.

The Grahams were frugal folk, I told the Firvale farmer and his wife. Uncle Will sold his extra produce and dairy products in town to regular customers. One day he took me along to learn something of the world of commerce. I could tell he wasn't much of a businessman. He often lost money on his transactions.

For example, sometimes his six cows weren't productive enough to supply requirements and rather than leave anyone short, he would buy milk from other farmers to fill his orders. His egg deliveries always contained a baker's dozen - thirteen. His rationale was that it was far better in the eyes of God to be reliable than to be rich.

Some days he would let me drive the horse that pulled his produce wagon. It wasn't difficult since the horse knew exactly where to stop, having been there so many times before. Uncle Will would become exasperated when the horse continued to stop at the same place long after the customer had moved away. "Get along with you, you silly old nag," he'd say. "The Jacksons haven't been there for months."

I had no such problem when in the second year of my stay at uncle Will's I was given milk route of my own. My motive power was "shank's pony" and a small red wagon. My customers were new-born babies, my product the milk from newly-calved cows. Almost yellow in color, it was believed that such milk was better than ordinary milk for new humans.

My short stumpy legs soon grew muscular from hauling the wagon up and down hills along a six mile route. In winter I pulled a sleigh through deep drifts that blew across the road. Despite these rigorous chores I managed to maintain high grades in school. My marks slipped only once to an A-minus and that was when the prim school teacher caught me reading something at my desk rather than concentrating on the lesson she was delivering.

"Ralph Edwards!" she barked. "Whatever that is you are reading, bring it up to me at once." I blushingly walked up to her desk amid a chorus of sniggers from my classmates. "Now," she commanded, "We'll see what you've been doing instead of concentrating on your Bible studies." I handed over the offending volume. It was the Bible. She looked surprised. "I got tired of waiting and skipped ahead to find out what happened to Lot's wife," I said.

I was often bored and impatient with school work and when aunt Annie was informed of my inattention she was upset: "Your parents have their hearts set on you becoming a minister, Ralph," she chided. "I don't care," I said defiantly. "I'm going to be a farmer, not a minister."

I was only fifteen but my mind was made up. Now I only awaited the right opportunity to inform my father of this resolution. Still, there was the agony of waiting to grow up and saving the money to buy a farm. Uncle Will was paying me fifteen dollars a month and, since I had no vices, not even those few allowed by the Adventists, I saved all I earned.

I had a considerable sum after two years and, more important, I had learned a great deal. Uncle Will had taught me carpentry and tree-pruning. Aunt Annie showed me how she preserved fruit, vegetables, jams and jellies. Still I was anxious to move on. Although the day to day routine of farm work never became tedious, I chafed under the constant directions of my two elderly relatives.

Every moment there was something to do. Even when I struggled with my homework there were interruptions: "Time to feed the pigs, Ralph." "Ralph, go fetch some logs for the fireplace." "Bring in the newspaper and check the mailbox." Occasionally the mail brought news from my parents. I tried to picture from the sketchy descriptions just what sort of life they were living. They and my brother Earle lived on borderline poverty with always a promise from father of a better day coming.

It was from my father and mother that I inherited dedication to learning and independence. Both had taken nurse training courses at Kellogg's famous sanitarium in Battle Creek, Michigan. As fully-qualified medical missionaries, they took the whole family to spend three years teaching and healing in India.

After surviving an earthquake and many other adventures in that land, we returned and father got his doctor's degree and set up a clinic for patients recovering from tuberculosis. He had already tried this before he got his degree at a tiny place called Hot Springs, Georgia, where I was born on July 19, 1891. He had only been able to attract one such patient and that didn't warrant us remaining there for long.

Jobs of any kind were scarce but father was willing to go anywhere that the call of God directed. At one place, Knoxville, Tennessee, it was doubtful if God knew that father had answered the call; it certainly wasn't a reciprocal arrangement at any rate. We almost starved to death. Down to our last penny, the family existed for a full week on nothing but a sack of walnuts that some kind soul had donated.

I had no intention of being as poor as that again and now that I was on my own at last I determined there would always be enough for tomorrow.

The Firvale farmer listened to that statement with a certain amount of amusement expressed in his eyes. "I like your enthusiasm, young fella," he said. "Reminds me of myself when I was your age and full of vinegar. God knows you are going to need it if you settle here. You seem to have your head on straight so you might just make it."

After wishing me good night, the couple directed me to the barn and I bedded in the hay for a deep sleep. I was awakened in the morning by the lowing of cattle and jumped to my feet, fully clothed, to help my host with the milking and chores. After breakfast they offered some helpful advice.

"Why don't you stop off at John Creswell's place?" the woman said. John Creswell, she explained, was what they called a "remittance man," a term applied to "second sons" of well-to-do British families who were given a small sum of money each month until they got established in Canada. Some never did get established but continued to live on their "remittance." The object of amusement and contempt by their harder-working neighbors, they did, if anything, add a bit of color to a drab social landscape. Many of them were Oxford or Cambridge graduates. Creswell was one of these.

"Come in, come right in, jolly good to see you," Creswell said when I knocked on the door of his little shack the next day. I refused his offer of a large tumbler of scotch, satisfying myself instead with a glass of cold water. "The place right next to mine hasn't been taken up yet," he said in answer to my question about availability of land nearby.

He hadn't done much to "prove up" his property. The rough one-room building he lived in was surrounded by tree stumps. A tiny weed-choked garden and the outdoor privy seen through heavy bush a few yards from the main dwelling appeared to be the only improvements.

"There isn't a great deal of open land here, I'm afraid," Creswell said in his clipped English accent. He brushed his wispy moustache with the back of his hand, sipped thoughtfully on his scotch, and told me of his struggle to clear a small patch out of the wilderness. "And the very devil it is to clear it too," he added. "Best idea would be for you to take a hike up to my east boundary and see it for yourself."

I left him contemplating the near-empty glass and fought my way through underbrush and huge trees to where I discovered a rag tied to a pole indicating where his property ended and the next acreage began.

The terrain was distinguished by huge Douglas firs and small cedars. The ground beneath was smothered in underbrush and windfall logs. Clearing it seemed a hopeless task. I felt closed in. There was no view of those beautiful mountains. Was this the homestead I had hoped to find after all those years of hard work?

I edged my way carefully along a fallen log, wondering if I would be doing the right thing in filing a claim on such a jungle. My thoughts were interrupted by crashing noises in the bush. I hoped it wasn't anything more than a deer; I hadn't thought to bring my rifle. It was more than a deer: It was a grizzly bear, the first I had ever seen.

I had heard they were gigantic animals, but this **Ursus horribilus** was even larger than the one I had read about. Typically dark brown in color, the grizzly is related to the brown bear of Europe but much larger and heavier and is very dangerous when brought to bay because of its great strength and fearlessness. I had no intention of bringing him to bay and fervently hoped he would have the same respect for me.

I stood shock still, scarcely breathing. I must have been downwind from him because he never even glanced in my direction but just scrambled over the end of the log I was standing on and crashed on through the undergrowth.

"You can expect to see those blighters around almost every day in this country," John Creswell said when I described the event to him. "Leave them be and most times they'll amble off about their business. But don't take any chances with a mother and cubs. Take to the nearest tree or - better still - shoot to kill. A dead grizzly is a good grizzly is what I always say."

I wasn't much impressed with that philosophy or with the land that lay above Creswell's. However, with no other choices open at the moment, I decided to apply for a homestead. I was informed in Bella Coola that the land office in Vancouver would take two months to process my application. Fall was on my heels. I had two horses to feed over the winter. I had no hay and no land and no prospects for a job.

While I was waiting for the application to be accepted or rejected, an acquaintance in Bella Coola told me two young men at a place called The Stillwater, about sixty five miles east of Bella Coola, wintered horses for other people as well as for themselves. I caught up to the two men in Firvale and Frank and Walter Ratcliff became lifelong friends who altered the course of my personal history.

A Dream Is Seen

"Not everyone wants to live in this kind of isolation. It's not exactly downtown New York." (Frank Ratcliff)

"Sure, we'll winter your horses for you," the Ratcliff brothers told me after I introduced myself to them at the Firvale home where they were staying. "It'll cost you fifteen bucks and you'll have to help us put up some hay first." " Sounds okay to me," I said.

Frank and Walter Ratcliff were true frontiersmen. Half-brothers, they were born near the coast of Oregon and had come to British Columbia as young men. Frank was the larger of the two and, at twenty eight, the oldest. I took to both of them right away: Frank because of his warm, jolly personality and Walter for his inexhaustible fund of amusing anecdotes. As I was to discover, if ever there was a lull in the conversation, Walter would soon fill it with a laugh.

Both men shared a reputation as experienced hunters and trappers and through them I learned more about survival in the wilderness than I could ever have managed on my own, no matter how long I lived.

After a good night's rest, we saddled three horses and each leading another horse, set off for the area called The Stillwater. At that time The Stillwater was a magnificent meadow of about seventy five acres of waist-high swamp grass. The weather was dry and warm but the mountains that rose straight up on the east and west were so steep and close into the valley that during these short fall days the early morning dew had scarcely dried off before shadows fell over the west mountain and a new layer of heavy dew began to form.

"Where'd a little fella like you learn to cut and stack hay like that?" big Frank Ratcliff asked as he rolled a cigarette. I knew that he and Walter had been assessing my performance on the business end of a pitchfork all afternoon. "It was a course in telegraphy that did it," I confessed. "A course in what?" Walter laughed.

I sat down on a pile of pitched hay, wiped my brow and explained how I learned to cut hay. "I was supposed to attend agriculture college at Corvallis, Oregon," I said. "Then I caught a fever, something like typhoid, and was laid up for quite a spell. I was living with my parents and during this time in bed I passed the hours reading books and newspapers and magazines. I've always been an avid reader.

"One day I came across an advertisement placed by a school in San Francisco that offered a course in telegraphy and a great future with jobs that paid up to seventy five dollars a month. I figured since I had missed the college fall session I might as well learn a useful skill and earn good money so I could buy a farm, which was what I wanted to do anyway."

I described to the Ratcliff boys how my father lent me the money for the course and, with the money I had accumulated working for uncle Will and at other jobs, I had the train fare to San Francisco with just enough left over to rent a cheap room. I found one in an old house south of Market Street, close enough to the school that I could walk to and fro and save street car fare. Despite scrimping on non-essentials, after I had purchased my books and paid my fees I had little left for food.

For several months I subsisted entirely on dates and day-old bread bought from a nearby French bakery. It was a rare treat to boil myself an egg in a metal cup over the gas jet in my room. I had no time for social life and no one offered me any. Letters from my parents and from Helen Cathie, a girl I had known since we were in school together in North Carolina, were

34

my only diversions away from my school work.

I spent all my energy mastering the Morse Code and by midsummer of 1907 I had learned about as much as I could about dots and dashes and decided I was ready to find a job. "And that's when you were issued with your diploma and pitchfork," Walter Ratcliff laughed. "Just about," I agreed.

I went to the instructor and told him I was ready for my first assignment. He told me to go try for work at the railway offices. "It's a big country," he said. "There's bound to be some place out there that can use your skills. Good luck."

"You mean to tell me that whole come-on to get people to take telegraphy was just a bunch of bunkum?" Walter asked. "Sure was," I admitted. "I applied at all the railway agencies in the San Francisco and Oakland areas but the answer was always the same. No jobs. It was quite evident that graduates of that school had been besieging those same offices for years, and with the same results."

I told Walter and Frank that my situation was becoming desperate. I had to have some kind of job or I'd starve to death. I was worrying about this one day when I met a fellow graduate on the street. He told me about a man named James Wilson who owned a ranch thirty five miles west of Redding, California. "Wilson is always looking for help during the haying season," he said.

The problem was how to get to Redding, which was in the Trinity Mountains area of northern California. "That's easy," this ex-student explained. "Go to one of the employment agencies here in the city and tell them you're willing to take a laboring job somewhere north of Redding. Then when you get to Redding, get off the train and hitch a ride into the ranch."

That seemed to be a pretty sneaky way to get a free ride but when my fellow student friend explained that these agents weren't above defrauding their clients, I quickly lost any qualms about cheating them. It seems the agents had a deal with the employers whereby they would talk the laborers into working for a certain length of time without pay to cover the cost of transportation. At the conclusion of the contract time the man would be fired over some hoaked-up offense and another worker would be sent out to replace him.

"Quite a racket," Frank Ratcliff said. "But how did you get the free ride without having to go all the way to the job site?" "I figured out how to beat these birds at their own game," I said. "With the last of my money I bought a second-hand suitcase and filled it with rags. To give it weight, I added a couple of rocks. I went to an agency and accepted a job in northern Oregon. A few hours later I was on the train."

Frank and Walter looked puzzled: "Why the dummy suitcase?" "Simple. I had to get off the train without arousing suspicion, you see. The agency had a representative ride in the railway coach with the employees to make sure they didn't try to jump off. When we got to Redding I removed my suitcase from the overhead rack and placed it on my seat, like I was saving it for myself. I even took off my old cloth cap and threw it on top of the suitcase. I gave a good imitation of a yawn and told the rep I was going to step off the train for a second to get some fresh air. He just nodded and hardly gave me another glance. I strolled leisurely off the train and a few minutes later I was a free man."

"But you still had to get to the ranch, didn't you?" Walter asked. "I hoped to hitch a ride with some farmer," I said. "A vain hope. Hardly anyone came along and those who did ignored me. I was darned tired by the time I'd walked the whole thirty five miles but when Mr. Wilson told me I could start work the next day and pointed me in the direction of the cookshack I felt fresh as a newborn colt and ready to go to work the next day."

Haying at the Wilson ranch was much different than it was at The Stillwater. The ranch produced about 100 tons of baled hay a year, plus a barnful of loose hay for their own horses and cattle. My main duty was to drive a team and hay rake.

Along with other teamsters, I "shocked" the hay with a horse rake, running down the winrows until the rake got so full it began to drag. It was then dumped and a "buck rake" came along to drag the hay to the stack where a man and horse stood ready to hoist it onto the stack with a contraption called a Jackson fork.

"I saw them using one of those old buck rakes in Oregon one time," Frank said. "It was a homemade affair of small logs bored to hold sharpened poles. The team was hitched ahead of the rake and about twelve feet apart so they walked on either side of the shocks. I think they dragged twelve shocks at a time to the stock." "That's right," I said. "Uprights were placed at the back of the buck rake which had handles to control the attitude of the teeth points."

"You didn't get much pitch-forking practice working a buck rake," Walter said. "No," I admitted, "but the hay for the barn had to be pitched on to a wagon, two men to a shock. And that was hard work. As well as learning how to pitch hay, I also learned how to swear. I never swore in my life before but the ranchhands there made sure that every new man drew the worst and orneriest team and the most broken-down rake. I had plenty of upsets and tangled harness before I learned how to handle them properly."

I could see that the Ratcliff's haying operation would have benefited from some of the experience I had learned at the Wilson ranch but I was not so presumptuous as to suggest their methods could be improved upon. At the Wilson ranch, horses did the majority of the work.

In the baling operation, horses were attached to a sweep which went around in a circle while a plunger pushed the hay in a hopper into an iron box. The plunger withdrew and the man feeding the machine pushed more hay into the hopper with a short-pronged fork. A couple of men on the stack kept the hay moving onto a table at the hopper-top level. When enough hay was compressed the feeder dropped a board with grooves on both sides for wires to be pushed through and tied. As the bales came out of the machine they were weighed, tagged and stacked.

"So that's how you used your experience to send telegrams," Frank Ratcliff laughed. "Well . . . I finally did get a chance to use my telegraphy," I said, but that's a story for another time. Right now if I don't get some sleep I'll never be able to keep up with you big guys on the hay field tomorrow."

At dusk the next day Frank said we had stored enough hay for the horses for the winter. "You say you're looking for a place to farm around here, Ralph. Well, Walter and I been keepin' our eyes on you and we figure you might have what it takes to stick this country. I know of a real choice chunk of property near the upper end of a long lake not too far from here. No name for the lake far as I know but if you want to come up to Turner Lake and help me haul out some traps and an old bed we got cached in our trapper cabin, I'll show you this piece of land."

I jumped at his offer. I had a rough idea where Turner Lake was from the maps I had studied in Bella Coola. It seemed to me that it was almost on top of the mountains and was drained by a huge waterfall. Could the lake Frank was speaking of be the one below that waterfall? That seemed too good to be true.

It was mid-October and dark closed in shortly after five o'clock so time was important. The next morning Walter headed back to Firvale for some more horses and Frank and I began the tortuous ascent up to Turner Lake. Our route took us over a series of paths that one moment led through park-like terrain, the next along six-inch wide footholds across mountain slides of broken rock. Then there would be miles where our progress would be impeded as we crawled over fallen logs brambled with vines and spiked with broken branches.

At last we came out on top of a plateau where late summer flowers still grew among outcroppings of rock. Turner Lake, deep and placid as a pond, is enfolded in gentle hills of dark green timber running up to white caps of eternal snow to the west and south. Streaks of gold and red indicated snowslides have kept the conifers in check but allowed the high country alders and mountain maples to grow.

"Best way to proceed from here is to build a raft," Frank said. My shoulders ached from the weight of the pack sack, rifle and axe but they soon loosened up as we chopped logs from green lodgepole pine for the raft. There was no dry timber available and Frank was dubious about the floatability of our rustic creation. We climbed on to test it and it sank like a rock. Dampened, we hauled it out.

"Got to attach another layer of logs," Frank said. More axe-swinging and we soon had added a second layer of logs and carved two paddles to propel us up the lake. The raft moved like a ton of iron. I told Frank how my brother Earle and I had once built a fifteen foot skiff, rigged it with a sail and took it for a trial run at our parent's place at Florence, Oregon.

"The boat had no centerboard and a short keel," I explained, "so we loaded it with rocks to keep it from skidding sideways in the water when the sail was up and the wind blowing at a good clip." We had caulked it with bits of cloth which soon got wet and the boat began to leak halfway across the lake. We turned around and bailed and rowed and sailed for shore. Since I couldn't swim I did more than my share of bailing. Finally we tied up to a barge alongside the dock just in time to feel the boat sink under us. Only the top of the mast could still be seen through the clear water.

"Yep. A sailboat would be real nice," Frank said. He dug his paddle into Turner Lake and grunted. "But we ain't got no sail material and we ain't got no wind if we did have one." I didn't reply but decided there must be some way to move a raft that was easier than with makeshift paddles.

At the end of the day my arms felt as though they were wrenched from their sockets and my knees were raw from kneeling on the uneven logs. Frank, toughened by this sort of life, turned around once in a while to see how I was faring. I smiled. My legs and arms could fall off but I'd be darned if I'd quit.

The moon was high when Frank pointed to an islet near the head of Turner Lake. "We'll camp over there," he said. "There's not much underbrush and no bears to step on us." I hadn't seen much wildlife, aside from birds, along the route. After building a roaring fire, we fried bacon, cooked beans and made sourdough biscuits. Washed down with coffee, food never tasted so good.

Then we rolled into our blankets and stared up at the moon while Frank described to me how his family decided to come to Canada. Like me, they were motivated by a desire to find a piece of land in a country where material rewards were only limited by man's willingness to work. Frank discussed how much man had to give in order to get something back and how much was compromise and cooperation with others and nature. "You are never totally self-sufficient no matter how independent you think you are," he said.

"But you've got a lot more control over your destiny out here than you have in the city," I argued. "And how else can you gain a foothold here if you don't force yourself in and lay a claim?"

Frank raised himself up on one elbow from his welter of blankets on the other side of the campfire. He looked me squarely in the eye across the embers. "There's a big difference between laying a claim and trying to be God," he said. "Ralph, I've been trapping and hunting and fishing this country for a good many years and there's one thing I've learned. The bush is boss. You can make your little marks from time to time, like slashing a tree with an axe to see which way to follow the next time by. But eventually the tree will heal her wound and you'll be lost.

"You can help yourself to whatever's out there in the way of food, clothing and shelter. Nature will provide, but it's a compromise, Ralph. Living with the elements, not fighting them, is what makes life possible in this wilderness. It's something we all have to learn - sometimes the hard way."

With that, Frank terminated the debate by rolling over. In a few minutes he was snoring. I lay awake for a while thinking over what he'd said. Soon the exhaustion of the day took over my whole being and I joined him in the arms of sleep.

After breakfast we re-launched the raft and continued paddling up to the head of Turner Lake. We beached the unwieldy craft and, taking up our burdens, hiked to the trapper cabin that the Ratcliffs had built years before and which now sat unused in a tiny clearing. In the windowless one-room log building were a stack of leg-hold traps and a bed of the type referred to as a Winnipeg couch.

We shouldered these extra encumberances and hiked to a low ridge overlooking the watershed of the Atnarko River. Coming out on the edge of a bluff, from where we could see down to the bottom of the Atnarko Valley, Frank pointed to the head of the unnamed lake he had been telling me about. As far as one could see, it was alive with birds: Geese, ducks, ravens, eagles, crows - I had never seen such a concentration of birds in one spot in my life. "They're only birds, Ralph," Frank said. I hadn't realized I was mesmerized by them. I have always felt communion with our feathered friends, as well as envy.

I could hardly contain my excitement. I wanted to get down to the lake as quickly as possible. I fell in behind Frank as he picked his way carefully down a timbered ridge. "Hell," he said. "It's a box canyon and that roar you hear is a waterfall. We'll have to go back and try another route." We clambered up and down several more deadends and each time Frank exclaimed: "Hell!" When we finally found our way out to an accessible passage to the valley, we had a name for the area: Hell Canyon.

Once down the heavily forested hillside to the lakeshore and around a big lagoon, we came to the river which was skirted by a well-traveled trail. "Nice well-trod path," I remarked. "Somebody live around here? Trappers? This sure is easy to follow."

"Yep," Frank said. "You'll find this trail easy to follow, all right. The grizzly bears love it." "Grizzlies?" I repeated, reaching back to make sure I still had my rifle slung over my shoulder and recalling my first encounter with one of the big beasts.

It was nearly dusk as we made camp. Far into the night ducks quacked by on their way to the lake. There were other sounds: Sudden crashing noises in the bush; softer, padding sounds, like little old men in slippers. Bears? I was too tired to ask Frank any more questions for this day. Besides, he was asleep already.

In the morning the ducks shot up off the lake forming V formations as they winged southward. There was a nip in the air and a mist on the river before the rising sun set the day on a warm course. "We have to walk south up river until we can find a place to cross over to the east side of the lake," Frank said. "Then we'll walk back up the east side to the end of the lake where you'll see this piece of land I was telling you about."

We walked about two miles before we found a log that had fallen across the river which we used for a bridge to cross to the other side. After another mile hike along another well-used bear trail we came into a natural clearing where the land sloped gently to the southwest.

It was surrounded by birch, poplar, willow and alder, with some cedar - excellent for splitting into shakes for roofs, I thought to myself. Douglas fir dotted higher ridges forming a gentle barrier before the steep mountain sides. Across the river several acres of natural willow and grass meadow separated the main river from the shallow big lagoon on the west. Downstream a mile the river and the lagoon opened into the deep waters of the main lake.

"Well," Frank said, "what do you think of it all?" "It's a perfect place for a homesite," I exclaimed. It was, in fact, almost identical to the picture in my mind, the one I had held there for years, the wilderness home I had yearned for. "Beats me why somebody hasn't filed on it before now," Frank said. "Course, not everybody wants to live in this sort of isolation. It's not exactly downtown New York."

That was a fact. There was not even a main trail into this valley. To get in and out meant following old trapper's trails, animal and Indian paths. When these scratch marks faded into oblivion or the traveler was faced by obstacles too large to crawl around or over, it was necessary to build rafts or bridges to get across streams, rivers and lakes. Was it worth it? Of course it was!

Frank and I built another raft, this one of dry cedar logs.

It was much easier paddling down the clear blue lake on our way back to The Stillwater. At the end of the lake there would be three miles of rugged trail to follow to reach the spot where the horses were pastured. We had hefty loads and the bed frame and springs hung up on branches and rocks slowed us but I couldn't have cared less.

Excitement grew and grew within me as I looked around this enchanting scene, in no way discouraged by the danger and discomfort of treading the mountain sides and the narrow ledges that led us to our destination. But the excitement was tempered with anxiety. What if someone had already pre-empted the land? Where else in the world would I find such an ideal spot?

4

A Lake For The Naming

*"I could see that progress in this country was going to be slow:
Two steps forward and one back." (Ralph Edwards)*

"Any mail for Ralph Edwards?" An agony of weeks had
passed and I still hadn't heard from the land office about my
application for the lake property. The man at the wicket in the
tiny Bella Coola post office looked up from his letter-sorting
and squinted at me through his thick glasses. "Got a whole pile
of books and magazines," he said. "You sure do a lot of readin',
young man."

People in the village gave me a ribbing about all the reading material I received. Some considered books an unnecessary
extravagance and carrying them any distance was a burden.
Personally, I don't think I could have gotten along without
them. They were more than an interesting diversion lightening
the long evenings; I gleaned a practical education from between their covers.

The clerk sorted through some letters in the pigeon hole
marked "E" and withdrew several addressed to me. One was
a letter from my brother Earle and another was from my mother. A third had an official-looking seal on it and was postmarked
Vancouver, B.C. I didn't wait to take it to the cafe to open it, as
was my custom. I opened it on the spot.

"Whooopeee!" I yelled, startling the clerk and several

people waiting in line for their mail. "I'm gonna get my land. I'm gonna get my land!"

It was two months almost to the day since I had submitted my application for the homestead rights. In their reply the land office informed me that there were certain legal requirements and formalities to be followed before the deed could be registered but since no one else had filed on it, the only hurdles to be overcome were paperwork.

I could hardly wait to tell the Ratcliffs. As I turned to leave the steamy little post office the clerk yelled after me: "Hey, Mr. Edwards. Don't forget your library." In my excitement I had forgotten all about the rest of my mail: Several seed catalogs, a mail order catalog from a Winnipeg department store and books on gardening and vegetable and fruit preservation.

I scooped them all up and after a quick lunch, mounted my horse for the twenty mile ride to Firvale. The horse was lathered with sweat as I rode into the yard of Ratcliff's farm. I was out of the saddle before the horse had stopped. "Hey, Frank!" I yelled, waving my letter. "I'm going to get the place at the lake."

"That's good news, Ralph," Frank said, pummeling me on the back. "Now I guess we can go back up there and get you started." I had been helping Frank ever since we returned from the exploratory trip to the lake. In exchange for my assistance in constructing a woodshed and workshop, Frank had promised to help me build a cabin.

I had been so positive that I would get the property I had already packed in some 600 pounds of supplies from Bella Coola to the Stillwater. On January 10, 1913, Frank and I rode up to the cache cabin he had built there and prepared to move food, tools, kitchenware and books the ten or eleven miles to my new home site.

At The Stillwater we built a large sleigh and braided moose hide harness which was hooked around the puller's shoulders. By the time I had pulled this contraption a few miles I knew what the term "work like a horse" meant. The pain from shoulders to calves was consistent. It was a relief to reach the lake where the strain of pulling would be less.

The lower part of the lake was frozen smooth and clear of snow. But was it safe? I hesitated before I set foot on it. "Don't worry, Ralph," Frank joked. "When you see only an occasional pressure crack it indicates you've got at least six inches of solid ice to fall through."

Toward the end of the lake the pulling got more difficult again; the ice was covered with a coating of pebbly snow. More important, Frank was concerned that the ice at the southern end of the lake might not be solid enough to hold our weight. But the slow-flowing Atnarko River was also a solid sheet of ice at that point and we were able to pull the sled right up to the eastern edge of the property.

From that point we looked back to where the lake disappeared around a jut of land and the mountains came steeply down into the ice. It was a majestic view: Towering peaks of green-covered mountains capped in white. Ice crystals sparkling as the sun made a supreme effort to climb across the cold winter sky.

"This lake has no name," Frank said, breaking the silence. "Have you decided what to call it?" To be truthful, I hadn't given it much thought. I had been too worried about whether I would be allowed to claim it without thinking about giving it a name. As we stood there, looking around us at all that beauty and serenity, I suddenly felt a deep sense of loneliness. I had felt loneliness many times in my life, particularly when I was young and separated from my parents. But this was different. This was not sadness. Was there such a thing as joyful loneliness?

"Lonesome Lake!" I blurted. "I'm going to call it Lonesome Lake." "Sound all right to me," Frank said. And so the lake had a name. There was no elaborate christening ceremony. Frank, ever the practical one, looked up at the sky: "It's going to snow tonight. Let's get these supplies up to the building site." We pushed and pulled the sleigh about 200 yards through the bush to the place we had first scouted for the cabin. We built a big fire and cooked supper.

The next morning a light dusting of snow had fallen but, thanks to Frank's efforts in keeping the embers of the campfire banked and alive, we were soon warm and moving about getting breakfast and planning the day. "A one-room cabin, about ten feet by fourteen feet, should do you for a while," Frank said. "No sense in building a dance hall until you've got somebody to dance with."

There were plenty of trees for a log cabin close by. Eight to ten inches in diameter, it was easy for two men to handle them once they were cut to the proper length. We notched the logs, placed them atop each other, and in a very short time the beginning of a cabin emerged in the wilderness.

Frank showed me how to use a froe, a cleaving tool with its handle at right angles to the blade, which can be used for splitting logs or shingles or shakes from a three foot long block of cedar. I soon had sufficient shakes cut to make a roof.

"Don't forget to leave a hole in one corner so the smoke from your fire can get out," Frank advised. The fire pit was built "Indian fashion" in the earthen floor. Above the hole, Frank showed me how to add a "super roof", an extension, to keep snow and rain from falling into the fire. It took three days to complete the windowless cabin. On the final morning there was six inches of fresh snow on the tarpaulin covering our blankets.

"The next thing we've got to think about is getting some fresh meat," Frank declared. "Why don't you go and shoot a nice fat doe while I get my traps ready for tomorrow?" Frank planned to drop by from time to time as he made the rounds of his trapline. In exchange for a hot meal and shelter, I could count upon his companionship and ready good humor.

I set off across the frozen river and up a hill covered with big firs set well apart. Almost immediately I spotted a deer and brought her down with one shot. I bled the carcass and dragged it across the river to the cabin. The meat problem solved for the time being, I turned my attention to clearing some land around the cabin.

I felled, piled and burned a large number of small trees

and when Frank returned, his pack bulging with furs for sale to the Hudson's Bay Company in Bella Coola, he remarked on my progress: "You're doin' a good job of gettin' rid of those bitty trees, Ralph. When are you going to start on the big ones?"

I told Frank I planned to cut the bigger trees down with axe and crosscut, then saw them up into manageable size for either burning or firewood. "If you're gonna cut them up for firewood you'll have enough fuel to keep hell warm for a long time," Frank remarked. "Come on. I'll show you a quick way to clear a forest."

We walked past the small piles of half-burned trees and ashes that my fires had formed in a half a dozen spots and stopped at one of the giant Douglas firs that rose nearly 200 feet into the air. Using a two inch auger, Frank began to drill through the tree at a point near the base of the trunk. The tree was so thick he had to go around to the other side and drill a hole to meet the first hole.

Frank then drilled a third hole at a forty five degree angle to meet the horizontal hole in the center of the tree. By the time he'd completed this operation I was mystified. "How can you cut down a tree by drilling holes?" I asked. Frank answered by gathering up twigs and branches of dry maple. He lit a blazing fire and, using a crotched stick, picked up hot coals and dropped them down the angled hole. "Now," he said, "blow down that hole until your face is blue and you've got a fire goin' in there."

I did as Frank commanded and blew into the lower hole until my face was the proper shade of blue and at last, hot air began to pour out of the upper hole. "Now, let's go on to the next tree," Frank said. We repeated the process, and then on to yet another large fir. For several days the hot air coming out of the upper holes was all that indicated heat within, then suddenly flames burst out and within a few minutes the trees fell over.

"That's a lot easier than cutting them down with a saw and axe, isn't it?" Frank asked. In two days a dozen forest monarchs around the cabin area had been dropped to the ground and were burning. In addition, we had burned out the heart of a twenty foot log, dousing the fire when it approached the outer part. We shaped the log fore and aft with sharp mattock and axes. The result was a heavy boat. With seats and oars it was a considerable improvement over a raft.

That particular boat didn't get launched until spring and I'm just as glad that Frank wasn't around to witness the proceedings. It was not a champagne affair. To get it to the water I peeled poles and slid and rolled the boat over them, moving the poles to the front as the boat proceeded to its watery welcome in the river.

That part of the launching went off according to plan. The next stage wasn't as successful. The boat stuck on a large rock as it began to move shakily down the boulder-strewn river. In an effort to try to pry it off with an oar, I slipped and fell headlong out of the boat; that is, part of me fell out of the boat. I managed to hook my feet over the gunwales and from this position, head and torso in the water, feet in the boat, I pulled myself back into the boat. It was the only time in my life I fell out of a boat without getting my feet wet!

After a mild January and February in my first winter at the lake, March came in like the proverbial lion. Snow deepened to three feet with a stiff crust. The horses at The Stillwater were finding it almost impossible to forage and they didn't care much for the half-cured slough grass that we had cut in the fall. Several horses and foals that the Ratcliffs owned or were tending refused to eat and collapsed in the snow. Frank gave up trapping for the time being to help Walter to get the horses back on their feet and eating again.

My two horses weren't faring any better than the rest. I couldn't afford to lose either of them. The old mare was in very poor shape so I packed all the oats and cornmeal I could expend and toted them back to The Stillwater. No matter how I coaxed and tried to force-feed the mare she refused even these delicacies and died shortly afterwards. I could see that progress in this country was going to be slow: Two steps forward and one back.

I turned all my attention to clearing land and when spring

came I had about two acres cleared. I removed the stumps with axe, shovel and "come-along" stump puller. After cutting the roots off the stump, the stump puller was attached by a chain to the stump and to a nearby tree or another stump. By pulling a lever which shortened the chain, the stump was wrenched out of the ground.

This device was only useful on smaller stumps; for Douglas fir and the larger cedars, fire and persistent cutting and digging was the only method. In order to get my garden plot ready for spring planting, I had to leave some of the larger stumps in the ground but still I ended up with about 400 square feet of garden space. I erected a pole fence around it to keep out the deer and bears and planted carrots, beets, parsnips, potatoes and turnips. I would have plenty of fresh vegetables when I returned to Lonesome Lake in the fall.

In order to expand my farm I had decided to earn money by taking a job during the spring and summer. Laborers were being hired to work on a construction gang stringing a telegraph line from Bella Coola through the Chilcotin to 150 Mile House, a 300 mile stretch of mostly uninhabited, hilly range country.

One gang was working in from the tiny community of Hanceville in the east while a second crew moved toward them from the west. The job entailed stringing a single line of cold-drawn, galvanized, number eight wire from tree to tree, and where there were no trees, to poles. Big coils of wire were put on turntables and one end was pulled over the rough ground from tree to tree. Linemen topped and trimmed the trees and sideblocks were nailed onto the trees or poles and insulators screwed into the side blocks.

I was given a variety of jobs to do. Because of my insatiable curiosity I soon learned everything I could about all aspects. During noontime breaks, for example, I learned from the linemen how to use climbing irons. These spike-like appendages strapped to their boots allowed the linemen to quickly climb up and down poles and trees.

When we ran short of insulators the foreman kept the crew

moving forward, hanging the wire on the side blocks until the insulator supply was replenished. I was delegated to go back and install the insulators and to tie in the wire. That was a fairly responsible job and I was pleased that the foreman had such confidence in me.

Another job I was given didn't require as much skill, but it did require confidence. It was very hot and dry and hornets were everywhere. Sometimes they had built their nests in areas where poles had to be placed or trees trimmed and right of way cleared. Both men and horses shied away from the nests. The foreman noted that I wore a wide-brimmed, western-style straw hat.

"Listen, Edwards," he said, "I want you to go in and get those hornets." I demurred. I wasn't anymore interested in getting stung than the next man or horse. "I've got just the rig for you," he said. He gave me a piece of fine mosquito netting which I wound around my face and tucked into my shirt, which I buttoned to the top. With my straw hat jammed down tight over the netting on my head, I was fairly well protected from the little stingers.

Working carefully around the nests, I cut through brush, dug a post hole or trimmed a tree, depending on the terrain we were working in. The hornets and I got along fairly well and I had only one close call. A big hornet wiggled its way inside the netting until it was about an inch from my face. I started to run. Suddenly it occurred to me that no matter how hard or far I ran the hornet was always going to be just as close to my face, if not closer. I took my hat off and the hornet and I parted company peacefully.

My next assignment was to help Tom Englebretson unpack and pack the horses and to keep them from wandering away at night. Tom was an expert horseman. He had fitted all the horses with bells to enable us to hear them in the dark and also to ward off any bears. He had some homespun philosophy about the habits of horses: "I don't know why it is but horses always seem to get restless around two o'clock in the morning, just about the time I feel like dozing off." It was true. I also

51

found it very difficult to stay awake at that time and nearly fell out of the saddle more than once. But, as novice nighthawk, I never lost a single horse.

We had now progressed to a place called Tatla Lake where a deal had been made with a rancher who offered to loan the telegraphers a wagon and team to use to haul poles. In exchange, two men from our crew would help him with his haying. Since I was known as a budding farmer, I was put on the hay crew.

It was a welcome change from the stringing of wire but it didn't last long and soon I was back at the hot, sweaty job of digging post holes in a long prairie covered with short grass and prickly pear cacti. Boulders fell into the holes almost as fast as we could dig them out and I began to long for the cool mountain greenery of Lonesome Lake. The only incentive was the money - three dollars a day, seven days a week. While we were not paid for overtime, we were not charged for room and board either.

Not that the "room" was anything special. We slept in tents but I preferred to sleep outdoors. It was only partly because I liked sleeping under the stars and communing with nature. I also liked fresh air. At the end of the day the more fastidious members of the crew headed for the nearest body of water to rinse off the day's accumulation of sweat and dirt.

Occasionally clothes would also be washed but this was considered by many to be an unnecessary waste of water and energy. They'd only get dirty again, wouldn't they? As the hot summer wore on, the atmosphere around the camp got worse. Fewer and fewer men bothered with the refreshing trip to the spring.

I suspected that the same circumstances prevailed at the camp of the eastern crew and no telegraph was necessary, just a strong breeze, to inform us that we were getting close to each other.

At last that day arrived and after a few words of congratulations from the foreman and several bottles of beer, the crews made ready to go their separate ways, east and west. It took several days to ride back to Bella Coola where we were paid off and goodbyes were said.

I spent only enough time there to buy as many provisions as my horse and I could carry. Then I collected my mail and headed home for Lonesome Lake.

5

Bears In The Back Yard

"I was faced with the possibility of facing two wounded bears in the woods. It was getting dark. The whole scene was fraught with danger." (Ralph Edwards)

The trail up the Bella Coola Valley in the two short years that I had been there was becoming a regular thoroughfare. Whereas it had been an event to pass another rider or a horse-drawn wagon every few hours, now many horsemen and cargo-laden vehicles passed each other, some going, some coming in. I knew a few of them. As we passed, they shouted weather information and road conditions to me.

I spent the night at Firvale where the Ratcliffs were busy getting ready for winter which, for them, meant trapping and the pasturing of horses. The second night I traveled as far as Stuie, a stopping place about forty miles from Bella Coola.

The three main tributaries of the Bella Coola River above Stuie drain another forty miles of terrain, each different from the other. The most eastern, the East Fork, comes from Charlotte Lake and is joined at the Hotnarko which drains the interior slough grass meadow country and is brown during the spring runoff.

The center tributary, the Atnarko, has a series of lakes on

it, including Lonesome Lake. Because of these reservoirs, the runoff does not reach its peak until June. The Talchako or Whitewater, joins the Atnarko at Stuie to form the Bella Coola.

This tributary drains the glaciers from the high mountain country to the south of the valley, an ice field with many peaks of 8000 to 10,000 feet. The Talchako is at its highest in July and August during hot weather. The melting glaciers wash out the pulverized stones they have been grinding, making the river gray and coloring the inlet for ten miles out.

Although it may appear that the Bella Coola Valley gets more than its share of water during any one season, nature has been kind. Were these tributaries to carry their runoff at the same time, the valley would be uninhabitable. As it is, an early snow followed by warm winds and heavy rains from the Pacific will bring freshets or floods almost every year and the early pioneers had problems keeping the road and bridges useable.

As I entered the Atnarko Valley, past the magnificent green and white fortress that is the Coast Range, Mother Nature had been at work here too. The leaves of the aspen, alders and maples were daubed with gold, brown, yellow and red. After leaving the horse at The Stillwater, I began the arduous hike along narrow pathways and over rocky ledges above the roaring Atnarko River.

Between the foot of Lonesome Lake and The Stillwater, the trail ran for three miles like a steeplechase designed by a lunatic mountaineer, up steep ridges and over cliffs and bluffs; down precipitous drops into wooded, brush-blocked bottom-lands, across creeks and rivers. During my many trips in and out of the lake I constructed numerous crude bridges which rotted away or had to be redecked. Some had been washed away since I had been home and, again, I spent valuable time replacing them, knowing I would have less time to do repairs when winter set in.

I climbed, crawled, stumbled and walked over this obstacle course until I reached the lake. A boat was cached there and, after the ordeal of the trail, rowing seven miles up the lake was a picnic. My heart was light as each tug on the oars brought me closer to my wilderness haven.

At last it came into view. The little log building looked forlorn among the towering trees. My clearing efforts, which had seemed significant at the time, were really just scratch marks. After beaching the boat, I half-ran up the short distance to the cabin. It looked secure enough; the door was still closed against any animal invasion.

The garden was my second destination. My second visible claim, after the cabin, to a part of the wilderness, should have vegetables ready to harvest. What a dreamer I was. Instead of a cornucopia of produce tumbling into my eager possession, the garden looked like a playground for giant rodents. Where I had left straight rows of flourishing turnips, potatoes, carrots and parsnips, only a few turnips remained. Everything else had been ripped out of the ground as if by huge hands.

Large holes had been scooped out of the soft black earth. Bears, I surmised. Curse them. Walter Ratcliff had warned me that bears love most vegetables, which is why I had built the fence - for all the good that did. "Bears like to dig holes and curl up in them," Walter said. I kicked dirt into the bear pits leveling them out for next season. All that work for nothing.

Up to now I had given the grizzlies and smaller black bears a wide berth, respecting their rights and expecting them to stay clear of my territory too. I had an insane urge to get my rifle and shoot every bear within twenty miles of my property. It wasn't long before reason returned. I was being foolish. After all, I had left a tantalizing food source for animals to be attracted to. I would have to be more cunning and careful in the future if I were to survive in this primitive world.

I walked dejectedly back to the cabin and pushed open the door. I hadn't barricaded it but left it so Frank and Walter Ratcliff could use it whenever they were trapping or traveling in the vicinity. The interior smelled damp and woody and of mice droppings, but my supplies and possessions were intact. The place was still windowless and at that moment the dark, cool interior seemed gloomy to me, having spent all summer out of doors. I would have to build a larger house.

I had never intended the cabin, with its smoke hole in the roof, to be a permanent residence. As soon as I could get time between hauling in the winter's supply of food and essential materials and clearing more land, I set to work to build a permanent home.

I selected a piece of level sandy land where a clump of big white birches arched out over a gurgling brook. The birches would supply shade in the summer and when the branches were bare in the winter, the sun would shine in. I decided to call the house The Birches.

The next day I began to dig a cellar, nine feet square and six feet deep. I walled it with split cedar logs which extended about two feet above the ground. I hadn't yet devised a way to get my one remaining horse up from The Stillwater to Lonesome Lake, so the heavy work of transporting logs to the house site was up to me. The logs were about 400 yards away and too heavy for me to drag or roll.

Instead, I designed a light "railroad", using alder poles for tracks held together with cross ties that were "nailed" on with square wooden pegs which I whittled myself. I constructed a rail car with wheels made from the ends of logs and flanged to fit into the alder rails. When I had moved all my materials to the site with the rail car I peeled the house logs with an adze and began placing them one on top of another, ends notched, in the regular fashion.

No space showed between the logs, especially after I "chinked" the cracks with mud and moss. To make the interior even more tight, warm and dry I felled some large cedars, peeled sections and split shakes. Smoothed and trued with a broad axe and nailed to the inside walls, they were not only functional but attractive as well.

The ceiling was made from large slabs of old-growth cedar and the floor of hewed birch, smoothed and trued with the broad axe. The two rooms, one twelve by twelve feet and the ther twelve by nine feet, were positioned so they "slid" past each other creating a twelve by six foot front porch and a nine by six foot back porch.

The half pitch roof was extended for eighteen feet to make a woodshed and workshop where I could build boats, furniture and other necessities of frontier living. The roof of the house extended two feet out beyond the whole building. From Bella Coola I packed in glass and set the sheets in window frames which I had cut out of the logs. With a Stanley forty five degree plane, I made rail and panel doors from cedar slabs.

The building of the house, along with land clearing and other endeavors, filled my days, The nights were less active. I thanked God for the printed word and each day the books and magazines which my Bella Coola friends thought were a frivolous waste, became a thumb-worn investment. There was little else to do after dark and I was too tired to carve or build furniture. I used the coal oil lamp sparingly, preferring instead to read by candlelight. As well as being expensive, coal oil was heavy to carry.

Until the house was completed, I continued to sleep in the little cabin and at night would occasionally lie awake listening to sounds and trying to determine what made them. The "little old men in slippers" were bears padding along a trail above the house, a trail that followed the river for more than a mile.

A variety of birds, animals and insects made their presence known. One creature kept me awake for many nights. It didn't seem to draw a breath but sang all night with a constant "oooooh, oooh, oooooh." At times it sounded like a bell on a horse in the lead of a pack train that never got any closer or any farther away. One night I couldn't stand the suspense of not knowing what this animal was, so I went outside and flashed a light into the branches of a tree where the sound was coming from.

There sat a pygmy owl (genus *Glancidium*), sometimes called the gnome owl, a rather dark-colored fellow with large, interested eyes. Although pygmy owls are known to be chiefly insectivorous, my little friend turned out to also be a good mouser. Now that I knew what he was, I found his breathless "ooooh" as soothing as a lullaby.

Usually I was so exhausted after the day's labors that lullabying owls were unnecessary to put me to sleep. But as winter drew on I had to spend more and more time indoors and there was little to do but sleep. The almost total lack of sound added to the loneliness. I mentioned this to Frank Ratcliff one day when I stopped in at Firvale on the way back from a supply trip.

"Why don't you learn to play a musical instrument?" Frank asked. "That's one way to pass the long hours and drive off wild animals at the same time."

"I can't afford one," I told Frank. "I've nearly spent the 200 dollars I earned working on the telegraph line this summer. Besides, I can't read music, although I can whistle a fair tune." Frank disappeared to the back of the house and came back with a violin. Although obviously handmade, it was expertly carved and shone like a mahogany floor. He played a lively jig on it.

"That's quite an instrument," I said, admiringly. "What's it made from?" Frank explained how he had fashioned the violin with an axe, a pocket knife, a small block plane and a piece of glass, which he used for scraping and smoothing. The bottom and sides were made of maple which grew in the woods in western Oregon. He wanted a piece of spruce but since there was none available he made the top, or sounding board, from part of a very tall fir tree growing alone on a windy ridge.

"I chose this wood from the top of the tree because I figured it would be more vibrant and resonant," Frank said. The bow was also handmade with hairs from a horse's tail. "I envy you your skill with that thing," I said. "It sure must liven up your evenings." Frank turned and walked into another room, returning a few seconds later with another violin.

"This one is store boughten," he said, "but it's a fair instrument. Tell you what, Ralph. You learn to play a tune on it and I'll give it to you to keep." That seemed like a good deal. Learning to play would give me something constructive to do and - who knows - if I became a virtuoso: Carnegie Hall? Royal

Command Performances? Dream on.

I sent away for a book of instructions and while waiting for it to come by mail I built a music stand. On each side of the stand I created impressions in which I could place candles. I knew the lessons would have to take place after dark. Everything was ready when the instruction book arrived.

When night came I opened the book, lit the candles, cradled the violin under my chin in the manner in which other master violinists did, and drew the bow hesitantly across the strings. The result was a sound somewhere between a wind blowing through a mountain tunnel and a cougar caught in a buzzsaw. Frank was right. With this sound emanating from my cabin, there wouldn't be any wildlife around for miles.

At least there was one benefit in that my neighbors were all animals. They couldn't knock on the door and complain, although I swear the coyotes and wolves some nights tried to drown out my concerts. Undaunted, I continued, although it soon became apparent that I wasn't going to give much conpetition to Fritz Kreisler, the Austrian child prodigy, who was then in his ascendancy.

From the music instruction book I learned to read notes by their places on the strings and not by the A,B,Cs. Years later, when my mother came to Canada, she taught me singer's notes: do, ra, me, fa, so, la, and so on. By matching the half-notes I managed to transpose pieces that were difficult on the violin to easier keys. I would never have made an instructor (I wasn't even a very good musician) but I did learn to belt out a few tunes. In due time, Frank Ratcliff made a formal presentation to me of the "boughten" violin. It filled the nights with something akin to music.

Frank also taught me more practical things, such as how to make hotcakes, sourdough bread and bannock. Everyone knows how to make hotcakes, or pancakes or flapjacks. Sourdough is the traditional bread of the camper in which both alcoholic and lactic fermentation is active. Bannock is a Scottish Gaelic word for unleavened bread of oat or barley flour baked in flattish loaves. In New England it was made of cornmeal and baked on a griddle. Generously laced with assorted dried fruits and coated with deer fat, it was a staple on trail and trapline. After the disaster of the garden, I ate a lot of bannock that winter.

Since I had already proved that a garden could be productive, if the bears could be kept out, I decided to transplant some fruit trees. Bill Graham, who lived in the Bella Coola Valley, had opened a nursery, proving that certain varieties of tree fruit could withstand northern winter. However, the temperature difference, due to milder Pacific air and other factors in the Bella Coola Valley, meant more experimentation at Lonesome Lake was necessary.

I bought a dozen apple trees and set them out along the creek bank in a well-drained location. My enemies this time were not the bears. Mice and weather combined to try to destroy my agricultural efforts. The mice chewed the tender bark of the trunks and when an early thaw started the sap flowing, a hard frost ruptured the moist tissues. Fortunately, enough apple trees survived and eventually I had fruit from them.

My training as a farmer with uncle Will and, later, as a laborer in California, was of some use as I searched to find a way to grow the vegetables and fruits I desired. Irrigation was a problem but I had already learned some lessons in this regard and after a great deal of hard work had water running from areas that needed draining and onto areas that were arid.

I wanted and needed the widest possible range of vegetables and fruit for I knew that dietary balance through the long winters must be provided. Trial and error offered the sole method to broaden the range of my crops; yet even that would not succeed unless abetted by an alert scientific approach. Year by year I experimented until I discovered what kind of corn, beans and peas and a dozen other vegetables could survive the opposition of the weather.

It took several seasons to score an emphatic victory for the string bean, and Golden Bantam corn was never able to beat the climate; the best this variety could manage was a few stubby ears at the end of summer. I finally settled for squaw corn, the kind that is distinguished by its muticolored kernels. The garden eventually yielded cauliflower, pumpkin, squash, broccoli, rutabaga, cabbage and even celery. Over the years I planted and experimented with more than forty varieties of fruit trees before I found an adequate number to survive the winter.

I began to correspond with directors of experimental stations in such diverse areas as Manitoba and Idaho so that I had pears from the Canadian province and other fruits from northern states. Also from Manitoba and Saskatchewan I recruited raspberries, strawberries and gooseberries. All flourished in the valley.

The days grew shorter and the mornings frostier as winter became more than just a threat and before long it was snowing. Even with the violin and more books, the evenings alone were bleak. I felt the need of some sort of companionship. I received many letters from my childhood sweetheart, Helen Cathie, in North Carolina, but these heightened rather than assuaged my feelings of aloneness. I hoped one day to go to her and bring her to the home I was building here in the Canadian wilderness. In the long winter days, as many of us have learned, a pet is the next best thing to human companionship.

Therefore, it was a joyful day when Walter Ratcliff announced that he was going away to join the Canadian army and asked if I would look after his dog Whitie. Whitie was a sensitive dog of doubtful heritage, which is to say he was of mixed breed believed to be, among others, Bloodhound, Airedale and Labrador. The result was a hound of good size and temperament - give or take a few points - with short, dense, cream-colored hair, similar in appearance to that of a deer.

"He'll make an excellent companion for you, Ralph," Walter said. "He's almost human." At that time my regard for humans was not above that for animals, so Walter hastened to add: "He's very sensitive so if you've got to bawl him out about something, do it in a kind way. Otherwise he's liable to sulk or run away."

Whitie and I liked each other right away. His worst traits

I would learn to live with just as he would learn to live with mine: Whitie had a habit of baiting coyotes; I snored and this caused him to howl. I think the result was mostly in his favor because I didn't like him causing problems for me by chasing coyotes and his howling at my snoring only caused me to wake up and lose sleep.

His fancy for coyotes became evident the very day I accompanied him in from Firvale. Just beyond the Stillwater he jumped a coyote bitch who had a batch of pups. Hardly before I knew what he was up to he had shaken her up and dropped her, half dead, among some rocks in a slide area.

I had to finish her off with my rifle. It wasn't something I had much stomach for. I was even less prepared for the sad prospect of killing her pups, a necessary piece of business since they would have starved to death without her anyway. However, there was a bounty on coyotes so I skinned them all out and stored the pelts until my next trip to town.

I soon learned that Whitie had a system of signals to distinguish between certain animals he was tracking. Wolves, bears and wolverines all were identified by a "boo, boo, boo." Coyotes alone were saluted with "ki, ki, ki."

He didn't use his signal system in the house and this led to several misunderstandings. At night if he went to the door and whined I never knew whether he wanted to chase a coyote or to answer nature's call. I was fooled many times. If I opted for a decision in favor of chasing coyotes and kept him indoors, nature's call would end up on the floor as Whitie's revenge.

Whitie's problem with coyotes was dangerous to him because he could not bring them to a confrontation. Coyotes, like wolves, often run in packs and seldom are far from their fellows. A pack fights wolf-like, circling and cutting off their quarry, then sending out a parry and thrust team which run past the victim, slashing at him with razor-sharp teeth. Whitie was at his best when he could corner a coyote in a coarse rock-slide where there was no place to retreat or out on a log in the river. He would then "ki, ki" me to come and help.

We had many adventures with coyotes; one almost led to

the loss of my hunting companion. In this instance he had run a coyote out onto the frozen lake and I finished him off with a couple of shots. As we walked back to shore, there was a sharp crack, and Whitie fell into the water. As he tried to clamber out, the thin ice collapsed under his weight. Even with a piece of willow tree extended to him, I could not get him into shore.

He dog-paddled around in the freezing water, yelping. I was dumbfounded at first about how to rescue him. I couldn't walk out too close to him because of the thin ice condition and I couldn't wait too long because he would soon die in the frigid water. I remembered there was a dugout beached nearby; as fast as I could I ran to it and hauled it back. As I left, Whitie shrieked, afraid that I was abandoning him.

In a few minutes I was back and after getting him aboard, rowed and oar-pushed the boat to shore. He howled with the cold. I attempted to wring the water out of his short coat but this intensified the cold so he cried even more. I dragged him, pushed and pulled him, making him move so that eventually circulation increased and he was able to warm himself through running and shaking. In a short while he was wagging his tail and licking my hands and face in the animal thank you.

When I say Whitie was a coyote baiter and caused me problems with his weird fascination for his distant cousin, I must give credit. Between us we got twenty five coyotes that winter which brought in 125 dollars in bounty money, a considerable contribution to our income and no doubt we saved many a poor deer from a slow, painful death.

Whitie's most endearing trait was his honesty. In my opinion, there are honest dogs and there are dishonest ones - just as there are humans in those categories. Shorty, who was a brother to Whitie and belonged to John Ratcliff, was a crook. Even his better qualities, such as the pursuit of squirrels, would often raise the ire of his master. He would stand for hours barking under a tree until his owner could come and collect a squirrel for dinner. Such diligence to squirrel-treeing became a pain to John who wasn't always in a mood to shoot a squirrel.

But Shorty's dishonesty outshone even this trait. One day

Ralph Edwards

Trumpeter Swans: the great white birds that he befriended by carrying tens of thousands of pounds of grain over rugged mountain trails to see them through the rough winter. Ralph, along with his daughter Trudy and her husband Jack Turner are credited by many conservationists as being a key reason why these magnificant birds started on the road to recovery from near extinction.

Trumpeters congregate on the tiny area of open water to accept life sustaining grain.

After years of feeding, birds have become tame. Here they herd around Ralph's granddaughter Susan Turner, even stealing grain from unattended sack.

The Birches—the family homestead. Note deer grazing in pasture.

Ethel and Ralph with part of their flower garden in background.

The famous—and sometimes infamous—frail little Taylorcraft floatplane that took Ralph all around the rugged coast and mountains of western British Columbia and parts of Alaska and the Yukon.

Ralph's hand-hewn hangar at Lonesome Lake.

Ralph Edwards being presented the highest Canadian award for conservation: The Medal of Service of the Order of Canada, in 1972 by Governor-General Roland Michener.

Ralph in latter years, now without aircraft or boat, is questioned by younger fishermen about his experiences of the past.

John (who was an uncle to Walter and Frank) and I were building a bridge to improve the trail between Lonesome Lake and The Stillwater. The dogs were hanging around the tent where the food was stored. Whitie came up to John and whined and shook his head, alerting John to the fact that Shorty was stealing bacon. Shorty got a spanking while Whitie was rewarded with a pat on the head and a piece of bacon rind.

If Whitie got his way at every meal time, he would have chosen bear meat. It wasn't always available, which is just as well: He got fat and lazy on a steady diet of bruin steak. During the bear-less days he subsisted on beans and rice, or whatever else his master was having, and he would again become lean and faster than a coyote. Somehow, I was lucky. I never managed to get fat and lazy whether fed bear or beans.

As good a hunter as Whitie was, he was absolutely useless when it came to mountain goats; he was terrified of heights. The one time I took him goat hunting he whined and became petrified on the spot. I had to carry him down to a lower elevation before he became mobile again. By then he had made so much noise the goat I was stalking headed for the high bluffs and that ended the hunt for the day.

From then on Whitie was commanded to stay home when I went for goats. Unfortunately, there didn't seem to be a word in his language or mine that meant "goat". Nevertheless, I tried it in English: "Stay home. I'm going for a goat today." When I climbed a considerable distance up the mountain, there was Whitie, skulking along behind.

Forgetting what Walter Ratcliff had said about Whitie's delicate feelings, I ran back and chastized him and give him a sharp smack on his well-padded rump. He took off for home, looking back from time to time to register his annoyance at my heartless action.

I continued my hunt and got a goat for the larder. It was late when I returned home. Whitie was not there. I kept calling him late into the night but he never came. Next morning I became really anxious because he had never run away before. I theorized that he probably headed for the home of his former master, Walter Ratcliff, in Firvale.

I found his tracks leading down the valley. Since it was time to go to Atnarko to get the mail anyway, I packed up and began to follow the dog's trail. Uphill and down they went. Across bridges and logs; across streams. They led past the Ratcliff's cabin at The Stillwater.

I wondered how far the hound would lead me. I was almost to Atnarko when my ears picked up the sound of a dog whining in pain. I raced across a log that served as a bridge across the river at that point and immediately saw Whitie. He was caught in a trap that Frank Ratcliff had set for coyotes.

Whitie seemed to have mixed emotions about seeing me. He was hopeful that I would get him out of his predicament but sensed that I was angry at him for running away. He had wisely chosen to wait quietly during his entrapment instead of panicking and jumping off the log into the river. "Good dog, good dog," I said to him as I eased the trap off his leg.

I quickly checked his leg to see if there were any broken bones. Aside from a bad bruise, he was uninjured. If he had tried to free himself he would have ended up with a nasty wound. He lay quietly while I checked him, then began to lick my hands and face. I hadn't the heart to chastize him too severely but I had to teach him a lesson. "You are not to do that ever again, Whitie," I said. "You are a good dog but you mustn't run away like that again. Do you understand?" Whitie hung his head, then looked sheepishly up at me, his tail between his legs. He understood perfectly. I patted him again and we started up the trail together to Atnarkò.

After collecting the mail and some supplies at the stopping place, Whitie and I began the return hike to Lonesome Lake. We were heading into an area of heavy cedars when the dog began to "boo, boo, boo,"excitedly. "Shut up, Whitie," I admonished him. "There are no bears around here." I should have trusted his superior judgment in this case because almost immediately a bear appeared in front of us.

I scarcely had time to take the safety catch off my rifle before the grizzly began his charge. The gun bucked and the bear fell down stunned but not dead. I hadn't time to examine him or get away another shot before Whitie began to "boo, boo, boo" again. I looked around and sure enough, there was another big bear clambering across a log in our direction from the south side. I fired at it without taking aim and it jumped off the log and went crashing off into the bush. By the time I returned my attention to the first bear, it too had disappeared into the thick undergrowth.

After a short interval of crashing and grunting sounds, the woods became silent. I soothed Whitie who was in a fever of excitement and fear. My own condition wasn't much better. I was faced with the possibility of two wounded bears in the woods. It was getting dark; the whole scene was fraught with danger.

I climbed a cedar and when I heard some grunting noises I fired a shot in that direction. All hell broke loose as a bear began to bawl and break through the brush in the direction away from the trail. I waited for what seemed an eternity, then climbed down from the tree. There was no more noise and Whitie and I cautiously continued our homeward journey.

A good hunter does not leave wounded animals to die a slow death or - in the case of bears - to turn into savage killers. But you shouldn't stalk a wounded bear at night, let alone two wounded bears. Next morning Whitie and I went back to the spot where the bears had entered the bush and began to search for remains. Aware that we were in a dangerous situation, we picked our way through the tangle of vines and fallen logs with utmost care. When I spotted some blood on a leaf, I offered it to Whitie to smell and he came alive with excitement, repeating his famous bear signal.

The next moment we found the bear. He was lying against a big log a few feet away from us. He was dead. Upon skinning him out I found that the bullet had passed through his stomach without hitting any bones. I surmised that this was the first bear I had shot at but there was no way to tell for sure. Where had the other one gone? Was it dead too? Or was it lying wounded somewhere around the next clump of trees ready to spring at us?

We tramped through the bush for several hours but could find no trace of the second bear. I assumed it had gotten clean away. I shouldered the heavy well-larded hide of the first grizzly and took it back to Lonesome Lake. It brought seventy five dollars on the fur market and helped finance necessities on the homestead.

As time went by my experience with the huge unpredictable grizzlies would become almost a daily event. Before that time, however, I was to sample a taste of what it was like to be shot at myself.

6

An Army Interlude

"I wished I was back in Canada and war was something that the history books told about." (Ralph Edwards)

A good horse, a faithful dog and a squeaky violin do not make a home. That was something I decided after spending another long winter alone at the lake. I knew something had to be done about it.

What was missing was a woman, someone who would be wife and helpmate, someone who would enjoy the pioneer life as much as I did and who would share gift of children. I knew, or thought I did, who that woman was: Helen Cathie had been my childhood sweetheart from the time I lived in Sylva, North Carolina. We had been corresponding regularly since I left and the moment seemed ripe for me to go there and bring her back to Lonesome Lake. I wrote and told her I was coming.

Helen had been the only woman in my life, aside from my mother and assorted relatives like aunt Annie. I just never seemed to have had time to get acquainted with women. I was always too busy getting established to worry about marriage and the details of learning to relate to the opposite sex. Also, I was shy around women, never knowing quite what was expected of me or what to expect of them. My religious upbringing had ingrained in me that premarital sex was as taboo as alcohol and tobacco so I lived an almost monastic life. There was no difficulty in maintaining this monk-like existence because I didn't know any eligible women in Bella Coola or anywhere else in the valley. And even if I did, I felt I had very little to offer someone - that is, until now. With signs of progress evident, Lonesome Lake was ready for a woman.

The train ride across the United States to Sylva, North Carolina was hot and boring and seemed to take forever. I was impatient to get there and back because there was so much to be done on the homestead before winter came. Nevertheless, I looked forward to seeing Helen. Her letters had become increasingly passionate and encouraging and I wanted to tell her in person about all the adventures I had faced and of those we would share.

I spent a lot of time rehearsing what I would say: I would be truthful. Life in the wilderness would be no bed of roses. It would mean long days of hard work and the loss of some of the amenities she now took for granted in the blossoming community of Sylva. There would be no dashing off to fancy shops to buy frilly dresses; no neighbors dropping by to gossip every day or so. There would be weeks alone while I hunted and trapped, days and nights spent with only the light of the candle and the sound of wild animals and the wind.

There would be the good things too: home-grown food, fresh air, the welcoming spring after harsh winter, the wonderful feeling of accomplishment. The independence; freedom to do just about anything with obligations only to yourself. It would take a superior woman to make a wife and mother in such a situation but our pioneer ancestors did it and the world was a better place for it.

When the train pulled into Sylva, I was in an agony of excitement. How did I look? Would Helen still like me? It had been years since we had seen each other. Would she look the same? I snatched a glimpse of myself in a small mirror in the vestibule. The view wasn't unpleasant. A rosy-cheeked young man with bright eyes. I looked less than the twenty four years registered in the book of my life.

I felt confident as I strode up the pathway to the suburban

home where Helen lived with her parents. She opened the door after I knocked. "Hello, Ralph," she said, hesitantly. "Hello, Helen," I said, feeling a blush come over my face. My hands were clammy and I couldn't seem to think of anything else to say. We touched hands but didn't embrace. "Come in," she said.

Her parents had discreetly stepped out somewhere and it was silent as a tomb in the cool parlor. I finally found my voice in the crevice where it had disappeared: "You look very well." "So do you, Ralph," Helen said. "How long can you stay?" "I hope to get back as soon as possible," I said. "There's a lot of work to be done on the farm."

After a long embarrassing silence, I blurted out my prepared speech. I told her all the good things and all the bad. In my own shy way, I explained that it wouldn't be an easy transition, but I loved her and wanted her to be my wife. I wanted to marry her as soon as possible and to take her back with me to Lonesome Lake.

"I'm sorry, Ralph," Helen said, tears welling up in her eyes. "I can't come with you to Canada. I'm really sorry, but I just can't." Her words cut through me like a knife. I was dumbfounded and my voice went back into its crevice. "I can't go, Ralph," she said. "I like it here in Sylva. All my friends live here. My parents live here. I'd never be happy in such a wilderness."

Perhaps I had painted too bleak a picture for her. I began to plead. "Helen, listen to me. Think of all the wonderful times we can have together. The things we can share. Don't you remember all the nice promises in your letters?" Have you forgotten what you wrote?" "I haven't forgotten," she blushed. "But writing words on paper and living them in real life are two different things."

"You've never experienced sunrises or sunsets anywhere that match those at Lonesome Lake," I said. "You've never tasted such vegetables and fruit. Why, you can grow almost anything there. And don't worry. There'll be neighbors soon. People are moving in all the time. And after the railway goes through, there may even be a settlement nearby with a store and a post office. Every day's an adventure. Please come."

My plea was of no avail. Her mind was made up. "I love you, Ralph," she said, crying. "But I'd only make you unhappy if I tried to be a pioneer's wife. I'm just no good at being alone. I like people around me. It's just not for me. This is my home. All this time I've been writing to you I've been hoping and praying that you would leave that forsaken wilderness and come back to Sylva. I never thought that you would ever seriously consider spending the rest of your life there." She paused and wiped her eyes.

"Why don't you come and live here? You can get a job and we can get married and live a normal life in a civilized world." The thought of living and working in Sylva, or any other city or town, was appalling. "I can't do that," I said. "I love Lonesome Lake. I like the independence and the challenge of doing something different every day. A routine job bores the life out of me. I'd be the one who'd make you unhappy if I was trapped in a city job."

We were at an impasse. I couldn't bear the thought of losing Helen, nor could I accept her plea to stay in Sylva. We both had tears in our eyes as we parted. For the next few days I couldn't think straight. It was a crushing defeat. I had loved someone half of my life and suddenly it was over in a few moments.

I had to force myself to concentrate on the larger goals. If Helen couldn't be happy in my country, I'd just have to accept the fact. It was easy to say at that time but impossible to accept. Perhaps some day she'd change her mind. I went back once more to talk to her again. We didn't even bring up the subject of her coming to the lake or my staying in Sylva. We vowed we would continue to write to each other and - after a teary farewell - I got on the train and went to Boston.

My mother and brother Earle were living in Beantown where Earle was working as a carpenter, supporting my mother who had separated from my father some years before. Since the thought of returning to Lonesome Lake without Helen was still very much on my mind, I decided to see if I could persuade Earle to join me on the frontier.

"There's a great opportunity for you there," I said. "Far more than there is here, nailing boards for somebody else. You can get yourself a good piece of land from the government and in no time you'll be a farmer like me." I must admit I poured it on a bit thick for Earle's benefit. I was optimistic, to say the least, about the future of the Bella Coola Valley.

But there was some solid basis for my optimism. There had been glowing reports about the potential for the district from government and private individuals who predicted that Bella Coola would become a railway terminal. "The railway has spent substantial money already surveying the area," I told Earle truthfully. "Options have been taken out on large tracts of land; in fact, there's a land boom on right now and real estate promoters are offering lots for 2000 dollars apiece."

I wasn't to know that these same lots would go for fifty dollars after the First World War, but this was the time for encouragement. "Get in on the ground floor," I urged Earle. I described to him exactly where my land was and where I expected the rail line to go through. "It's not beyond my expectations that some day trains will stop near my place and take my produce to Bella Coola for sale." "Okay, okay," Earle said, "you've convinced me you've found the garden of Eden, Ralph. I'll come with you. I don't care much for this carpentering job anyway."

My disappointment at going home without Helen was lessened somewhat by this good news and even more by the announcement by mother that she and my other younger brother George (we called him Bruce) were also coming to Canada. In a few days we were on the Union Steamship's Camosun and three days later arrived in Bella Coola. We found a house for mother to rent and Earle and I went immediately to look at the Lonesome Lake property and to scout a likely homestead for Earle at Tenas Lake, three miles south of my place.

Earle filed on the land and during a trip to town to get supplies we heard that a family named Mosher had decided to leave the valley and wanted to sell their homestead. It might be a good place for mother and Bruce.

The Moshers lived in an isolated log cabin in a small clearing about fifty miles from Bella Coola on the horse trail to the Interior. "I need 900 dollars to pay off my bill at Christensen's store in Bella Coola," Mr. Mosher told us. "I don't suppose you've got that kind of money since you're homesteading. But if one of you was to take over my job as lineman for the telegraph company you can pay off the store bill and I'll turn over the deed to this place to you."

It meant another spring, summer and part of the fall away from the farm but someone had to devise a way for mother to have a permanent residence and, since we couldn't afford rent, this seemed an ideal solution. With my experience with the telegraph company as a laborer behind me, it wasn't difficult for them to accept me as a replacement for Mr. Mosher.

As well as 178 acres of land and the improvements, such as they were, the Moshers left behind a large amount of food and other items: two rifles, one shotgun, ammunition for each, enough food to last a family of four for a year, blankets, a phonograph with a wooden horn and cylinder recordings. The record that got the most play was "Red Wing". The most curious item in the Mosher stockpile was two gallons of almond cake flavoring. To say that the Moshers liked almond was an understatement.

This should have been a happy time for me now that three-quarters of the Edwards family was in British Columbia and were holding land. I had Lonesome Lake, Earle had secured his place at Tenas Lake and mother was ensconced at the Mosher place. However, what ruined that summer of 1917 for me was the receipt of a letter from Helen Cathie.

"Dear Ralph," it read. "I know that this will come as a great surprise to you but I have met a wonderful man and we plan to be married next month. I know you would like him. He is a little like you in some ways, independent and strong. But he wants to live and work in Sylva and that makes the difference. I hope this does not come as a shock to you. I know that you

82

will be happy to know that I will be happy. Please try to think kindly of me. I wish you all the best of luck and hope you too will find someone to share your life with. With love, Helen."

I was stunned. Although I had thought I had accepted the fact that Helen would never come to live at the lake, I couldn't help harboring a small hope that this would change. To learn that she was going to be married cut all the pins out from under this ridiculous expectation.

Alone at the lake, I was depressed and angry. How could she do this to me? I began to brood about it. I never like to give up and it seemed unjust that my happiness should be snatched away by some other man. I tried to get her out of my mind by working from dawn to dusk but despite slaving at land-clearing and barn-building I still found my thoughts concentrating on Helen in another man's arms.

Rather than go crazy thinking about something that couldn't be changed, I decided to leave Lonesome Lake. Canada had entered the war against the Kaiser in 1914 and the Ratcliff boys had long since joined the army. Earle was ready to go any day now. Lonesome Lake had lost its enchantment for the time being and it wasn't long before I was on the boat for Vancouver and at the door of the enlistment office.

Another disappointment: I had less than 20/20 vision in one eye and failed the physical examination to get into the Canadian airforce. That was a surprise because I was far healthier than most of the recruits I saw around me. I was determined to get into the air war so I crossed the border into Washington State and applied at the recruiting depot of the United States Air Force. "Sorry, you don't have enough education," they told me.

That may have been true, but what I lacked in education I more than made up for in enthusiasm. I had been fascinated by planes all my life and occasionally got chided by fellow workers for gawking at every plane that droned by. That was in the early days of flight and I was working at odd farming jobs in the States. It wasn't until September 1939, the month the Second World War began, that I actually got my first plane ride. I was hauling some hay when a plane flew over and landed at the head of Lonesome Lake.

I rowed across in a boat and down a channel in the river where there was a narrow island covered with willows and grass. The plane had slid into the mud and the pilot was in his underwear in the water trying to turn it around.

"Where the heck is this?" he yelled. I told him it was Lonesome Lake on the headwaters of the Bella Coola River. "Well where's One Eye Lake? I've been trying to find that forsaken place for two days now." I pointed out it was just a short flight to the southeast of us. He climbed out of the muddy water and sat on a pontoon, mopping his brow.

"Say . . . how'd you like to come along with me and show me exactly where that darn place is?" I told him I had a lot of hay to get in and should stay and tend to the job at hand. "Won't take but a few minutes," he persisted. "I'll bring you right back soon's I drop these guys off. You see, I got three hunters in here who want to get to the lodge on One Eye Lake and I already wasted one day of their hunting time trying to find it."

I felt sorry for him and besides, the prospect of a plane ride excited me. I tied the rowboat up on the shore and soon I was aboard, riding in the co-pilot's seat. What elation! Nothing I had ever read or heard had prepared me for the joy of flight. I could hardly suppress my feelings. Why had I waited half a lifetime for such an experience?

I was in the most advantageous seat in the aircraft and could look around below and at the same time observe the pilot operating the controls. I asked him what type of plane we were flying in and he replied, laconically: "It's a sort of a hybrid. A little bit of this and a little bit of that."

In a few minutes we swooped down and landed on One Eye Lake, also known as Tenas Lake. One Eye had apparently been an Indian who had lived in the area. The passengers, Americans who were hoping to shoot bear and moose, trooped up the aisle to the door, packing some of their gear with them.

A dinghy was waiting to pick them up and take them to a dock at the lodge, a rustic-looking building set back from the water. In another minute the plane was off and I was looking down at the specks the hunters had become as they trudged up the ramp.

This was my first plane ride. An opportunity to own and fly my own plane was a long way in the future. I would do a lot of standing around and gawking at airplanes before that dream became a reality. The "hybrid" I whetted my appetite aboard was a streamliner compared with the aircraft used by the Allies and the Germans in the First World War. The closest I got to any of them, however, was looking up at planes "dog-fighting" over the muddy trenches of France.

At least I was working at something I knew something about: Wireless operation. Finally my course in telegraphy paid off. I had learned the Continental Code, which is slightly different from Morse, at Fort Mason, on the north shore of San Francisco. When I mastered it, I became a corporal in the U.S. Army, Company A, 8th Field Signal Battalion.

At this time the apparatus we used in radio transmission was extremely primitive: Open spark transmission and a "cat's whisker" centered on a sensitive point on a piece of mineral. It was good only for short range transmission and uncertain even for that. When we got to France the caliber of equipment had improved considerably.

While still in the United States training for service overseas, I spent one day hanging long range antennae on a high power tower, exposed to cold wind. When I came down I felt feverish and trembly in the knees. I was soon flat on my back at the base hospital with what the doctor diagnosed as a combination of measles and bronchial pneumonia.

Men in the hospital who could move around had to look after themselves but I was unable to do so for a few weeks. My fever quickly abated so I was out of danger but the bronchitis created so much mucus in my lungs I could scarcely breathe. I lay with my head over my bunk so that the stuff could run into a sputum cup.

Many men were far worse off than me. A few were taken dead out of the ward every day. Others lay crying for their mothers and praying for relief from their misery. An elderly nurse was finally assigned to our ward and for the first time since I was admitted we were given sponge baths. There were no proper bathroom facilities in the hospital. If this was the United States in wartime, I wondered what it would be like in Europe.

It wasn't long before I found out. After two more moves within the United States, I found myself on a troopship bound for France. We landed at Brest on the Brittany coast where our accommodation was in some ancient Roman barracks with stone floors. Thin straw mattresses and a couple of army blankets were our beds. It was as cold as Satan's heart but a soldier was expected to be tough. I had learned to sleep in worse conditions in the north and did not feel the discomfort as much as the other young men in my group.

We were moved into the Soissons-Rheims area, 100 kilometers from Paris, moving towards the Belgian border. German airplanes dropped bombs in the woods where we were sheltering and it was decided that a night march to a re-grouping area would be advisable. In less official language it meant a disorderly retreat. Casualties were high on the forty five kilometer trek; we were all weak from dysentery; dead men and horses were lying everywhere and more kept falling until only five of our group reached the rallying spot.

During the next few weeks I bellied my way through mud and dead bodies to set up wireless equipment while shells burst all around me. When one shell-burst blew out the candles lighting the culvert I was working in, I began to think that facing grizzly bears in British Columbia was not such a dangerous piece of work.

The news from home was encouraging. Mother wrote to tell me how lovely the Bella Coola valley looked in the spring and how lush the grass was for the cattle and horses, although she didn't think she would be able to stay there forever and hoped one day to return to the States. She kept me informed of small events that cheered me through long days spent in muddy trenches and in stinking, dilapidated buildings. I longed for the sweet pure fresh air of Lonesome Lake.

I pictured the green valley misted in rising dew and the clouds that hung over the snowy peaks. While I had the smell of cordite and death in my nostrils I kept alive the visions of the farm. In my mind's eye I saw the hay field; piles of burning stumps; Whitie and I tramping the trail to The Stillwater.

Dreaming was a relief but we didn't have much time for it. Orders came through for our company to take part in the invasion of Metz, a city in a triangle between Luxembourg and the Saarland, that much-disputed piece of territory that has been tossed back and forth between Germany and France for centuries.

I went forth with a strange feeling of anxiety and expectancy. Although I did not now practice my religion, I wished I were back in Canada and that war was something that the history books told about. Wishing comes pretty close to praying sometimes and may be as effective. At any rate, our big test at the Front never came. On November 11 the big guns fell silent on both sides of the lines. The war was over.

We in our company, being wireless operators, were among the first to get the news. We also got the news that we were to stay on during the long occupational march into Germany. The incident was not without its lighter sides, such as my first bout with the fermented grape.

Almost anything would have been better to drink than the terrible dysentery-giving French water, so many soldiers drank wine or beer, if they could get it. After the Armistice it was much easier to acquire because we were allowed more contact with the civilians in the villages we passed through.

The water and the wine were both excellent in Germany, although experience with the latter was new to me having been a teetotaler all my life. One fine afternoon some buddies asked me to come with them for a stroll through the countryside where the wine was only surpassed in quality by the beauty of the local girls. We soon found an inn where the wine indeed was potable and the girls pretty and flirtatious.

It only took two glasses to turn my head slowly around to

thoughts of imminent illness. I didn't like the feeling of unsteadiness and my tongue was like a piece of felt. After stumbling and seeing double on the way back to the barracks, I vowed never to touch wine or intoxicants again. But before long I witnessed a new use for wine and several of my comrades owed their lives to its use.

More particularly, they owed their lives to a fine old German woman who used the wine to save them from certain death from the 'flu. Like millions of others, soldiers at the end of the war were dying from influenza which had spread around the world. One after another, men in my company fell ill. They were taken away to hospital from the old farmhouse where we were billeted and never returned. The old German woman who owned the farm asked me what happened to the men from her house. I told her they had died.

When the next soldier in her house became ill, she refused to let him go and instead asked me to bring him down to the kitchen where she put a goose-down quilt around him and seated him in front of a roaring fireplace. She placed the feverish man's feet into a tub of hot water up to his knees then administered mug after mug of a strong potion.

When I asked what was in the medicine, she smiled. "Wine," she said in English. "Moselle wine . . . very goot." I couldn't believe it. All wine did for me was to make me feel woozy but the soldier was soon sweating heavily and we took him back upstairs where a second heavy quilt was put over him on the bed.

By the morning the 'flu symptoms had disappeared. I was astounded that a simple home remedy could cure such a serious illness. I have never had much faith in doctors or hospitals; perhaps there is a time when we all feel the need of them. I know that my own father was a doctor of a rare breed. He was a healer who had great respect for folk remedies and often used anything at hand to effect a cure, if it was at all possible. All I know is that the old German woman treated my friend John Schoenberg, who lived, while Karl Christensen went to the hospital and died there.

I had a renewed respect for the Germans. When we first moved into the occupied country my attitude had been: "If they want to talk to me, let them learn to speak English." I soon found it was logical to learn some German and with a German-English dictionary and the help of the people I soon had enough command of the language to communicate with the natives. I discovered the Germans were very much like the people back home.

At long last the Treaty of Versailles was signed ending the "War To End All Wars" and the Allied soldiers were "demobbed" and allowed to return home. I was first put aboard a train, then a large troopship which landed me at Newport News, Virginia. Officially discharged with the rank of sergeant at Fort Lawton, Washington, I climbed aboard a train to Vancouver where I bought myself a suit of clothes to replace my uniform.

With some of my discharge pay, I also bought a new rifle and a one-way ticket to Bella Coola. It would be a long, long time before I would leave the valley again.

7

Peace
And Almost Quiet

"A man travels the world over in search of what he needs and returns home to find it." (George Moore)

"Hello, Ralph! Welcome home from the wars!" Max Heckman ran the stopping place at Atnarko. A one-armed trapper, Max was a good conversationalist who could keep you up all night with his yarns. "You're a sight for sore eyes," Max said. "You've put on some weight though. A good hike up the trail will get rid of that in a hurry."

I debated whether I should stay the night at Atnarko or try to make it to The Stillwater and stay over in the little cabin there. I chose to remain. A night at Max's place was the surest way to catch up on the latest gossip.

He told me about the men who had gone from the valley to war and had been killed and of others who would ultimately spend the rest of their lives in veteran's hospitals. I told him of my own meagre contribution to the war effort and before long it was dark and I was eager for a good night's sleep before tackling that ding-blasted trail to the lake.

The meal at Max's was typical of what I had eaten there many times before. It was simple but adequate and only cost fifty cents. I ate sourdough biscuits, dried fruit, potatoes and venison. In the winter it was venison; in the summer salmon. Aside from that, the menu never varied.

The accommodation was also standard and hadn't altered or improved since I had been there last. A smoke-begrimed room in the attic was where all the guests slept. Two double beds were covered with bedclothes that were permeated with the smell of sweat and smoke. As a special consideration for the next lodger, it was etiquette that everyone hang the bedding over a rafter so that mice wouldn't set up housekeeping in it.

The cookstove and wood heater downstairs kept the building cozy. I would sit on a mouse-proof box that doubled as seat and storage area and pore over all the correspondence that had come in since the time I had been there last. I would read and answer letters while Max yammered away. Seed catalogues and books and magazines were all treated with respect and often I sat up all night reading by candlelight. Replies to letters were completed by morning so they could go out on the earliest mail.

Next morning was bright and clear with just a halo of mist around the mountain tops. I said goodbye to Max and began to walk up the roughest part of the trail. Improvements had been made since I had been away; some had begun before the war. Settlers worked on the trail from the junction of the Atnarko and Hotnarko Rivers to The Stillwater. A large bridge had been built across the Atnarko just at the start of a granite cliff which rose steeply at that point.

More bridges were required upstream in order to return the trail to the east side of the valley. The bridges, large and small, were eventually washed away, the largest one lasting until a huge flood in June 1948. The three mile section of trail between The Stillwater and Lonesome Lake was not completed when I returned in 1919. It now runs on the west side of the valley and is on river level most of the way except for two short stretches of about fifteen feet. It is very dark here and the sun has to battle its way through shadows cast by towering Douglas firs, cedars and cottonwoods. It always gave me a creepy feeling going through that area that I dubbed The Valley of Shadows. It felt good to get out into the sunshine again.

On this return home, nothing could daunt me. I climbed around stumps and fallen logs, under dipping branches and through dense underbrush, over rocks and roots. I could see however that a great deal of work would have to be done to improve the trail so it could be navigated safely year around by man and beast.

Later on, I expanded this old trapper's trail to make it possible for horses to negotiate. In 1926 I cut out a horse trail around the west side of Lonesome Lake for five miles. Then I swam the horses across a narrow place in the lake to where the trail continued on the east side to the farm. During freeze-up, but before the ice was thick enough to cross, horses could not be moved in by this method so I scratched a rough trail out of the rocky hillside the rest of the way to the south end of Lonesome Lake on the west side.

I was walking now in my army boots, the only footwear I owned. In winter I would follow the pattern I had adopted before: Strap nail-studded wooden platforms to my rubber-soled boots. These platforms were removed after I had passed the icy areas.

About noon I came to a sparkling creek and set my rifle against a log while I knelt to drink. I had my mouth in the water when I suddenly thought, what if a grizzly came along right now? I looked up just as a huge head poked around a stump in front of me. I leaped back and grabbed the rifle. The sudden movement startled the bear so he turned and ran off up the trail.

I heaved a sigh of relief and finished drinking. This was not to be my last bear sighting of the day. I had learned by experience that sharing game trails with these huge brutes led to frequent encounters. Sometimes the bears just lit out into the bush; other times they charged. As I have noted, they are extremely unpredictable beasts and should always be approached with utmost caution. To cut down on the element of surprise, I used to whistle or sing or smack at stumps and trees with a stick to create noise.

At the lake at last I fashioned a pair of oars for a hastily-built raft. There was no sign of the dugout I had cached there when I went away. Just as I shoved off, I spotted two small black bears on the shore. I shot both and put them aboard. They had been living on berries on the mountainside and would be good to eat. I was thankful for this bounty because now there would be fresh meat for several days, grease for cooking and for waterproofing my boots and the hide would bring some money when sold to the Hudson's Bay Company.

Some people find it amusing to learn of the many uses I found for bear grease. It is a fact that I made quite edible doughnuts with lard from the bear. I even used it for medicinal purposes and rubbed it on to ward off mosquitoes and black flies. I was telling Lester Dorsey, Len Butler and Andy Christianson about this one day and described to them an incident in which I had been chased by a bear while generously coated with bear grease.

"I was walking on a narrow trail and didn't have my rifle with me," I said. "I looked over my shoulder and saw a bear behind me. I quickened my pace and the bear kept up. So I dived under a fallen tree and the bear kept going. You know, "I said, "I don't think that bear smelled me." Lester said: "On the contrary, Ralph. The bear **did** smell you!"

Well . . . they could laugh if they wanted to. I only wished all my encounters with them had been as amusing. This particular day was eventful but there was no danger involved. Then about two miles from the head of the lake I saw another small bear walking on the beach. I was too far past him to get off a sure shot but in my eagerness I fired anyway. I saw the bullet hit the water and richochet. I couldn't see if I'd hit the bear or not.

Although I hated to have to row that overloaded raft all the way back to shore, I felt duty-bound to find out what happened to the bear. It would serve me right for being greedy. I didn't really require another bear, although the hide would be worth a few dollars. The best reason for going back was to make sure the bear was dead and not just wounded. As I've already stressed, a wounded bear is neither good for himself nor others.

I was relieved to find his carcass where he had dropped, a few feet away from where he had been hit in the back of the neck by the richoceting bullet. Now I had three bears on the raft, food for a few weeks, hides for sale or warmth, and about six inches of water to sit in. It was a very unstable craft that I arrived home in.

What a homecoming! No one had been near my place in the two years I had been away and already Mother Nature

93

was making plans to take over again. Second growth trees were making appearances in the fields and the garden looked like a weed display. A large number of fruit trees had been nipped by the frost or killed by animals nibbling at their trunks.

All in all, the homestead had weathered well. The house and the big birch trees around it were sound and secure. It felt good. The nearby babbling brook, which I called Home Creek, was swollen with the runoff from the snow that melted up 7500 foot Mount Kappan.

Almost immediately I began to clear more land and to get my traps ready for the trapline. A week later Earle joined me. He brought with him a black and tan collie named Snoops. It was an appropriate name because the dog had an insatiable curiosity that often got him into trouble. But he was excellent company.

We decided to scout my trapline. It had not been touched for nearly two years and the area was well-stocked with beaver, muskrat and mink. Another of the dugouts had broken loose and drifted down the river so Earle and I duplicated our feat of many years ago and built a boat from lumber we sawed from a cedar tree.

We put in a centerboard well and a clamp to hold a mast near the front of the boat so we could either sail it or pull up the centerboard and row it. What a far cry it was from the primitive craft Frank Ratcliff and I had rowed down Turner Lake when I first came to look at Lonesome Lake.

After we had done a tour of my trapline, and Earle had picked up some firsthand knowledge on how to bait and unload a trap, we made plans to establish another trapline for him. It was January and in our snowshoes we trooped over the mountain to the west and down into the valley of the Talchako which is the real head of the Bella Coola River. It comes out from under a big glacier and snowfield.

We were weighted down with traps, bait, axes, rifles and enough food for a week. We carried a light blanket each but that was not enough to keep us warm so "night trees" had to be found. The Ratcliffs had taught me how to prepare a "night tree" which was better than any fireplace for sheer comfort. The trick is to find a large, hollow-hearted balsam.

We found one easily the first two nights but on the third night we had to settle for a huge dead cedar. The problem was it would only burn as long as wood was piled around it. We took turns on wood detail which had to be done by firelight but even taking it turn about, it was a long, cold night.

Then next morning we followed up the valley until we were halted by the perpendicular edge of a forty five mile tongue of glacial ice, 200 feet wide and sixty feet high, an offshoot of a gigantic glacier miles away in the distance. A stream of thick, gray pulverized rock and water flowed from the depths of the cavern beneath the ice, the source of the Talchako River. There were stories of gold being found in the area but I was never able to substantiate any finds and never had the time to go looking for anything so elusive as gold at the end of a glacier.

The timber on the lower slopes and along the river bottom consisted of large balsam, cedar, spruce and an undergrowth of young cedar and Douglas fir. It was about a half a mile from the ice to big timber through a spread of glacial boulders and gravel. "I think this is about as far as we can go," I told Earle. "Let's set the rest of the traps and head for home. With the traps we've set out in the Atnarko and Eastfork, we should have enough to keep both of us in fur money for the year."

We rested for a couple of days then went out to check our separate traplines, Earle to the line set in the Talchako and I to the Atnarko and Eastfork. I got back early because I was well acquainted with the line and while waiting for Earle continued to burn down trees and clear brush. Each day I looked up the river to see if Earle was in sight, but he never showed up.

After two more days I began to get worried. The next morning, after a sleepless night, I decided to go look for him. Just as I was getting my gear prepared, he strolled in. "Where have you been?" I asked. "I got lost," he said. "There was a heavy mist and I must have circled around and around for a couple of days before it lifted and I got my bearings." He had been on a divide between Kidney Lake and a creek leading down into the Talchako Valley.

"I was just coming out to look for you," I told him. "It's just as well you didn't," Earle replied. "It snowed heavily as I was baiting and unloading traps and it was quite a while before I realized I was following in my same footsteps. If you came along you probably would have gone on circling too."

We agreed after that to give each other a few days extra time before starting to panic. If one person is lost and another person goes looking for him and gets lost, it does not accomplish much. That particular trapline continued to be hazardous because of its sudden and mysterious mists and snow storms, so we called it "Circle Divide".

As predicted, our packsacks bulged with furs that winter and with prices high, we each were able to put aside some money for the next year and for acquisitions. I badly required some horses to help me work the land and to carry in supplies so in the summer of 1920 I decided to walk east across country to where Tom Englebretson ran some horses at a place called Towdystan Lake. Tom and I had become good friends while working together on the telegraph line before the war.

I hiked up the valley of the East Fork of the Atnarko River to near Charlotte Lake. I climbed a ridge from which I could see a butte at the back of where Tom's homestead was supposed to be located. I decided to test my skill with a compass, and crossing the land of meadows and ridges, laced with old Indian trails, I came out on a telegraph line only about a mile south of my destination.

"Well, I'll be a ringtailed polecat!" Tom exclaimed when I arrived at his doorstep. "Look who's here. Old Ralph Edwards. I'd heard you had gone back to the States to make a career out of the army." "Not me," I said. "I couldn't wait to get back here and settle this land for good and all."

We went inside his small cabin and while he boiled some coffee we exchanged stories. "Is this a social visit, or are you after something?" Tom said. He knew how practical I was and that I wouldn't walk this far just to spin a yarn. "I'm looking for a good horse, " I said. "Well," Tom replied, "I got lots of them. Some are better than others. You're welcome to take your pick but it'll mean a lot of ridin' 'cause those critters don't stay long in one place and right now they're all over hell's half acre."

Early in the morning I saddled a pony Tom lent me and began to comb the range looking for a likely horse. After a long day in the saddle I settled on a dapple-brown colt with a white tail and mane. He was just over a year old with lots of spirit.

My first job was to curb some of that spirit and in the high-walled corral near Tom's house I soon had him coming when I called, instead of showing me his heels, which he preferred to do at first. Next, I got him to allow me to lead him to water.

There is something to that old adage about leading a horse to water. This colt reared up and refused to drink, falling over backwards and rolling his eyes. He did that several times until I made him understand that he was not going to get anything to drink unless he did it with a rope around his neck.

He then drank thirstily and our first argument was over. Satisfied that I had found the right horse for me, I paid Tom ten dollars and led the horse to the Atnarko. The problem now was to get him across the lake. There was only one solution and that was to float him over on a raft. I had built his confidence in me by then and by taking it slow and easy and giving him many pats and crooning in his ear, I got him safely to the other side.

Tom had warned me that the horse had been born late and had suffered through his first winter. However, he matured well on timothy and clover and blue grass in my pasture and when I met Tom on the trail a few months later he could scarcely believe that this fine big horse I was riding was the skinny runt he had sold me. "What are you calling him?" Tom asked. "Ginty," I said.

Ginty became the most important animal on my farm for many years. I will detail more adventures with him later on. First, I would like to recount some stories about "Snoops", the collie that Earle had brought to the lake for me.

When Snoops arrived I had one room in the house which

I used to store pelts awaiting sale in Bella Coola. It was a twelve foot by nine foot room which had not yet had the windows cut out of the logs. Snoops, who had a very amiable disposition at most times, had a keen sense of smell and one odor above all others nearly drove him mad. At the smell of bear he went into a frenzy.

I went into the room where the hides were stored one day and the dog nearly had a fit barking. He was terrified. To soothe him, I reached toward his back and touched him on the neck. He must have thought a bear had him. When he realized it was just me, I swear that dog laughed in relief. They say that dogs are the only animals other than humans aware of the ludicrous. I believe it.

We had many a good laugh together, but one adventure was almost his last. Aside from Whitie, who had gone back to Walter Ratcliff, Snoops was the first dog to stay at the farm. Before he took up residence I had placed oatmeal soaked in strychnine all around the house and barn to control the increasing mice population. When Snoops arrived I carefully went around and collected the poison but obviously I missed a little piece which the curious dog ate. He went into convulsions and fell down with his head thrown back in the classic pose of the strychnine victim.

Knowing that the poison paralyzes the diaphram, I applied pressure at that point, then relaxed it, then applied pressure again, as with a drowning victim. The dog responded but in a few minutes he had another convulsion and I had to repeat the treatment. This was done several times before the convulsions finally subsided. Sick as he was, he was so well housebroken that as soon as he could stand without convulsing, he ran outside to relieve himself.

Like humans, dogs and other animals have to be given some guidelines to modify their behavior. Some learn; others never do. Stealing food from a wilderness stockpile is a serious offense. I placed a chunk of bacon on a bunk in one of my trapline cabins one day and while I was frying a few slices from it over an open pit fire, Snoops gobbled up the uncut piece.

I gave him several sharp smacks and bawled him out for such greedy behavior. This taught him a lesson and I never again had to take such action, for that particular crime. From then on he never took anything that was not given to him. He complained, of course, and sometimes if I was cooking a delicacy which he could share, I gave him some. But there were things which he could not or should not eat and when it was something that he especially fancied, he would give a loud sigh and purposely turn his head so he would not be tempted.

When I acquired cattle, Snoops kept a close watch on them for me, learning hand signals which he could discern even while in full pursuit of the herd. He was also incredibly patient, faithful and obedient and whenever I was down the valley visiting friends, all I had to do was whisper: "Go way back and sit down" and he would immediately withdraw and stay there until I told him to leave, his mournful eyes fixed on me, waiting for a signal to come forward.

I became extremely fond of Snoops but unfortunately one night when I had to camp on the lake in the boat, Snoops was shivering violently, which was not like him. Thinking it was too cold for him in the boat, I put him ashore. He cried for a while, but then was quiet.

In the morning I couldn't find him despite a thorough search. I concluded that he might have started for home around the lake. For days I watched and waited for him but he never showed up. I hiked along trails calling his name and whistling but no Snoops came running. I finally had to accept the truth that he probably was suffering from distemper and had been killed by a wolf or a bear while he was in his weakened condition. Poor old Snoops. I missed him dearly.

Although Snoops was gone, I still had Ginty and added to my animal kingdom by buying two more horses. When my nearest neighbor, John Ratcliff, abandoned his homestead at the upper end of The Stillwater, I was able to buy a little bay mare called Queen and a coach horse named Blue. Blue had once pulled stage coaches on the old Cariboo Wagon road through the Fraser Canyon.

I now had a three horse pack train and with a trail gouged out of the rock and some adequate bridges, I could bring in supplies farther than I could before and in greater quantity. My homestead was rapidly taking shape. I also acquired, through the agency of John Hober, a merchant who lived at Firvale, about forty miles from Bella Coola, a one-horse Massey-Harris mower and horse rake, a twelve inch plough and other pieces of farming equipment. In order to get them to Lonesome Lake I had to dismantle them and load them on the horses. I didn't bother with any wooden parts but made them at the farm when I reassembled the rest.

Old Blue had been out of work for a long time and getting him back into shape was worse than working with a new horse. When I say he was like a mule, I mean it literally. Mules have a tendency to inflate their lungs so it makes it difficult, if not impossible, to saddle or harness them properly. They are able to hold the air in their lungs so no matter how tight you make the cinch, when they let out their breath, the rigging is loose. Smart mule packers would give the mule an unexpected kick in the abdomen and tighten the cinch as they expelled the air in a grunt.

Old Blue was like that. A number of times his harness fell off like an oversize brassiere. Then at a crucial moment, he would exhale loudly and buck his load all over the landscape. On the day I moved the machinery in, I chose Ginty to carry the two rake wheels because he was the tallest of the three horses. Blue was elected to pack the mower wheels and Queen was given some of the smaller pieces to haul. The ropes were damp when I loaded up and as they dried out in the sun they lengthened and became loose. Blue decided - in his traditional fashion - to unload.

I was leading Queen and driving Ginty ahead of me, Blue bringing up the rear. He began to run and buck. Queen stayed with me. I couldn't abandon the other two horses just to find Blue so was reduced to whistling and cursing. After a time he returned, his saddle under his belly and the pack ropes trailing behind him. The wheels were gone.

Ornery critter that he was, he then lowered his head and charged through the pack train and down a trail that led to a surveyor's camp in a clearing below me. The surveyors, recognizing a runaway nag from the trailing gear, caught and held him until I got down to their camp, after securing the other horses at a safe place along the trail above. Blue expected a good beating but I fooled him. I packed him up with the stuff he'd dropped and made him continue the journey with the rest of us.

The trails and roads - if you can dignify them with those terms - were mostly of broken rock that horses could not travel very far on without developing sore feet. With no blacksmiths between Lonesome Lake and Bella Coola, I had to learn to shoe horses myself. At first they didn't like having nails pounded into their hooves and resented the heavy objects on their feet but once they found it was easier to walk on rock with steel shoes, they submitted to my rather clumsy shoeing procedure.

In May 1920, after a successful winter's trapping, I loaded old Ginty with furs to take down the valley to sell. I was leading Ginty by a halter and short tie rope. Suddenly he stopped and threw up his head, his ears straight ahead. Anyone who has seen a horse or mule with ears pointed straight ahead recognizes an animal on standby alert.

I looked in the direction of a brown mass in the grass and brush on the lower side of the road. The trail at that point ran along the bottom of a very steep hill and directly ahead a huge rock marked the start of a game trail leading up a mountain. The brown mass raised its head and I saw that it was a grizzly grubbing for skunk cabbage.

Thinking the bear would do as many did when I yelled and waved my hat at them, I employed this tactic. Instead of running up the hill, the bear jumped into the road and started for me. I continued to wave my big straw hat and yell but he came on regardless. Ginty decided to be elsewhere. Back up the road we went, horse, followed by man, followed by bear.

The lead rope was short and I was in danger of being pulled under Ginty's pounding hooves so I let go the rope and turned my body so as to roll across a large fir log that was lying in a swamp. The upper end of the log was in a mass of willows and alders and I dove straight in, burying my face in my arms on the ground.

I recalled the old advice about the way to outfox a bear is to play dead. It might be true, I thought. I hoped. As I lay there, scarcely breathing, I could hear the oncoming grunts. When last I looked, he was about three bear jumps behind me but I was not going to look up now to make new calculations. It was obvious he was very close to the log I was behind. I could almost smell his breath. "Grunt, snort, sniff, sniff," was followed by sounds of breaking sticks and underbrush as he moved away.

After a short but discreet wait, I got up and walked back to the trail, expecting to have to go about six miles to locate Ginty. I had gone perhaps 200 yards when I saw him coming back looking for me. He whinnied. His pack of furs was still miraculously in order.

It was a six mile ride to Hober's place where I would be spending the night but we seemed to fly down that stretch of moonlit emptiness and soon I was comfortably seated in their livingroom recounting my close brush with the bear.

The elder Hobers, flanked by children of various ages, listened intently. The eldest, an attactive teenager named Ethel, was particularly attentive. "That brute was within biting distance of any part of my body," I said. "At one time he was so close I could hear his grunting and sniffing. How he ever missed me is anybody's guess."

My tale was not having the expected response. Clearly, the Hobers were not impressed. "Really," I stressed, holding up my arms, "that bear was no more than a foot away at one point." "Sure, Ralph," old man Hober said. "We believe you. Millions wouldn't." He was grinning ear to ear.

I shrugged my shoulders and the subject was changed. Mrs. Hober came into the room and announced that dinner was about to be served. I was glad that I had worn my Sunday best. While it was not the store-bought suit I had brought back from the war with me, it was the runnerup - a brand new pair of blue denim coveralls.

As I walked into the kitchen, one of the Hober children suddenly yelled: "Hey dad, look at this!" Mr. Hober looked where the child was pointing. It was at my left pant leg. Seen clearly in the yellow dust from the road was a huge bear paw mark on the cloth.

No more words were necessary to describe my close brush with the grizzly bear!

8

No Longer Lonesome
At Lonesome Lake

"When you meet a young lady you like, you naturally commence to get interested." (Ralph Edwards)

Although I had gotten over my feelings of regret for the loss of my first love, Helen Cathie, I still had moments when loneliness was my only companion. I worked an eighteen hour day, made trips to Atnarko for mail and sometimes went all the way to Bella Coola for supplies. Still the emptiness in my life cried out to be filled.

The companionship of Snoops and Ginty helped; I often found myself talking aloud to them about things they would have no knowledge of, but they were good listeners. But nothing could assuage the terrible longing for the missing element - a woman in my life.

More and more I found excuses to visit Firvale, ostensibly to see the Ratcliffs, but I also spent a good deal of the time at the Hobers. John Hober reminded me of some of my relatives, particularly of uncle Will, although he was younger and spoke to me as an equal. We spent long hours talking about religion and politics.

Although I had long ago stopped practicing the teachings of the Adventist religion, I could still argue its merits and defects and frequently my views clashed violently with those held by John Hober, himself a devoted Adventist in a community established by members of that faith. However, he never lost patience with me, perhaps hoping that one day I would return to the fold.

I admired the valley Adventists. They were successful farmers, honest, clean and orderly. It was Bill Graham, another Adventist, who sold me the first fruit trees I planted at the lake. But as much as I tried to convince myself that I was taking these long trips into Firvale to talk religion with John Hober and to keep in touch with the Ratcliffs, the real reason was Ethel Hober.

Ethel was eighteen, while I was thirty one, quite an age span. However, she carried herself with such lady-like grace and spoke with a maturity that belied the number of years she actually claimed, that I couldn't help admiring her. And when you meet a young lady you like, you naturally commence to get interested.

The problem was, how to get Ethel to like me? She didn't seem particularly interested. Why should she be? There were many younger men in the valley and I was also slightly shorter than she was. Not that these considerations stopped me from pressing my case. Ethel was a challenge and I enjoy a challenge. Occasionally she would come into the parlor while John Hober and I discussed politics or religion but she never took part in the discussions. Once or twice I caught her smiling when I scored a point and frowning at me when she found something to disagree with.

The incident over the bear paw mark on my coveralls seemed to make an impression on Ethel that nothing I had said or done to date had been able to accomplish. She laughed outright at my protestations and defense of the close encounter and later, when the truth was revealed, she looked right at me with eyes full of merriment. I felt myself blushing several times during dinner whenever she regarded me.

Ethel continued to intrude on my thoughts during the next few months. It was frustrating being at Lonesome Lake without her and not much better seeing her but not being able to talk to or touch her at her parent's place. The Hobers were very strict. No parlor romancing; no hand-holding; no touches or stolen kisses in darkened hallways. In short, no rewards for all that hiking across mountains, fording of streams or rafting of lakes. To say nothing of braving blinding snow and freezing rain in the wintertime. Although Ethel slowly began to show some interest, I suspect it was her mother who understood that the bearded pioneer from Lonesome Lake had more on his mind than just discussions with her husband.

I felt I had to take some dramatic action so one weekend in the fall of 1922 I asked Mrs. Hober and Ethel to come spend a week at The Birches. They agreed. I came down to Firvale to escort them by horseback to The Stillwater and then along the rugged trail and up the lake to the farm. Mrs. Hober, of good pioneer stock from Ponoka, Alberta, fared well on the trip and Ethel also took it in her stride.

My original doubts about whether she would be too frail to handle the job of pack horse - which she would have to become if she were to be mistress of Lonesome Lake - disappeared. Her long legs and strong, broad shoulders indicated her body was as strong as her spirit.

Both women loved Lonesome Lake and were enchanted with the view. A thoughtful chaperon, Mrs. Hober left us alone when it was propitious to do so, but was on hand when it was convenient - when meals needed preparing or other mundane chores had to be completed. Meanwhile, Ethel and I began to get to know each other. I took her for long walks and on short hunting and trapping trips. She seemed to know a great deal about flora and fauna for a "town girl", and I was impressed with how quickly she learned.

As the week drew to a close, I felt I had to make another move - and fast. I rehearsed a half a dozen ways to ask her to marry me. To be truthful, I don't even recall what I **did** say. I'm sure my proposal was as clumsy as any delivered by a smitten swain in the history of man. I must have communicated my request in some fashion because when we tramped back along that treacherous trail and the long ride back to Firvale, Ethel and I had somehow become engaged.

Mr. and Mrs. Hober were pleased and on August 23, 1923, we were married in the Hober's home. Everyone within miles of the little settlement came to wish us well. It was a simple Adventist ceremony and a few hours afterward I helped Ethel into Ginty's saddle, climbed aboard my own horse and we headed toward home. Lonesome lake was not going to be Lonesome any longer.

Before long Ethel got her first opportunity to test her mettle as a wilderness bride. During the next few months she wielded a scythe and fork alongside me in the hay field. She ate, slept and cooked in the cool, tiny cabins on the trapline, faced total insolation while I was away, and faced the ever-present danger of attack from wild animals.

Although I had been in the bush for a long time now, I never stopped thinking about the danger of attack. It was always there in the back of my mind; if I hadn't thought about danger constantly, I wouldn't have been alive to tell this story. This caution had nothing to do with being either courageous or afraid. It had to do with being careful. In the bush you develop a sense of awareness, like an animal, that is almost as much a part of you as your shadow that you can't shake off.

I was often concerned for Ethel and for her safety and happiness but if she was scared she never showed it. She proved to be a remarkably self-possessed woman. She had work to do and she did it. In time to come she milked cows in an open unfenced field where she could hear grizzly bears grunting and snorting only a short distance away.

Adventurous and dangerous times were ahead of us. Right now more romantic matters were on the schedule. Our "honeymoon trip" ended at The Stillwater. I planned to winter the horses on the natural meadows there and while Ethel built a fire and made Johnny Ratcliff's cabin cozy, I went off to hunt for something appropriate for the honeymoon feast.

With a choice of bear, moose, deer or goat, I chose mountain goat, a delicacy because it was the most difficult to get. The area I chose to scout was the heavily-treed and rocky face of Mount Marvin, a 7500 foot protrusion in the Coastal Range, a good long hike from The Stillwater cabin. I hoped it would be worth it. Nothing would be more galling than to go back to my bride empty handed.

Within two hours I spotted a goat, its head peeping from behind some rocks, almost in front of me. I aimed my rifle and fired; the goat disappeared. At first I figured I had missed but after clambering up the crags to the spot where she had been, I discovered more than I had bargained for. The mother had been killed instantly and so was her kid, who must have been standing directly behind her. The bullet had passed cleanly through both bodies. My jubilation at getting the goat for Ethel was modified by a slight twinge of guilt, a feeling . . . I couldn't quite define.

I dressed the animals, packing the kid inside the mother's carcass, tied them up with straps made from the leg skins and carried the game down to the cabin. Ethel was delighted. "What a beautiful surprise," she said. "We never had much meat at home. My parents were practically vegetarians, you know. This will be delicious." And it was. "Just like young chicken," Ethel exclaimed.

She had already learned how to fish and was adept at coaxing trout onto her line. She was willing to experiment with most wild and domesticated meats. She had a knowledge of herbs and spices and could blend the seasonings so all dishes tasted just right. But one thing she would not abide was pork, taboo to devout Adventists. It was still too warm in the season to stock the larder with bear or venison so we had to eat other types of meat, such as bacon, which would not spoil.

"I will not eat bacon. Nor will I cook it for you to eat," Ethel declared. "It's against my religion to eat animals with cloven hooves. And that is that!" It was our first quarrel. Not so much a quarrel but Ethel's declaration of independence.

I didn't argue with her. I had to leave for a week-long tramp of the traplines and didn't want to depart with bad feelings between us. As I was packing my supplies, I casually mentioned that I was leaving behind a good-sized portion of the bacon supply. "I can come home to it if you change you mind about cooking some for me," I said. She didn't reply. We said our goodbyes and off I went.

When I returned I noticed a large piece of the bacon had disappeared. Obviously sometime during my absence Ethel had pitted her religious scruples against pork and her hunger for meat and the bacon had won. After that there was no more talk about religion and pork.

Ethel and I disagreed on very few things. We were too busy cutting six month's hay to bicker over silly trifles. Our joint effort made quick work of the job and when the hay was dried and stacked, we packed as many supplies as we could into our rucksacks and trudged up the trail to Lonesome Lake and The Birches, the house I had built for the woman I would spend the rest of my life with. My dream was all coming true.

Ethel had seen the house before, of course, during the visit with her mother. It was different now. There was no chaperone and a distinct change came over Ethel. This was **her** house and I could sense the difference in her attitude toward it and me, as part of it. With the addition of a few wild flowers in jam jars, handmade curtains and a table cloth from sacking, a chair angled a certain way - the feminine touch I suppose you call it - and the house took on a feeling of permanency.

Although we carried in most of the wedding gifts - coffee pot, roasting pan, assorted kitchen utensils and tools, we still had one large present to bring in to Lonesome Lake. Ethel's parents had given us a part-Ayrshire milk cow name Maybelle. We decided to go back together to get her.

We rowed down the lake, hiked over the trail to The Stillwater, collected two horses in the hay meadow, then rode to Firvale to claim our milk, cream and butter supply: Maybell, a four-legged package of dairy products who would sustain us through many a winter. At first she followed along the trail behind us without much hesitation. Cows are not as good at walking as horses but some are better than others. Maybelle was one of the good ones.

After we left the horses at The Stillwater she maintained her pace like a veteran. Then we reached a place where we had to cross the Atnarko River. It was wide and deep and Maybelle did not like the look of it at all. She balked, rolling her big brown eyes in fear.

We had cached a boat there but it was out of the question that all three of us, or any combination of cow and human, could travel together in that fragile craft. Maybelle was fated to swim and that was all there was to it. She braced herself, hooves anchored in the gravelly shore of the river. Ignoring her protests, I tied her to the stern; Ethel jumped into the boat and placed the oars in position. I pushed the boat off from shore and at the same time leaped in, giving Maybelle's rope a vigorous yank.

Ethel rowed into the fast-flowing stream. Maybelle plunged suddenly forward and thrashed about trying to maintain her footing. For a few moments she touched bottom, then as it fell away from under her, she went beneath the water and came up snorting. Under she went again. She got short of air and came up a third time. She now gained confidence, along with buoyancy, and began to swim like a muskrat. Ethel rowed as hard as she could and Maybelle stayed right with us.

That old milk cow ended up liking the water - as did all Ayrshire cattle we later purchased or raised - and often we milked her right from the boat. We would take a bucket down to the head of the lake where Maybelle was on range and just run the boat under her udder. She would stand perfectly still in knee-high water while the milking was performed.

We added more cattle over the years until the herd reached a total of fourteen but long before then we decided to get a shorthorn bull. I ordered one from a ranch in Golden, B.C., a yearling from a good family. The bull arrived at Bella Coola on the boat and I picked up Ginty at The Stillwater and rode out to bring the bull in.

Before we were half way back to the farm, poor Ginty and the bull were worn out, the bull from straining against the lead rope and Ginty from leaning into it, forcing the bull to follow. I too was exhausted from superintending the operation. That night at camp Ginty was too tired to eat and just fell into a heap. After eating a light supper, I made sure both horse and bull were well-tethered, then became my own heap. Next thing I knew it was daylight and time to hit the worst part of the trail.

That trail, as already noted, had some narrow spots where

there was only room for one man or beast to pass over at a time. When packing in provisions, kegs of nails, bulky rolls and assorted wheels, barrels, sacks and bales, a single wrong step by the animal could mean a long drop to the rocky river below.

One of our horses did take such a tumble but he was so heavily loaded and cushioned that he slid more on the stuff he was carrying than on his hide so he was not badly injured. Getting him back up onto the trail was harder on him, and me, than the fall.

The yearling bull had more luck. He led better after I got him to The Stillwater where Johnny Ratcliff was in residence. Johnny got behind and pushed the bull while I pulled him. Unlike the Ayrshire cattle, the bull would not swim the river. This meant a fifteen mile detour up the valley beyond the route where we had taken Maybelle in. It was a delaying tactic; he could not avoid getting his feet wet eventually. On account of some unscaleable bluffs at the foot of the lake, he had to swim a short stretch of water behind the boat.

Johnny held the rope while I manned the oars. The bull came snorting and kicking into the water, nearly drowning himself repeatedly. How else can you explain his ridiculous tactics? He stuck his head under the water and kept it there and it was all that Johnny could do to force him to raise it so he could breathe. I had never seen such an obstinate creature. Finally, when he must have been bloated with water, he floated on his side, all four feet above the water, looking like a leather bag full of wind.

Even when we grounded the boat and the water was only six inches deep at the end of the rope, the bull tried to get his head under again. With a few well-aimed kicks and shoves we got the ornery cuss out onto the dry land. The next spring I began to wonder if he had been worth the effort. He ate water hemlock (poison parsnip) and died. We eventually lost three cattle to this noxious weed and Ethel and I became so fed up we put on our gumboots and went about with gunny sacks, gathering up all the plants we could find, not only at home but on range up the long valley.

111

Poison parsnips grow underwater. Some animals seem to have no trouble digesting them. Beaver, for example, eat the tops and roots but reject the bulbs. Growing as they do at the edge of the water, they are among the first plants to show new growth in the spring, tempting the greenery-starved cattle to eat them. The foliage is harmless, but to cattle the bulbs are fatal.

There were other duties to attend to with the long winter coming on. Luckily we had good luck with the garden that spring and summer and after packing in flour, sugar, salt and other commodities necessary for canning produce, Ethel bottled jar after jar of precious preserves for winter dining. Meat, fish, vegetables and fruit all went into quart sealers. The root cellar under the house stored potatoes, turnips, carrots and other vegetables that tasted as fresh as store-purchased when revived in Ethel's busy kitchen.

While we were taking breathers from these chores I cut down trees and cleared out deadfall for wood for the stoves, hunted, fished and built fences. We also took advantage of the salmon spawning period in which vast numbers of these incredible fish with the retentive memories return to the tiny stream and creek pools in British Columbia where they were born. They lay their eggs, fertilize them, and die. Their rotting bodies literally clog the creeks for several weeks every fall.

We would row up the Atnarko River and with pitchforks Ethel and I would spear the boat full with dead, bloated, mottled salmon. Buried in the soil, they made excellent fertilizer. Such planning was essential. The soil was rich but its richness must be maintained. We continued this practise for many years and as our garden plot and orchard increased in size, so did our food production.

Winter was at our door again and it is cold on Lonesome Lake, particularly in January when the temperature goes down to -16°F. and on the coldest days the mercury can plummet to -46°F. I continued to service my trapline, spending long nights in the small cabins Earle and I had built or inherited from earlier trappers. For various reasons, bad weather delays sometimes, I would be forced to sleep outdoors. A "night tree" or an open fire was the only source of heat and either cedar or balsam boughs became my bed. If I had to snowshoe along the trapline, I used my snowshoes for the bed.

Many people caught outside in very cold weather fear they will freeze to death in their sleep. I never got so cold that I didn't wake up first. I learned the knack of cat-napping and had no trouble dropping off to sleep in short order. But there were many nights when it was too cold to sleep and I would lie awake, stoking the fire and listening to the voices of the forest: The sonorous hooting of owls, the querulous yapping of coyotes and the eerie, long drawn-out howls of timber wolves.

I thought often of Ethel, nineteen years old and never alone before in the winter in the woods. What could she be doing and thinking to pass the time and to keep from worrying about me? I always made a point of getting back on the day or night I had told her to expect me but this was not always possible because of weather or other unpredictable events.

My departures and arrivals, especially in the early days of our marriage, were important occasions. There was warmth and comfort in the cabin and in each other. There was conversation. Alone for a week, even the most dour of men become loquacious. Ethel and I were seldom garrulous but after a trapline trip we unwound our vocal chords and chattered like chipmunks. We would lie awake talking long after the candle had been snuffed out.

One of Ethel's most heartwarming customs was to accompany me to The Stillwater and stay in the cabin there while I trekked into Atnarko to get the mail and carry in supplies. Sending me off and greeting me with warm food and warm arms made that journey considerably more pleasant and something to look forward to.

To quell her loneliness Ethel devised ways to fill her time. There were things to do: Sewing and weaving, knitting and cleaning and cooking and baking and canning and - if the weather permitted - sawing and splitting wood. In summer and spring Ethel took the initiative and worked at everything from plucking insatiable tent caterpillars from the fruit trees to fishing and caring for the animals and learning to shoot. She became a good marksman with a small bore rifle and once had to use a larger one to shoot a grizzly that invaded our garden.

These were real life adventures but in the early days making-believe was part of Ethel's way of passing the time while I was away. She started by pretending that I was only going to be away five days instead of seven. After all, it was not necessary to count the day I left, no matter how early, nor the day I returned, no matter how late. She peopled the house with family and friends and imagined she was entertaining them with stories of our adventures, some real, some not. Some of these adventures she dared not think about.

One day I was running along the trapline; I seldom walked. As well as getting finished earlier, I stayed warm. I wasn't paying much attention and it was some time before I noticed I had dropped a mitt, probably back at a trap where I had recovered a fat, dead muskrat to store with the others in the pack on my back. In addition to a very cold hand, I was suddenly aware of something on the trail behind me. I whirled around. Four wolves were nearly upon me.

Two of the large, gray predators were ready to spring by the time I raised my rifle as far as my hip. I was lucky enough to nail both of them. Their bodies landed in the snow only a short distance away. The other two smaller animals hightailed it off the trail and into the bush. I regarded that lost mitt as a lifesaver. If my trigger finger had not been free, I might have been the bloodied heap in the trail instead of the wolves. At the very least I would have been badly slashed and bleeding by the time I had gotten into a position to defend myself.

I avoided telling Ethel about some of my adventures and misadventures; she had enough to worry about without being overly concerned with my welfare. I preferred to concentrate on positive events and on the present. People who dwell in the past or try to live in the future don't have much time for what is happening now. Also, I was more interested in her delightful chatter about what had transpired since I had been away.

She soon had quite a menagerie to care for: Chickens, cows, cats and dogs. Looking after them became almost a full-time job, but field work also had to be done. The fields that we began to open up with axe, saw, stump puller and bonfire were sweet with honey-bearing plants that blossomed almost as soon as the trees fell and the sunlight flooded in.

We sent away for books on apiculture and after learning what we would require as equipment, purchased foundation wax, smoker, gloves, veil and honey extractor and proceeded to build bee hives from home-sawed red cedar lumber. We built "Kootenay cases," boxes three inches larger than the hives, and filled the spaces between with wood shavings for insulation.

Bees in well-protected packages arrived in Bella Coola and were installed in the hives. Ethel and I enjoyed working with our buzzing friends, probably because we appreciated their industrious nature. They seemed to know that we could be trusted not to harm them, despite the fact that we stole the major portion of their output.

Only once did we have to return a swarm to its hive after the queen bee escaped and led the workers off the job into a nearby tree. Capturing them at night led to the only stinging I ever got and that was because one bee got loose from the gunny sack I placed over the swarm to return them to their cosy little home.

Bees provided us with all the honey we needed as well as increasing production in orchard and garden through pollination. We learned there are several varieties of bees in the wild country. Little gray bees, big black bees that work along the ditches and banks and the big, clumsy-looking bumblebees. They are not as clumsy as they appear and are much more efficient than the honey bee, if time spent on the job means anything. When a bumblebee lands on a flower, it goes to work immediately with no waste movements. The honey bee, on the other hand, spends quite a bit of time buzzing around before getting down to business.

In order to obtain some darker honey for variety from the pale stuff, we planted a patch of buckwheat, hoping our bees would pasture on it. They may have done but they got very

115

little nectar because hornets, blow flies and other insects worked the blossoms so assiduously that there was very little left for our domesticated variety to bring to the comb.

Our beekeeping came to a sad end years later when I foolishly forgot to put a pad of insulation on top of the hive to keep the bees warm during their winter solstice. They froze to death and we did not send for more.

Long before then, another tiny resident was to make his presence known at Lonesome Lake. Ethel informed me that she was expecting a baby. We both looked forward eagerly to the arrival and began to make plans for the new addition to the family at The Birches.

9

The Population Grows

"Fire is the test of gold; adversity, of strong men." (Senaca)

"Ralph," Ethel said, "I think it's time to go to Bella Coola."
At that particular time "going to Bella Coola." meant only one
thing. "You mean you're going to have the **baby**?" "Not right
away!" she laughed. "Soon." "How soon is soon?" "A week,
maybe more, maybe less. Probably by the time we get there."

I jokingly chastized Ethel about having a baby in the winter instead of the summer when the trip to the Bella Coola hospital would have been a lot more comfortable for her - to say
nothing of the child. Just how uncomfortable this journey was
going to be for the baby we had no way of knowing then.

It was the fall of 1924 and some snow had already arrived,
although it hadn't lasted on the ground. Warm rain and wind
often remove the November snow as soon as it lands. The most
severe weather at Lonesome Lake is likely to come after Christmas and then the snow begins to pile up and drift. This year
there had been warnings of heavy snow but to date there had
been only rain, buckets of it. It was uncomfortable but warmer
to work or travel in than snow.

Ethel made up two packs of supplies to carry with us along
the road and we scheduled how far we would walk or ride each
day. At The Stillwater cabin we would rest and get two horses
to ride to the stopping place at Atnarko, then to Stuie, the
Hober's home at Firvale, friends at Hagensborg and finally

into Bella Coola. That was our plan.

We placed enough feed and water out for the domestic animals and secured the house against the wilder varieties. Ethel seemed fit as a fiddle and cheerful as a Highland tune. She chatted gaily about the event she was about to experience, conversation being possible only on the wider stretches of the trail where two could walk abreast. On the narrower parts of the trail she followed "Chinese fashion", her stride measuring mine. Now and then I looked back and she would smile.

We caught two horses at The Stillwater and spent the night there. At dawn we saddled up and left for Atnarko. Our progress was good and the weather was fairly mild. At Firvale, John Hober insisted his daughter ride in his wagon to the hospital. Ethel felt worse in the wagon than on horseback. Neither was an ideal way for a pregnant woman to travel to deliver her first child but she bore up under the strain of the bouncing and bumping of the wagon exceptionally well.

Although the Bella Coola hospital was small and continually understaffed, it was a cheery place. There was never more than one nurse there at one time and sometimes there was none at all. An overworked, harrassed doctor was expected to handle every form of emergency from a smashed hand to a mild epidemic of whooping cough. Both Indians and whites had their babies there in an atmosphere of congeniality and friendly confusion.

"I'm not expecting any complications from this birth, Mr. Edwards," the doctor said. "No sense in you hanging around. Go to your friends' house and get some sleep. We'll let you know when the baby arrives." I felt a bit guilty leaving Ethel alone but there was no room for anxious husbands in the cluttered waitingroom.

It seemed only a few hours after I fell into a deep sleep that someone was shaking me and telling me to come to the hospital at once. "He's a fine healthy lad," the doctor said. "Not a thing to worry about. Now where is this place you're taking him to?" I told him about Lonesome Lake. He was aghast. "You mean you're going to take the mother and that new-born

118

child all the way in there in this weather? That's insane, man. You'd be better off to wait until spring and the mother and child are stronger."

I assured the doctor that there could be no waiting until spring. At least, not for me. There were animals to be fed and a trapline to be tended. After a few more cluckings from the doctor I was ushered into the room where Ethel and baby were in bed. The baby was a solemn, fine-featured chap of average size and weight. "He's in good health," the nurse said, "if the strength of his lungs is any indication." She was quite right. Stanley Bruce Edwards - the name we conferred on him - had a good set of bellows.

After a short visit at his grandparent's home at Firvale, Stanley Bruce and the other two Lonesome Lakers got ready to make the long haul home. It was now mid-November and it had turned colder, although the precipitation in the Bella Coola Valley was still in the form of cold rain. While Ethel picked up hints from her mother about bathing and feeding the baby, I collected some maple saplings and wove them into a sort of basket which I could put Stanley in when we left the horses at The Stillwater.

That first morning we stepped out into a wind that blew frozen rain like shingle nails into our faces. Stanley's first horseback ride was in his mother's arms, wrapped tightly in a flannel blanket with a heavy woolen blanket pinned around that. Almost immediately he began to fret. I asked Ethel if maybe it would be better if she stayed behind with the baby after all. "Certainly not," she said. "We're coming home now."

She continued to fuss over him but Stanley registered his protests loudly all the way to the tiny community of Stuie. Here some friends offered us the use of a vacant cabin which was as cold as the devil's heart. It sooned warmed up when I got some kindling crackling in the old wood stove. Loosened from his bindings, Stanley relaxed a little. He still was not comfortable. "What's the matter with him?" Ethel cried. "He won't stop crying." Stanley's red, perspiring face was pathetic and Ethel's persistence in trying to calm him seemed to annoy him

119

more than anything else. I wished there was something I could do to make things better for both of them. I stayed awake to make sure the cabin was warm.

In the morning it was apparent that the weather was going to get worse. This was not going to be one of those winters in which the valley snow might not appear in quantity until January. Pellets of frozen rain hit us as soon as we emerged from the warmth of the cabin. The lead horse turned its head sideways as I pulled it and its burden of supplies onto the icy trail.

Stanley began to fuss at once, his muffled moaning heard through the blankets his mother held snugly against her breast. We stopped frequently along the way to Atnarko and spent another restless night trying to comfort the squalling infant. The next day, on the way into The Stillwater, I debated whether to go back now while we had the chance. What if the baby really was ill?

The only respite in his crying was whenever Ethel changed his diaper - and this should have been a clue to his discomfort. During this procedure, Stanley would stop crying, but Ethel figured it was because he was enjoying the warm, soft dryness. Bathing him, even in the warmth of the cabin was out of the question, Ethel decided. Now, swaddled again in clothing and blankets and smothered in his mother's frantic caresses, he was like a clenched fist, anger as much as pain in his cries.

Ethel tried all day in The Stillwater cabin to calm the child. He had reached a point now where he would scarcely allow himself to be nursed and fear was in Ethel's eyes as she attempted to offer him the sustenance necessary to keep him alive during the next, most crucial part of the journey. None of us got much sleep that night. Stanley coughed and choked fitfully whenever he started to doze off and Ethel would awake with alarm. I would restoke the fire and look outside at the steadily deteriorating weather.

Next morning the cabin was warm as a sun ray and Ethel felt confident enough that she could completely unwrap Stanley for the first time since leaving Firvale. He almost sighed with relief. That day he slept like a worn-out colt. Ethel begged me to stay another day. "Stanley seems a little better this morning after that long sleep. I hate to take him out again in that awful cold." Although I feared the weather would get worse, I had to agree that the little tyke seemed to have gained back some of his strength. We spent another fairly relaxing night and next morning got ready for whatever lay ahead.

Ethel wrapped Stanley even tighter than ever, afraid that the next part of the trail would be a severe test for us all. There would be no horse to ride and the narrow thread of footpath along the mountainside was covered in six to eight inches of new snow.

Gingerly, I felt out each footstep, my face covered in scarf, beard and sou'wester. Stanley, strapped to my back in the hand-woven basket, was jammed around with blankets so he could not move. Ethel plodded behind, clutching her scarf about her face, occasionally patting the well-packaged bundle ahead of her. Although she said she felt strong enough to carry my pack, I decided to leave all the supplies at The Stillwater for transfer to Lonesome Lake later. The important thing was to get Stanley home safely.

I could feel his sobs penetrate through the basket into my very backbone but I had to ignore my mounting concern. I had to retain a clear mind and make sure I didn't slip. If I hadn't known every inch of this three mile obstacle course I might have miscalculated and we would all have been swept off the ledge into the river.

I breathed a sigh of thanks as we safely traversed one particularly steep bluff where the trail drops off 150 feet. The path that was somewhere under the snow was totally wind-swept and invisible. In the swirling snow I was a blind man leading the blind.

Somehow we reached the top of Lonesome Lake and I untied the straps holding the basket. Stanley was quieter but it was the quiet of exhaustion and not of peace. Although I felt I mustn't betray my anxiety to Ethel, who was already agitated enough, I was starting to get really worried.

"We're going to stop here for a while until we get warmed

up and rested," I told her. "Prop yourself up against that big log out of the wind while I fetch some dry twigs for a fire. "I soon had a blaze going and in a short while Ethel loosened the clothing around his little body. She attempted to feed him but he only nudged half-heartedly against her breast and did not stop whimpering for more than short gurgling intervals.

Snow began to fall heavily and we still had a long way to go. It was the worst time to travel on the lake; it was only partly iced over, not solid enough to walk on but with enough ice to make rowing a boat between the floes a near impossibility. Along the shore I located some logs suitable for a raft and after lashing cross pieces into place, chopped out a rough pair of oars. I then returned to the fire to let the heat steam some of the water and cold out of my sodden clothing.

It was late afternoon when we shoved off from shore. I was wet again as I settled everyone aboard and balanced our bodies for maximum floatability. Ethel insisted I warm up again before we finally cast off. "We haven't got time," I insisted. "Don't worry about me. Rowing this thing and beating through the ice will soon warm me up." I wasn't exaggerating. Sweat poured between my shoulders as I stroked the unwieldy raft homeward.

I hoped there were no ice packs but it was a vain hope. Rounding a bend, the news was clear: Ice in the form of a solid block. It brought us to a halt. It was thick, but not thick enough to trust to human weight. I beached the raft, hoisted the baby and basket onto my back again and, with Ethel single-filing behind me, plunged into a trackless area of rock slides and foot deep snow. We trod this route as close to the lake as we could until we reached a point where I decided the ice was solid enough to bear our weight.

The sidewalk of ice was only safe for a short distance and open water again was the only trail home. We were so near and yet so far. I didn't want to take precious time to build another raft. "Ethel," I said, "I'll build a big fire and leave lots of wood nearby for you to stoke it with while I walk around the shore and get the boat." It was cached a mile or so away. Ethel simply nodded and pulled the baby closer to her.

I don't know what thoughts might have been going through her head but she must have had a great deal of faith in me. Here I was leaving her in the wilderness with a seriously ill infant. What if something happened to me and I couldn't get back to her? What if the boat had drifted away or had been crushed by a wind-downed tree, as sometimes happened to our boats? "I'm leaving you the rifle," I said and turned my back on her so she couldn't see the fear in my eyes. "I'll be back as soon as I can."

Brandishing the axe as a balancing tool and to clear away snow-laden branches, I fought my way through to where the boat was cached. "Thank God," I said aloud. It was safe and sound. Several hours later I oared my way back to where the blaze from Ethel's fire was like a lighthouse beacon. I scooped the baby from her arms and nestled him into his basket again, then handed it to Ethel as she climbed aboard. Almost before she was settled, I began to oar the craft up the dark lake.

It was after three o'clock in the morning when I finally pushed open the door to the freezing-cold house. I had kindling all set to get a fire going and before long it was snapping in the grate. That done, I turned my full attention to the baby who had stopped crying, his eyes popping feverishly out of his head.

It was still cool in the house when Ethel unwrapped the infant and saw for the first time how wet and clinging the clothing next to his tiny body had become. Right away his heart-rending sighs began to subside. The rolling eyes glazed over, eyelids drooped and - I swear it's true - Stanley began to snore!

"Oh, Ralph!" Ethel moaned. "How could I have been so stupid? It's all my fault. I wrapped him up so tight he couldn't breathe properly. He nearly suffocated because he was so hot." I consoled her as best I could. I could scarcely do otherwise. Should I have scolded her? What did she know about caring for an infant in such primitive conditions? I should have known something too. I hadn't been of much assistance, even though I had grown up with younger brothers and a sister and had worked as a volunteer orderly in the army.

"There's nothing for you to feel guilty about, Ethel," I said. "He just needs a good rest and he'll be right as rain. You better get some sleep yourself. You haven't had a good night's sleep for four or five days. I'll stay up and keep the fire going and watch him. When he wakes up you can give him a bath and you'll both feel better."

I stoked the fires and made a quick foray outside to make sure the animals were all right. Everything seemed quiet and when I returned to the house Ethel was asleep. I sat down by the fire and looked for a long time at the sleeping occupants. Stanley had come through his baptism by fire and survived. He'd make a welcome addition to the growing family at Lonesome Lake.

10

Farming For Fur

"By this story it is shown how much ingenuity avails and how wisdom is always an overmatch for strength." (Phaedrus: The Fox and The Raven)

The arrival of Stanley made it even more necessary than ever for me to earn a steady income to support the family. Although we had become almost self-sufficient in vegetables, fruits, fish, fowl and meat and - thanks to Maybelle and her growing herd - dairy products, we still had to have money for the non-essentials.

Books, magazines, stationery and postage were a vital part of our existence and we did not consider them frills. They were our only entertainment. They were almost all of a practical nature: We soon collected hundreds of volumes on a wide variety of subjects: Books on mechanical subjects provided us with information on all aspects of our surroundings. They sat side by side with texts on the arts, philosophy, music and a well-worn Webster's Unabridged Dictionary.

We had a large collection of reference works on plant identification, bacteriology and other scientific subjects. Periodicals around the house included **Saturday Evening Post, Time, Reader's Digest, National Geographic,** various farm newspapers and two or three women's magazines. We excused the purchase of all these items on the basis of their being necessities, as indeed they were. A home medical journal, for example, was our only doctor.

There were other items, such as bits of machinery, particularly those made of steel, which I could not fabricate and which had to be paid for with hard currency. In order to do so, it was necessary to have an income of some sort and fur trapping was the source. It had several aspects which made it undesirable. For one thing it meant leaving Ethel and Stanley alone at the lake for periods of a week or more. Ethel was a resourceful and courageous woman but it was unfair to expect her to face every emergency that might arise alone. God knows there were many emergencies ahead of us.

Often while I was tramping the trapline I would worry about what might be happening at home. I do not like to be distracted from my work and in the wilderness it is vital to keep the mind alert and prepared for the unexpected. In addition to my being absent from home so much, there were two other factors which caused me to alter my methods. First, when one traps, one must take what one gets. Often it is young animals which bring only a small reward compared with that obtained for a mature pelt.

More important than this is the humane aspect. Catching animals in leghold traps had bothered me for some time and it grew to concern me more and more as I matured and my outlook toward conservation and the killing of animals changed. I realized that in order to survive in the wilderness we had to kill other animals, just as they in turn kill to exist and thus maintain the food chain.

I have little patience with people who live in urban comfort and sit in judgment on those who have to kill animals for food and clothing. They do not have a full understanding of the facts. They do not live with nature. Content to wear fur and eat meat that someone else has killed, they claim some sort of immunity from it all. It is a most amazing rationalization.

My pangs of conscience came not so much in the taking of the animal's life as in the way it was taken. Many times the animal, such as a bear or a wolf, would have taken mine except I was swifter of foot or had superior strength or weapons. What bothered me was to come upon an animal in a trap that had not been killed instantly and painlessly.

126

Too often I found animals that survived in a trap for days, their legs or back broken; I found animals in my traps that had been half-eaten by predators and these predators had not given the trapped animal the same quarter that I would have done: A quick paralyzing blow or a shot in a vital spot.

I tried designing a new trap but my ingenuity failed me and none was successful. At that time I could not obtain any other type of trap than the leghold variety. At any rate, the question was not whether I would stop killing animals - I had to kill to feed and clothe my family - but how to do it humanely?

The answer came to me one day when Ethel and I were walking along the lakeshore. "What's that grunting noise like an old man talking to himself?" Ethel asked. I laughed. That's an old man beaver talking to himself. Come on. I'll show you." We turned a bend and there was the "old man," pushing a piece of brush in front of him in the shallow water. He turned to regard us, slapped his tail in annoyance, and continued on about his business.

"He seems tame as a dog," Ethel remarked. "And about as easy to feed," I added. "Quaking Aspen is their main diet and there's plenty of that around here." "They also like our vegetables," Ethel complained. "I've had to chase more than one of them out of the garden. Imagine having to chase Canada's national symbol out of your garden!"

Remembering this conversation a week or so later, I made a decision, then asked Ethel for her opinion. "What do you think about farming for fur, rather than trapping it?" Ethel was enthusiastic, but puzzled: "How do you go about farming fur? Do you really think those beaver are that tame that they'll stay in the backyard?" "Not exactly," I said, "but we could build a dam in such a way that they can't escape. It will mean a lot of work getting a dam built and pens made." "Is there anything we do that doesn't mean a lot of hard work?" Ethel sighed. "We're working eighteen hours a day, seven days a week now. Maybe we can squeeze it in during our spare time."

I reminded Ethel that I would not have to be away for weeks at a time but would be here at the farm and able to accomplish more with less effort. But before we could engage in

127

this bold and inventive experiment we had to pack in the suitable materials. The first item would be metal fencing. We dragged out our hardware supply catalogues, pored over them, and made a selection of what would be required.

On my next trip to the post office at Atnarko I sent off my order for the wire for the fences. It came in widths of two and three foot rolls weighing 100 pounds and 150 pounds respectively. It would take careful planning to get it into the lake. We now had a rough horse trail hacked through from The Stillwater so we wouldn't have to carry it ourselves. A horse carrying its load on a saddle can manage about 250 pounds so two rolls to a horse seemed all right. Since the bales were of different sizes I reckoned a short roll on one side and a long roll extending over the other side would be advisable.

The long rolls had to be on the outside of the load so as not to strike the overhanging rocks and other obstructions along the mountainous trail. If a horse loaded the other way came around a curve and its load stuck an abutment, it would push him off the trail and over the cliff. Even with this planning, we still had trouble.

As the horse trail approaches The Stillwater it climbs about 300 feet above the roaring Atnarko River. It continues around a seventy degree mountainside of small bluffs and rock slides. Near the top of the climb there is a gully down which rocks roll and into which the trail bends. The rocks had accumulated in this bend and when old Blue, loaded with an ungainly pack of wire came around it, he stumbled, his burden struck the rock pile and over the cliff he went.

I watched in helpless horror. Down and down he went, heading for the river in a shower of rocks and gravel. Then the cinch around his middle broke and horse, saddle and wire began a mad race for the bottom of the cliff. I was on my way down a few moments later, stumbling, sliding on my backside, kicking and scratching and trying not to gain too much momentum. Blue and his cargo had rolled to the bottom, just short of the river. He whinnied painfully as he stood up and looked at me.

I checked him over and decided he was not badly injured.

I left him there with the material while I climbed back up to where the rest of the pack train waited. Unpacking Ginty at The Stillwater, I rode him back to a point in the river where I could cross and avoid the bluffs that led to the accident. Blue hadn't wandered far. I put the load on Ginty and led the battered Blue to The Stillwater.

Imagine my chagrin when, after all that effort, I discovered that what I had ordered was hog fencing, which was completely unsuitable for our purposes. The squares were too wide and a beaver could crawl right through and escape. "Darn it, Ethel," I said. "What am I supposed to do with this bunch of useless wire? What a waste of time and effort and hard-earned dollars."

"Surely it can be adapted in some way," Ethel said. "Maybe you can make the holes smaller by threading pieces of wire through the squares." It was worth a try. I ordered some straight, soft, galvanized wire from Woodwards in Vancouver and when it arrived I weaved pieces of it into the hog fencing which made the holes the right size to contain beaver. Or, so we hoped.

That done, I began the next task - moving in large quantities of huge rocks to build the dams. Ginty and the wagon were engaged for several weeks in hauling the rocks, the result being two ponds, one in front of the house, the other behind it on another creek. We would have beaver neighbors on both sides of us.

All I had to do now was to capture some beaver. The first two I caught by snaring them upriver about fifteen miles from The Birches. I carried them home one at a time (they weighed about forty five pounds each) in a case on a packframe which I had constructed for that purpose. They lay quietly most of the time, except when I had to cross fast-running water and they became agitated with the noise and began to thump around in their box. I almost lost my balance crossing logs over streams.

Once released in their new home, the beaver set to work and play. It was fascinating watching them. They were very systematic and determined. One determination was to escape by cutting holes in the fence which I had anchored under the water with big boulders. Bending the wire back and forth in their powerful teeth, they managed to cut through a strand at a time. I was kept busy just repairing the holes the beaver made in my fences.

Despite their plans to escape, we had to admire them. We loved to watch them emerge from the water, clamber up onto the dam shaking their shiny wet coats and flat tails. One would wipe his beard with his paws and, standing together with one paw on another beaver's shoulder, present a picture very like two humans chatting over the day's events.

Once the beaver were settled as comfortably as possible into their new home, we waited for nature to take its course and deliver us with pelts which would make the whole time-consuming and costly venture worthwhile. While this was taking place my brother Earle and his wife Isabel came to visit.

Earle had met Isabel when she came to visit her sister in Bella Coola one summer. The sister was married to Vincent Clayton who lived in an old, rambling, twelve room house on the river bank. They married in 1926 and moved to Portland, Oregon. Planning a six month visit to Bella Coola and area, they finally succumbed to the beauty of the place and have remained ever since, finally settling on a small farm in Hagensborg.

Earle and Isabel couldn't contain their amusement at our venture into the fur farming business, particularly at our insistence on absolute silence around the beaver dams. We did not want to disturb them in their cosy lodges when babies were being expected. "Should we whisper in the house too," Isabel laughed. "You can joke about it," I said. "We'll have the last laugh yet."

Earle suggested since we were going to farm fur, why didn't we try mink as well. "Mink pelts are selling at a high price right now," he said. "And if you can get them to bunk in with you too, you might end up with a pocketful." "I have no intention of sharing my house with mink," Ethel said indignantly, "Earle was speaking figuratively, Ethel," I said. "But that's not a bad idea. Maybe mink should be the next cash crop in the Edward s menagerie."

One requirement that the beaver did not need which the mink would want in quantity was a guaranteed source of meat. It was illegal to kill game for mink feed so the solution was to find horse meat. In Atnarko I looked up an old Indian named Honelin who sold me two yearlings for ten dollars each and two older horses for five dollars each. They were skinny critters, not worth much as beasts of burden or for riding.

With a meat supply assured, I built some simple wire cages and went looking for specimens to fill them. The first one came easily, albeit unintentionally; she was caught in a steel trap at the foot of what we called Third Lake, one of the chain of lakes that gather in our valley, about six miles from home. I should have let her go because she wasn't worth the trouble she caused me.

She was in good shape, having only been caught by a couple of toes. I had no conveyance such as I had devised for the beaver so I simply held her down as gently as possible with my foot and freed her. Holding her by the neck, I headed for home. At one point, when I wasn't paying close attention, she worked some slack loose, whipped her head around, and bit my hand. Her teeth burned like a red hot needle.

I put her on the ground again and held her with my foot while I wrapped a handkerchief around my bleeding hand. I could feel the powerful muscles in her neck expand as she struggled to get free. After a time she relaxed and I got another neck hold. At home, I placed her in a pen and although she bred successfully with male mink I acquired, she always destroyed her young as soon as they were born. Her hatred for me was so fierce I eventually had to pelt her.

I was more successful with four other females and two males who did not develop the same hatred and fear and bred well in captivity. I caught these mink in wire box traps which I

131

weaved myself. They prospered on a mixture of ground horse meat or squaw fish mixed with carrots.

With beaver and mink established on the farm, it seemed only natural to add another little animal which formed part of my annual income - the marten. The marten is an extremely beautiful, yet nervous, alert animal consumed with curiosity and playfulness. A slender-bodied carnivorous mammal that is larger than a weasel and of somewhat arboreal habits, it has a long tail and a coat of soft, fine fur which is light colored below and rich brown or gray above.

While highly intelligent, the marten is not very smart. Let me explain: On my trapline I came to a trap set at the foot of a large cedar tree growing at the edge of a spring swamp. There was a small cleft between the roots of the tree on its trail side that made a cubbyhole for the bait with the trap set in front. A marten was in the trap and he had dug back under the tree and when I tried to pull him out, the trap slipped off and he was free.

I re-set the trap and put on my packsack again. Instead of running to the other side of the tree, which was wide open to the water, the marten stuck his head out of the hole and scolded me with a chatter like a large squirrel. When I found he was still there I took out a spare trap and set it down in the hole near him and he stepped into it. "That'll teach you to talk back," I said, as I slipped off the trap. I took him back to the farm where he became a good father and husband to another marten already there.

For marten-raising we used two mink pens measuring three feet by ten feet, with one pen flat on the ground and the other standing on end against the flat one. A passage was constructed between them and a small tree, with a nesting box in its top. To catch more marten, I set homemade woven wire box traps on the mountain east of our place at about the 6000 foot level and visited them every day until I had three females and two males.

The females were already bred and one raised a family that summer - a family of one. He was very tame and we de-

132

lighted in watching him sit in his feeding bowl, twirling it around. The fun of watching marten ended when it came to breeding time. The males and females fought continuously with each other and it became evident that it was impossible to breed them sucessfully in the conditions I was providing. We decided to give up marten-farming.

The farming of beaver also ended when our house burned down (a tragedy described in the next chapter) and we were unable to give full attention to their constant attempts to escape. However, mink-raising was carried on successfully for some years until the price of fur dropped so low that it was unprofitable.

Although my fur farming experiment was not an unqualified success, it provided income when we badly needed it and at least one indirect result altered life on Lonesome Lake.

We did not have a large enough herd of horses to practice selective breeding so the supply of fresh or canned meat that the mink consumed every day posed a problem. This was especially true in the summer when nature did not provide us with a free deepfreeze. Additionally, grinding mink feed was an arduous task. To make it easier to reduce the meat to edible portions for the mink, I built a waterwheel to generate power to operate the meatgrinder.

I had been fascinated with waterwheels since I had constructed my first one as a small boy on a relative's farm in the States. All the ingredients were at the lake; it just required some ingenuity to put them together to generate power. A creek, about eight feet below the house, would be the water source.

I placed a couple of logs across it to support the waterwheel axles. I had no lathe to shape an axle but an axe, adze and carpenter gouge worked as well. I bored holes in the axle to hold poles which I attached to wooden boxes which I built from hand-sawed cedar lumber. As the flowing water filled each wooden box it moved the wheel slowly; as more boxes filled, the wheel began to revolve at considerable speed.

To get the water to the wheel, I hollowed out logs cut in half. One inch manila rope was used for drive belts but the constant spray wet them, causing them to shrink and break. Also, the half-log flume did not carry enough water to produce sufficient power to operate the meatgrinder.

I decided to rebuild the whole layout with a flume made of lumber and larger water boxes. Ten inches by ten inches and mounted on a large circular slab cut from a huge log, I had a seven foot diameter waterwheel, two feet larger than the earlier variety. An endless rope ran between grooved pulleys, one of which had a heavy rock counterweight to take up all slack that developed in the system so all ropes pulled equally.

The ropes broke continually and after many frustrating days of stop and start operation I decided to use strips of cowhide braided in eight strands. To keep it from slipping as it rotated between the pulleys I covered it with grizzly bear grease which softened it and at the same time provided good traction.

The water wheel turned at forty revolutions per minute when running free and the thirty inch saws I bought were supposed to turn at 1200 r.p.m. A circular saw has a bulge pounded into it so when it turns at a certain speed the centrifugal force will straighten it out. If it runs too slow the bulge will rub against the wood and cause the saw to warm up and bulge still more until it stops the saw.

I had to make a countershaft at 200 r.p.m. to give the saw the correct speed. At first I had the main bearings of the waterwheel turning on birch pillow blocks and sheathed in sheet metal. The countershaft turning at 200 r.p.m. began to smoke and burn and I corrected that by making roller bearings of three-quarter inch steel shafting cut in four inch lengths and turning in sheet steel boxes. The ends of the axles were covered in sheet steel as well. The machine worked fine then.

Although the mink and other fur-farming experiences were less remunerative than we had expected, the positive result was the waterwheel which generated enough power so we could cut a year's supply of stove wood in a few days by using a tip-up carriage which the operator simply levered up with his leg as the log was pushed forward and into the saw blade. I built a shed to house the wheel and the saw with lumber cut in the mill.

All things in life, I believe, have a balancing positive effect. The problem is, some of these positive aspects are only apparent in retrospect. In the next few months, it often seemed that life had only its negative forces working for us.

11

One Thing After Another

"Leave Lonesome Lake and Ralph? Never . . . it's our home!"
(Ethel Edwards)

The year 1926 started out well enough. Stanley was growing into a fine, strong lad. Ethel was busy and happy to have the extra company and diversion. We were all enjoying good health and the farm was taking shape as more and more acreage was opened up for crops. We had completed a horse trail all the way to The Stillwater, making civilization a little closer. Then a series of large and small events occurred to mar the peace we thought we had found forever.

Like all children, especially between the ages of two and four, Stanley could be a trial at times. He could get into more mischief in ten minutes than a dozen squirrels in a peanut factory. For his peregrinations about the house, barn and the yard between, he was rewarded with a variety of cuts, bruises and sprains.

"Ralph, we're going to have to do something about Stanley's disobedience," Ethel said. "Maybe if we built a corral for him he'd stay in one place for a minute. I have to leave whatever I'm doing to go looking for him. He's a regular little pest." I had never seen Ethel so upset, but she was under a strain what with looking after all the domestic animals, the house and the child. There was the additional worry that all mothers have, that a child might get seriously hurt. This was more of a worry to us than to someone who lives where doctors and hospitals are only minutes or hours away.

We were so vulnerable that everyone had to be constantly aware of the possibility of accidents. Stanley had already established a reputation for getting into trouble but I was loathe to curb his initiative. Corralling him may have been desirable but - as I pointed out to Ethel - he could find more ways to escape from an enclosure than the beaver from their dam.

He yelled and squealed if fenced in, throwing his toys about and making himself so obnoxious it was almost preferable to let him run loose - within reason. He would learn his boundaries soon enough.

"It's time the little jasper learned some responsibility," I said. "I've got to get back to the plowing. Call me when lunch is ready." I wasn't back in the field long before I heard Ethel calling. From the tone of her voice, it wasn't for lunch. "Ralph, Stanley's missing," she said breathlessly. "I've looked everywhere and I can't find him."

It was true. We both went through the house and barn including the hay loft, but could not locate the child. We stood in the yard, perplexed. "What's that noise?" I asked. It was the loud quacking of ducks down by the river, about 150 yards from the house. "Good heavens," Ethel cried, "he's down by the water!"

She flew down as fast as she could just in time to catch Stanley wrestling with an oar, all set to take off in the boat which he had somehow managed to untie from its mooring. Ethel hauled him out and gave him a good smack and talking to. The warnings seemed to bounce off his hide like rain drops off the ducks who stood scolding from a safe distance, obviously enjoying the come-uppance being given to this recalcitrant little human.

Adding to the pressure put on Ethel by the domestic chores and the naughtiness of her first-born, was the fact that she was pregnant again. The second child was expected in about six months. Mindful of the near-disastrous first trip to and from Bella Coola, we decided that she would not be put through that ordeal again, even though the delivery date would be in the summer this time.

I wrote to my father in the States and he persuaded a doctor from Eugene, Oregon, to come into Lonesome Lake for a holiday. The doctor brought along his daughter, who was a nurse. We had as complete a hospital staff at home as any to be found at Bella Coola. The problem was, Ethel was not quite ready to deliver and our medic's holiday was nearing an end. Much to our misgivings, the doctor induced the birth with drugs. The baby was delivered quickly - too quickly in fact - and it scared us all. I swore then and there that if we were to have any more children, I would learn to deliver them myself - with Ethel's assistance of course!

Our second child, born in July, 1927, was also a boy. A delightful, chubby fellow we called John, although he was known mostly as Johnny to everyone. He had a sunny personality and added another dimension to our family circle. He and Stanley were as opposite as two brothers could be.

The doctor left shortly after delivering the baby but before he did he recommended some books on the subject of midwifery. I glanced through them after they arrived in the mail about a month later. I wasn't really expecting to have to put them to use for some time, if ever. Two strong boys for future assistance on the farm was all that was really necessary. However, I wasn't counting on Ethel's desire to have a daughter.

"Ralph," Ethel said casually, as we sat reading around the fire one evening. "You remember those books the doctor recommended in case I had another baby?" "Yes," I answered, still concentrating on my reading. The **National Geographic** certainly had some interesting articles and photographs.

"Ralph," Ethel said again, "Where are they?" "Where are what?" "Where are the books on child delivery at home?" "I dunno," I said. "They're in the library somewhere. Top shelf, I think. Why?" "Because you better dust them off. I'm going to have a baby."

"Oh, no," I said, dropping the magazine on the floor. "You can't have another one. You've just had two." I was caught between two emotions: Fear and delight. I looked across at

Ethel. She was slightly flushed. Obviously she had been hesitant about telling me about this latest "good news." I stepped across and put my arms around her. "That's great," I said. "Maybe now you'll get the daughter you wanted."

In March of 1929 Trudy arrived, without benefit of doctor or nurse assistance. Although I had delivered calves and foals and didn't expect the delivery of a human being to be that much different, it is impossible to be that objective. It was a traumatic moment both for Ethel and for me. Probably for Trudy as well. In any event, her entry into our lives was a joyful and rewarding experience. I don't know if it was because of, or in spite of, my bumbling help, but from that moment on a link was forged between that child and me that nothing could break.

Like me, Trudy grew up to be short and a bit heavy across the shoulders. She had a light complexion like her mother with the rosy cheeks of her father. Robust at birth, she grew strong as a bull. Almost from the time she could stand she was by my side, working with me when most girls her age would have been playing with dolls.

I was pretty much of an authoritatrian, reserving my respect for things and people who worked for what they got. My own inventiveness, tenacity and hard work enabled the family to live in almost total independence. My conviction that dogged determination plus a peck of imagination and energy could overcome most obstacles infected the others. I also expected a lot from them.

Trudy was the youngest but she had the largest amount of my "got to know" compulsion. From the time she was able to contribute her physical energies to getting chores done, she was expected to do so. Even as a small child she was given the job of milking cows and training them to lead.

She was always rather a loner who never had much companionship from her brothers. I doubt if she ever gave much thought to loneliness, however. Horses were her love and right from the start - as soon as she was able to sit up straight - she was in the saddle. Her favorite was a mare named Topsy and,

139

at three years old, she could ride like a veteran.

While Johnny too had a natural kinship with nature, it was Trudy who grew to love the wild environment quickest and the only one who chose never to leave it. As a child she learned to imitate the calls of many of the wild creatures around home and generally elicit a reply from them.

Trudy's help was very valuable and we could use all the help we could get. The land clearing was progressing well; by now we had nearly forty acres cleared and free of stumps. A variety of crops were sown for the animals and a huge garden and orchard supplied us with almost everything we required. The root cellar under the house fairly bulged with canned and fresh produce, fish and meat. The years passed quickly and quietly.

Then one day the bad cycle began: "Come quick," Ethel cried. "Ginty kicked Johnny in the face." It was all my fault. I had told Johnny, who was eight or nine at the time, to chase Ginty out of the carrot patch. Instead of shouting at him, he came up behind the horse and gave him a smack across the legs with a willow switch. Surprised, Ginty let fly with one hoof that struck the child in the face.

By the time I got to him his face was almost unrecognizable - a mass of blood and broken bones. His nose was smashed flat and one cheekbone was protruding through open, bloody flesh. Some teeth had been knocked out. I took quick note of the damage, then reached into his mouth to make sure he could breathe and to retrieve the teeth. It was obvious his nose was going to be out of commission for some time.

That taken care of, the important thing now was to keep Johnny as calm as possible to prevent him from hemorrhaging. I thanked God that I took the time to read and digest books on first aid. I carried the poor little guy into the house. He whimpered like a puppy all night as he lay in my arms. It was difficult to keep him from squirming but I knew these next few hours were crucial. For the first time in years I found myself praying, asking God to make the bleeding stop.

In the morning, Johnny was still awake and in terrible

pain. The snuffling noises he made trying to breathe made Ethel wring her hands in despair. "Take over here," I said, cradling the boy into her arms. I'm going to Atnarko and phone the doctor. We can't handle this on our own." How I got to Atnarko so fast I'll never know. The horse must have had the wings of Pegasus.

Over the phone I was given instructions on how to dress the wound until Johnny could be attended to in hospital. Some disinfectant was in stock in the Atnarko store and that was a blessing. By the time I returned, Johnny was in a deep sleep and it appeared that the greatest danger was past.

Johnny recovered despite our clumsy ministrations but before then we had many bad nights. He suffered even more in later years because his face was so badly scarred. When he grew older and was able to earn some money, extensive dental repairs and plastic surgery made the scars less obvious.

Bad luck seemed to dog us throughout the twenties, although there were fair times too. I had some good years trapping and with some of the cash rewards laid in extra supplies of coal oil and even splurged on two cases of canned pumpkin, my favorite pie filling, a commodity we would later grow ourselves. As fall drew into winter in 1929 there were six sacks of potatoes in the cellar, a 100 pound sack of cooking onions and Ethel canned over 500 quarts of vegetables, fruit and meat. She had learned how to can milk so it would keep for months without spoiling. We knew vaguely about the stockmarket crash, but it was so remote from our world that we hardly gave it a thought.

I was in the potato patch digging up the remainder of the crop when I heard Stanley yelling from the house. I didn't pay much heed because he was always yelling about something. When he continued in this way for some time I finally looked up. Smoke was curling out of the area where the house stood in the clump of birches. I dropped my fork and ran. The quickest way to the house was up the field and across the creek to the back door. As I approached, a bullet exploded somewhere. Then more shots followed, richocheting in all directions. The loaded rifles in the house!

I kicked the door open and was met with a tongue of flame. Where were Ethel and the other children? I ran around to the front of the house and found Ethel standing there with the children clutching at her legs, eyes wide with fascination. "Get the children out of here!" I yelled. "Get out in the field away from here." There was no hope of entering the house, which was already an inferno.

Ethel had thrown out a few blankets before retreating from the house after some sparks started the fire by falling onto tinder-dry cedar shakes near the chimney. The heat was unbearable. I threw the blankets a few yards further away from the flames and falling sparks and stepped back where I nearly stumbled over something. It was the cashbox which Ethel had thoughtfully tossed out. It contained some important documents as well as our life's savings - a few hundred dollars. The box was so hot it scorched my hand but I managed to throw it away from danger, then I ran to join the rest of the family in the field. From there we witnessed the destruction of nearly fourteen years' efforts.

Within minutes, the house, lined with cedar and building paper, crumbled into the cellar. The blaze was briefly renewed as sealers popped, coal oil exploded and vegetables and meat hissed, steamed and cooked. It is possible that no house ever smelled so good. As the ashes cooled, the smell drew the children's attention to the fact that they were hungry. It drew my attention to the fact that we were stuck in the wilderness without food, clothing or defense against wild animals.

"Well, Ralph," Ethel said, fighting back the tears. "What do we do now?" I thought for a moment. "It's pretty bad," I admitted. "But let's look at the bright side. There's still plenty of spuds in the field and I can kill that calf out in the pasture. We won't starve to death." I found a heavy sledge hammer in an outbuilding and an hour or so later we all gave thanks for the provision of the fatted calf. Cooked beef and potatoes were served around the ashes of our dream home.

Appetites satisfied, the next thing was to find a roof over

our heads. "We'll move into the old trapper's cabin that Frank Ratcliff and I built," I told Ethel. "Let's get busy and make it liveable. We may be there for a long time." The cabin wasn't far away and was still dry and warm inside. The fireplace stones were still in place and the hole in the roof soon let out its first smoke in many years.

Ethel and I scraped through the coolest areas of the house remains to try to recover some utensils to cook in. Among the still useable items were several mis-shapen pans which could be used to hold milk and water. Ethel found an empty vanilla bottle where the children had been playing and used it to feed Trudy with, utilizing a piece of cloth for a nipple.

The heat had reduced a heavy cast-aluminum kettle to a lump of metal and our wedding silver and Ethel's gold watch had fallen into a large enamel pan and fused. We continued to use that pan for several years, a reminder that life's fortunes can change with the flicker of a flame.

Next day I set off for The Stillwater and recovered a cache of blankets and some old clothing I had left in the cabin there for those occasions when I slept over on my way to pick up mail or supplies. I found an old coal oil lamp as well. It had some oil in it and although the base was broken, the fount operated and it was a source of light.

I took these supplies to Lonesome Lake and at daybreak was on the trail again, this time to Atnarko. With its telephone in operation, "the stopping place" brought Bella Coola and other parts of the world within the sound of the human voice. I ordered groceries and cooking utensils from the Christensen store in Bella Coola where my credit was good. I stayed at Atnarko until the supplies were delivered by wagon and then loaded Ginty and Blue and headed for home.

Along with the purchased goods came some unexpected bonuses: The good citizens of the Bella Coola valley had heard of the fire and donated 100 dollars in cash, blankets and household items. We were thankful to them all. One gift I will never forget was a suit marked, "From a good friend." I never discovered who that good friend was but he knew my size and I was proud to wear that suit. My father, who was still living in the States, heard about the fire through relatives and sent 100 dollars in cash. Two hunters I had guided previously sent us a supply of books. This was a most thoughtful gift because the loss of our beloved library was probably what we felt most keenly of all.

It almost made me cry to think of the years it had taken to save the money for, select and haul in those books, which must have weighed several tons. Hardly a trip back to the lake was made without books being a choice part of the burden in pack-sack or horseback. Gone were textbooks on inorganic chemistry, plant physiology, cryptogamic botany and dendrology. We would have to replace **The Home Physician And Guide To Health; Chemistry And Cooking; Human Development And Learning; Walden Pond** by Thoreau; **The World's Great Wonders; The Story of Mankind; Working in Wood;** and dozens of other volumes dealing with everything from how to witch for water to making toys.

Since we were all voracious readers, the books sent by the hunters would be a God-send in the long hours we would be spending in the little trapper cabin. With the problems of what to eat, what to wear and where to live solved, at least for the time being, we turned our attention to determining what could be salvaged from the ashes of the old house to build a new one. I recovered most of the nails and spikes; lumber could be cut with the saw powered by the waterwheel; logs were still close by enough to make transporting them a comparatively simple task. Ginty was skilled at pulling them into position, having had experience in the construction of a new hen house.

Since the heat from the house had killed the lovely birch trees we decided to find a new site. After considerable debate, Ethel and I selected a spot across a field to the north where fir and birch trees would shade the building, just as the birches had done for the old house.

Winter came on early and since I had to trap again to make a living, the actual building of the house would have to wait until March. The family had to be content with the little ten by

144

fourteen foot cabin with its earthen floor and smoke hole for six cold months at least. The temperature could be expected to plunge to about -30⁰ F and a family of five crammed into a space so small had better be prepared to get along with one another.

Although cramped and sometimes cranky with each other, we managed to stop short of inflicting any serious wounds. I built a double bed of cross poles and balsam branches for Ethel and me to sleep on; the boys shared the bunk that was already built. Trudy was content to be in a basket set beneath a drop-leaf table placed against the cupboard. There was about three feet for us to navigate past each other so there were frequent collisions.

The song says: "The Smoke Goes Up The Chimney Just The Same." Don't believe it. The composer of that song obviously never observed smoke, certainly never in a wilderness cabin in a valley vented by capricious winds. It lazed its way up, around, through and down the hole so the cabin was always subject to major and minor degrees of smokiness.

That wasn't the worst discomfort. Boredom affected us all. I had installed a single, three-paned window so we could read and the children could see to play during the daylight hours, but there was precious little daylight at Lonesome Lake some winter days, which was a mixed blessing. It kept us from irritating each other too much; we all slept a lot.

Ethel, resourceful as ever, invented games to keep the children occupied. I told them stories about my parent's missionary days in India. They were particularly fascinated by my account of the earthquake. We were in Calcutta living in a compound within a wall that embraced several residences and an Adventist meeting house. A variety of sects, including constantly warring Muslims and Hindus, held noisy street parades and protests against each other and the ruling "Raj".

One day Earle and I were playing in an upstairs room of our two storey house when it began to shake violently. We ran down stairs to where mother and father had converged in a hallway leading to a back door. "It's an earthquake," father cried, gathering us together. "Come on, quickly, let's get outside in case this building collapses."

We were in the street only seconds before the front half of the building neatly separated from the back portion. Further damage resulted from the second, or aftershock. Although nearly paralyzed by fear, we weren't injured or in any danger. The rest of the compound escaped heavy damage but parts of Calcutta were in shambles. Huge chasms had opened in the streets, swallowing humans and animals. Whole city blocks tumbled into the cracks, some of which closed up again, entombing everything and everybody, as though they never existed.

The children were amused by my description of a servant who worked for my parents. Called a "punka walla", his duty was to squat on the floor outside our bedroom door and keep the "punka" swinging back and forth to keep Earle and me cool in the sweltering weather. The punka was a two foot by twelve foot parallelogram of stiff material hung from the ceiling with a rope that passed through a hole in the wall to the punka walla outside. I often wondered if the punka walla had a punka walla of his own, or if he ever fell asleep on the job. The closest we came to such comfort on the farm was the hammock-like arrangement that I often slept in over the barn.

I told Stanley and Johnny about the time I got a leech in my mouth while drinking water from a forbidden - and filthy - source. My mother cut the little bloodsucker off my cheek with a scalpel then told me to "run around outside and let the air get at it so it'll heal."

Not all the adventures that Earle and I got into were as serious as leeches in the mouth or earthquakes. In the market square in the Himalayan Mountains near Darjeeling, where my parents had been allowed a short vacation, we watched a fakir, or magician, perform tricks for a small crowd of Indians. A cobra wound its huge flat head out of the basket he had set in front of him as he sat cross-legged in the dirt.

The serpent continued to uncoil to the flat notes that the fakir blew on his ancient flute. (I learned later that it isn't the music that makes the snakes uncoil into the air, swaying and

146

apparently hypnotized. It is "charmed" by the drumming of the man's foot on the ground and mesmerized by the motion of the flute and the man's body.)

The magician saw us watching his magic act and motioned us to come forward. Earle and I approached warily. The turbanned fakir said something in his own dialect which we did not understand. "Come closer, little one," he said to me in accented English. "I want to see what you are hiding in your pants." I hesitated until I was given a gentle shove by Earle. "Why are you keeping this up here?" the man said, quickly sliding his hand up the inside of my short pants and withdrawing an egg. The crowd roared and Earle and I ran away in embarrassment.

The boys giggled at the thought of their dad having an egg taken out of his pants and begged me to tell them more funny stories, but I had to do chores and get ready to go out on the trapline the following morning. I would be away for a week. I hate to admit it but the minor hardships on the trapline were often a welcome relief from that crowded domestic scene. Poor Ethel and the children were confined almost entirely, particularly when the weather got severe in January.

Friends and relatives were urging her to take the children and stay with them until a new house could be built. Ethel was aghast at such a suggestion: "Leave Lonesome Lake and Ralph? Never. Why . . . it's our home!" She stayed - and I'm glad she did. By constantly keeping the children occupied with useful tasks and gainful enjoyment, she earned a certain amount of pleasure and they certainly benefited through learning independence and responsibility. With our Adventist backgrounds, Ethel and I had been schooled in the old proverb that idle hands make for idle minds. We were seldom idle when there was light to work by.

The boys were old enough to help out with chores and young Stanley in particular showed a natural skill working around any kind of machinery. He had the natural touch of a born mechanic and was always taking things apart to see how they worked and then putting them back together. Sometimes he didn't always get it right but doggedly he worked at it until the parts were back in place.

November and December were deceptively mild that year so I left the cattle out on the range between Elbow Lake and Knot Lake. Knot Lake is the division of the watershed of the Atnarko and Klinaklini Rivers where the slough grass is good feed for cattle as long as the snow doesn't get so deep they can't forage for it.

Snow fell heavily in January so it became necessary to bring the cattle home. The herd consisted of an old milk cow, her two year old heifer, a crazy wild milk cow, her big, two year old, unweaned bull calf, and a three year old Holstein bull. Although the crazy cow could be a pest, she wasn't dangerous. As I had already learned, the Holstein bull was.

At the ranch one day I caught the bull trying to drive its head through Ginty's mid-section and probably would have done the poor horse considerable harm had I not given him a kick where it hurt him most. Another time he chased Laura, Ethel's sister who had married one of the Ratcliff boys, around the field. This was no way to treat a visitor so I put a stop to that by whacking him across the snout with a stick.

They say bulls have better memories than elephants, who apparently have notoriously poor ones. I have never had to draw upon an elephant's memory for anything but I suspect this ornery cuss of a Holstein bull had a long-standing grudge that went back to the time I tried to castrate him and he broke loose from the ropes I put around his legs. Altering his mood from brutal to neutral was one of those assignments that got put off for more urgent matters. Such procrastination almost cost me my life.

Bringing the cattle home, I put a lead rope on the old milk cow and another one on the heifer. They led like two lambs. I expected the bull and the crazy cow and her offspring to follow. The bull sullenly fell in behind but the crazy animal refused to budge and stood staring vacantly in our direction a few hundred yards up the path. I tied the milk cow and her calf to a tree and went back to get the slowpokes.

As I nudged my way past the bull he swiped at me with his horns. De-horning him was another job that never got attended to. Fortunately I had snipped the tips off. I decided that Mr. Bull had better have a rope on too. After I had made a lasso out of the end of the heifer's rope I leaned across her and slipped the loop over the bull's horns.

He took exception to this and lunged at me, knocking the heifer up against my legs and stomach and catching my clothing with one horn. The heifer scrambled across my feet and slipped clear so the bull could advance another foot and drive me backwards, slipping and sliding in the snow.

The next thing I knew I was flat on my back, pinned to the ground, the bull's horns driven into the snow-covered ground beneath me, one prong on either side of my chest. At that moment I had reason to feel grateful that I was not a larger man. I tried to squirm under him but his head and throat were only inches away and the pack I had on my back with grain in it acted like a misplaced pillow. I brought my feet up and kicked him but I couldn't get much leverage from my prone position, and the rubber-soled boots had little effect on his tough hide.

The bull's breath steamed into my face as he pushed ever downward, crushing my head into the snow. In desperation, I bit him on the eyebrow with all my might. He drew back in surprise, which quickly turned to rage. I rolled away but he hooked me with his horns again and tossed me. I rolled over and tried to get up. He advanced and threw me a third and fourth time.

I managed to stagger to my feet by wrapping my right arm around a slim alder. My left arm was stretched out toward the bull's head. The right pack strap had come off and the left strap was all twisted around my left wrist. The pack itself hung over the bull's eyes. I let go of the tree and slipped the pack off my wrist, an action that possibly saved my life because the bull became distracted as he swung his head around trying to shake it loose. It gave me the opportunity to run to a tree and climb to safety.

For a moment I was too dazed to see clearly. Then I spotted the bull in a little hollow ahead of me, trying to grind the packsack into the ground. Sliding painfully down to the ground, I ran back to where I had dropped my rifle. I moved in to where the packsack battle was rapidly drawing to a close and felled the bull with one shot. He never knew what hit him. I left him there and went back and untied the cows.

After the shock wore off, the pain set in. I gave up all thought of taking the cattle to the farm. I felt I would be lucky if I could get back there myself. I trudged painfully toward the nearest trapper cabin, a distance of about six miles. Each step was sheer misery. I made frequent stops to take rasping breaths. Twice I nearly fainted from the pain. At the cabin door I was overcome with nausea and fell inside.

I collected my wits long enough to reel to my feet and get a fire going. I stripped off my sodden clothing and let the heat draw some of the soreness out of me. I brewed some tea and sipped it slowly while I examined the extent of my injuries. To start with, I had two broken teeth. I probed my chest with my fingers and determined there were a number of cracked ribs. My arms felt like two chunks of lead. They were scraped, bruised and bleeding in several places, but not broken. Having judged there were no serious injuries, I stoked the fire, crawled into a bunk and slept for ten hours.

I felt better the next morning and, after some hot tea, I closed up the cabin and began the trek back to the lake. It took most of the day to get there; I was weak from hunger but when I tried to force something down my throat I nearly gagged on it. I could feel the injured ribs grating together.

Ethel took one look at me as I staggered up to the cabin about four o'clock and nearly dropped in fright. I was dead on my feet and almost collapsed at her feet. "Good heavens, Ralph," she cried. "You look like you've been run over by a grizzly. Whatever happened to you?" I explained to her in a croaking whisper the details of my encounter with the bull. The effort of talking was dreadful; my voice was like wind whistling past each crack in my ribs.

After I gasped out the last detail, she asked: "Where's the bull now?" "He died," I said. "How did he die?" she wanted to know. "Well it sure wasn't fatty degeneration of the heart," I growled. "It was lead poisoning."

Ethel was in no mood for my gruff attempt at humor. She toted up the prospects at that moment: She was crammed into a tiny cabin in no-man's land with three small children to care for. She had an assortment of farm animals to look after. There was wood to be cut and packed in and a fire that must be kept alive in the freezing cold. We had just lost a valuable breeding bull that we could not afford to replace. The worst of the winter was yet to come, and now she had an injured husband to nurse back to health.

No, jokes were definitely not welcomed at Lonesome Lake that day.

12

Keeper Of The Swans

"There's a double beauty whenever a swan swims on a lake with her double thereon." (Thomas Hood)

"Fire, Ethel, I'm on fire! Get the children out!" "It's all right, Ralph," Ethel said, gently pushing me back down on the bed. "You're not on fire, you're just having a bad dream. Now go back to sleep and you'll feel better in the morning."

I may not have been on fire, but that is not to say I wasn't hot. I was burning up. Ethel had fortified some patent medicine with her own concoction of herbs, spices and secret ingredients. I had also been rubbed with liniment and my ribs bound up in a bedsheet that Ethel had torn up for that purpose. Tanked up with hot tea laced with some other cure-all from her witch's cupboard, I was in my own private Hades.

"A few days of this and you'll be right as rain," Ethel soothed. "I could use a little of that rain right now," I countered. "I'm going to die of the heat." "Now just lie back and relax for once, Ralph," Ethel said. "The world won't stop just because you're laid up for a few days."

Ethel knew how much I hated to have to stay in bed; we rarely had colds and then only if someone brought one to us. I couldn't just lie there. I had better get up and get going. Set an example for the children." You are not getting up in that condition," Ethel commanded. "We can manage perfectly well without your help for a few days while your wounds heal. What do you think we do all the time you're away on the trapline? Sit in the house and sip tea?"

I could see there was no point in arguing with her. She is a very determined woman and once her mind is made up there is nothing on earth that can change it. Nothing. Besides, she was right. I wouldn't be much use hobbling around in this condition. I couldn't sleep on my sides or my stomach because of the pain from the broken ribs. Ethel had said she'd go for a doctor if I felt it was necessary and I had vetoed that idea. The alternative then, she said, was to lie still and let her nurse me back to health.

Well . . . I'd do it. But I sure as heck wasn't going to like it.

After three days of Ethel's combination witchcraft and home-nurse treatment, I began to feel much better. I could move around without too much pain and the tightly wound sheet around my chest seemed to have helped the ribs and got them mending. They were still sore to touch but there were no rasping sounds when I breathed. I had been keeping everyone awake. "Daddy", Stanley said, "you sure can snore." "Lying on your back all the time will do that to you," I explained. "The tongue flaps around in your throat like a loose fan belt. I can't help it, son. Give me a few more days and I'll get up and wrestle a bear for you."

The children had been very patient. Ethel had organized them so well with duties and games they found little time to quarrel. Once in a while one of the boys would tease Trudy, the baby, and get an angry look from his mom, but most of the time peace reigned in the cabin. I felt duty-bound to do something useful and since Ethel forbade me to get up, even to haul in wood or feed the chickens, I decided I might as well tell stories to the boys.

"Did I ever tell you boys when I was in India I saw a shoe walking without a foot in it?" I asked. "No, dad," the boys chimed. "Well . . . this day I was sitting on the veranda and along came this shoe belonging to my dad, only my dad's foot wasn't in it. It sure looked strange." "What **was** in it, dad?" Stanley asked. "Not even an old sock," I said. "I picked it up looked it all over and put it down again. And away it walked. I thought for sure I'd found a ghost shoe. Then I looked underneath, and there was a great big beetle, black and about two inches in diameter. It had got its head caught under the instep and was just plunging blindly along." "What did you do then, dad?" Johnny asked. "I pulled its head out and it went its way and the shoe went back to its mate in the bedroom."

"Tell us another story," the boys pleaded. "Well . . . there was the time my mom threw me and my toads out of the house. You see, in India they have a lot of strange animals. Scorpions, cobras, and all kinds of lizards. Like some of the ones you've seen in the **National Geographic.** I had a large collection of toads - all different sizes. One day my mother came storming into my room. 'Ralph Edwards,' she said, 'you'll be the death of me yet. I went into the market today and when I opened my purse to pay a shopkeeper, one of your toads leaped right into his face. Now what do you think of that?' I told her I thought it must have seemed pretty funny. But she didn't see any humor in it and that's how I found myself outside with my toad collection."

"Did you put the toad in your mom's purse, dad?" Stanley asked. "No, I didn't," I said. "I've always had a sneaking suspicion it might have been your uncle Earle who did it, but I never could prove it." "Did your mom let you back in the house?" Stanley asked. "Yes, she did. But she never let my toads back in. My bedroom was never the same after that."

Ethel was grateful for the respite of looking after the children and spent more and more time outdoors. After a week I was well enough to do some household chores and even cooked a few meals. But I was soon chomping at the bit and wanted to get back to work. First, I had to get those cows home. Reluctantly, Ethel agreed that I was well enough to tackle that assignment as "long as you take it easy and don't strain yourself."

The weather had warmed up and for that time of year very little snow had fallen. I put some grain in my pack as an inducement to the cattle to follow me home and shouldering my rifle, took off up the trail in their direction. The walking did me good and eased the stiffness. By the time I'd got to the valley

154

where I left the bovines, I was feeling more like my old self. Whatever had been in Ethel's witch's brew, it had worked a miracle.

The good milk cow and her heifer started bawling as soon as they saw me and I was still a half a mile away. They had found shelter among the trees and enough exposed grass to forage for. A nearby lump of frozen blood and guts was all that remained of my attacker; predators had done a fair job of rendering him to skin and bones.

There was no sign of the crazy critter and her bullish youngster - I never did locate them until spring - and it was just as well. I was feeling better, but not so well that I could control ornery livestock. The cow and heifer were enough as it was and by the time I got back to the farm I was exhausted. But I was darned if I'd let Ethel know it.

"You need some more of my potion," she said, when I limped in. "You look dreadful. Take off those wet clothes and let me put some of this on your chest." I never did find out what it was that Ethel put into her chest rub; it smelled like turpentine and looked like it was mixed with lard. At any rate, it was hot! "Feel better?" she asked. "Feel great!" I choked. "Feel like a new man."

It wasn't until many years later, when I had a full medical checkup that a doctor told me that sometime in my life I had broken my back. It had healed; in fact, had become stronger. I'm not so sure about my head. Whether I broke it at that time, when the bull gored me, or later when I fell off the horse rake onto a pole lying on the ground, I don't know. I do know what cured it. Ethel's back rub. It fused the bones together - under great heat!

After another day or two in bed, I was up and around again, considering the jobs at hand and debating with myself which one to tackle first. While I was thus engaged, nature dealt us another blow. A high wind blew two huge trees onto the barn roof. The log sides burst out so the structure looked like a child's game of pick-up sticks.

I wondered how many more things could go wrong before

our luck changed. I wasn't long in finding out. When I picked up the mail at Atnarko, one of the envelopes contained a check for a shipment of mink pelts, our major fur crop of the season. Mink prices, which fluctuated between twenty and thirty dollars a pelt, had plummeted to less than three dollars. The Great Depression had hit Lonesome Lake at last. There was no escaping its insidious grasp.

The next morning the sun came out and spread its rays across the lake and, despite our seemingly endless string of bad luck, I felt grateful. We didn't practice our Adventist faith as we should have done. Perhaps God was punishing us for our lapse? Certainly we didn't break many of the ten Commandments. We said grace when we ate our meals and refrained from alcohol and tobacco. Was there more that we should be doing? Perhaps we hadn't been thankful enough. I made a mental note to try to be a better Christian.

As the day continued to improve, I walked over to examine the barn damage and to look again at the site we had picked for the new house. On the way I stopped to check the unfinished hen house. No damage had been done to it by the wind. This was going to be a good-looking building, I thought. Then I had another thought, one which I expressed to Ethel a few minutes later: "To heck with the chickens. They can stay where they are, Ethel. That new building can be adapted to make a darn good home for us. For the time being anyway." Ethel agreed. Neither of us realized it but that hen house was going to be our permanent home as long as we lived on Lonesome Lake. The most difficult part of the construction was already completed. The plates were thirty eight foot logs and to get them in place I had employed Ginty and a block and tackle in a tree at the end of the structure. The long log slid on end on skid poles. As it went past Ginty he thought something was wrong. I had quite an argument with him. Every time he started up, the log went in the wrong direction, according to his reasoning, so he would always come to a dead halt. I finally convinced him that regardless of his calculations everything was all right and would work out in the end. After that he worked with a will, which was just as well: I was still plenty sore and didn't feel like arguing with a horse, or having to do any more physical labor than I had to.

What we ended up with was a log cabin, ten feet by twenty four feet, with a roof of dry cedar shakes extending over another twelve feet which would be used for a woodshed. By early spring I had the roof on and about half the floor laid. We moved in at the end of March, wheelbarrowing over our meagre belongings from the trapper's cabin. Ethel was forced to cook outside for several weeks until a stove and a heater were installed but she preferred that to the crowded conditions she'd been accustomed to for nearly six months.

"I really love this house," Ethel said, as final construction was within sight. "We never really gave this site enough consideration. You were right. It is far too good for chickens. Look at that view!" We had a magnificent, unobstructed vista southward across our entire clearing to beautiful green and snow-capped Walker's Dome. A Douglas fir, 150 feet tall, stood near the house, casting a dark shadow on the south kitchen wall at noontime, letting us know without benefit of clock or radio that it was time for lunch. We called it the noontime tree.

The warm summer sun brought the promise of a good year at Lonesome Lake. The barn was gradually constructed. The house was completed. I built new furniture to replace that burned in the fire. The boys lent a hand in the fields and from the spring onwards, Ethel canned vegetables, meat and salmon in the sealers we hauled in from Atnarko where supplies came from Bella Coola. This time we were taking no chances on losing everthing in a fire. The root cellar was separate from the house.

Day by day I saw subtle changes in the children. Although Stanley and Johnny took orders and carried out their duties, they lacked the personal initiative shown by their baby sister, Trudy. Young as she was, she thrived on work. Growing like a willow tree, I could see a lot of Ethel's and my spirit: "If you try long enough, there's always some way you can lick a problem."

While we were convincing ourselves that we could take anything that Fate could throw at us, while being thankful to the Lord for providing the bounty we had, we weren't certain that other creatures in His care were faring as well. For the past several years I had been becoming more and more concerned about the welfare of the trumpeter swans that landed at Lonesome Lake in the winter.

I had, of course, been aware of the swans since my first winter at the lake and had always been attracted to their trumpeting which reminded me of the little instruments that youngsters played tunes upon. The first year in the country, Frank Ratcliff shot one of these magnificent birds. We fried it in a pan like a steak and found it tasted quite different from goose. It was more like liver: Very rich and filling.

At that time there were no laws governing the shooting of trumpeter swans nor was it widely known that they were an endangered species. These beautiful snow-white birds with a wingspread of up to eight feet once bred from the Pacific throughout Canada and the United States as far east as Ontario and northern Quebec. They wintered on the U.S. Atlantic coast, in the Ohio-Mississippi valleys and along the coast of the Gulf of Mexico.

During the 19th century, however, swan skins became an item of trade. Powder puffs were made from them, muffs filled with swan's down were popular, garments were trimmed with swan skin and the hard, yet elastic quills made excellent pens. Between 1853 and 1877 the Hudson's Bay Company alone sold 17,671 swan skins in London; in 1828 it sold 347,298 goose, swan and eagle quills for pens.

In 1912 the famous American ornithologist Edward H. Forbush warned: "The trumpeter swan has succumbed to incessant persecution in all parts of its range and its total extinction is now only a matter of years." In 1916, just a few years after Frank Ratcliff and I were devouring one of this fast disappearing flock, a well-known Canadian biologist estimated there were only about 100 trumpeter swans left in the world.

Unknown to me at that time was the fact that about one-third of that number was wintering each year at Lonesome Lake. They had always come here. An old Indian in his nineties living in Bella Coola told me that his grandfather noted that as a young man he had seen swans congregating on the lake in winter. They ate in the spring-fed, ice-free areas of the Atnarko River and other rivers in the valley.

One day in 1926 a man name Ken Moore from Tatlyoko Lake in the southeastern Chilcotin, south of Tatla Lake and Kleena Kleene, brought some hunters over the mountain to our valley to hunt for bear. He asked Walter Ratcliff and me to guide for him and his party and we were both glad to get the chance to earn some money. More important, something resulted from that meeting that changed my life and influenced my attitude about a lot of things. The source of this inspiration was the introduction to John P. Holman of Connecticut, a member of the Audubon Society, one of the hunters in Moore's party.

Holman asked many questions about the trumpeter swans as we sat around the camp fire at night. He became enthusiastic on the subject of the wintering flock at Lonesome Lake. We became close friends and began a correspondence which lasted for many years, some of which he later published in his book **Sheep And Bear Trails.**

On his way home to the United States, Holman called on the Provincial Game warden, A. Bryan Williams, who, upon learning of our wintering flock of trumpeter swans, immediately communicated with J.A. Munro, Chief Federal Migratory Bird Warden for British Columbia. Munro wrote to me asking for details about the size of the flock and whatever other information I could give him. Ethel and I began to keep a log of all swan flights seen during the winter and extending up to the time that the swans left in the spring.

This was not an easy task because we were not trained then to spot trumpeters from the smaller whistling swans which sometimes traveled in close proximity with them. To further confuse us, both the trumpeter and the whistler are gray in their first juvenile season and white in their adult plumage, so close observation was necessary. I felt a real kinship for the birds and envied their ability to fly. I yearned to join them. But I was to remain earthbound for a long time yet.

We also became aware of the natural predators of the swans. In addition to wolves and coyotes, which occasionally harrassed the flocks, they had eagles to contend with. But cold weather was the worst enemy of the rapidly diminishing flock and in the spring of that year, after all the swans had left for nesting areas, I mailed a copy of the swan log to Mr. Munro. He insisted on paying us ten dollars for our trouble and next year appointed me part-time Assistant Migratory Bird Warden with a stipend of ten dollars a month for the five month period November to March.

Ethel and I did not feel right about making money off our beautiful neighbors so we decided to use the money for a sort of home improvement fund. We bought a typewriter to use in making out our reports and correspondence with the Canadian Wildlife Service, a Webster's Unabridged Dictionary and an encyclopedia. The latter was to help us answer the children's questions. Although neither Ethel nor I had much formal education, we had garnered much from books and magazines and through experience so that we had practical knowledge on a wide variety of subjects. Nevertheless, the children came up with queries that would have stumped a Harvard professor.

In her book **Fogswamp**, Trudy summed up her formal education this way: "I began correspondence school at the age of eleven and went through grades four and five in the first year. Then, because of having so much time taken up with farm chores, I slowed to one grade per year. Formal schooling stopped at Grade 9, although I started some Grade 10 courses. Of course, the correspondence school work did not comprise the total intellectual stimulation to which I was exposed. I grew up with books and truly cannot remember ever being unable to read."

The winter of 1932 and 1933 was severe and in the course of my trapping and on trips to Atnarko for the mail I came

160

across eleven dead swans. A three day downpour of rain set off landslides that raised the lake level and dammed up parts of the river, slowing its flow so that it froze over and deprived the swans of vital feeding grounds. The flock was reduced to nineteen.

In my annual report to Mr. Munro I suggested that it might be a good idea to feed the swans during bad winters. This idea was first broached by John P. Holman. The result was that I was given authority to purchase twenty five dollars worth of barley to feed the starving flock. That amount of money in those days bought 800 pounds of barley in 100 pound sacks. The problem was how to get it into Lonesome Lake?

Like it or not, the only way was to haul it by horse back and human back. Teamsters from Bella Coola brought it with our regular supplies to Belarko at the junction of the Talchako and Atnarko where the "good road" ended. It was left in piles, covered with tarpaulins to protect it from wildlife and the elements. Taking as much as possible at a time, I gradually moved it three miles to Atnarko where it was stored in a cabin. It took most of a week to complete the haul and another two to three weeks to move the winter's supply of grain and our own supplies to the north end of The Stillwater. Here I had built a mouse-proof grain bin.

The swan feed eventually was moved another three miles by horseback to the outlet of Lonesome Lake where it was another seven miles up the lake to where it was finally stored at the ranch in grain boxes that I had constructed.

Although we became fairly well organized in this delivery system, at the beginning it was learn as you go. From Mr. Munro and through our own experience we learned that for best results the soaked grain had to be poured into about two feet of water. Swans, tipping bottoms-up, reached with their long necks for aquatic plants, roots or insects from the river and lake bottoms. Similarly, they tipped for the grain we deposited. I would place a sack of barley in the river overnight, tied to a stake, so it was soaked by the time I was ready to distribute it. The swans would frequently fly over me while I was preparing the grain in this fashion and soon came to understand what I was doing.

At first they were wary but got to know I meant them no harm and became confident, bold even. Once while I was on the trail to Atnarko, they broke open the coarsely woven sacks so when I came back to the feeding site I was greeted only with empty sacks. "You sneaky devils," I said. "I'll fix you." After that I fed them the grain without soaking it first.

The important thing was that the grain did not float away but sink immediately to the correct depth for the swans to reach it. Three feet was the maximum depth their long necks could stretch. Deeper than that and it became food for the hardier, diving ducks. Feeding them once a week was not sufficient but as time went by we built up our supply of grain at a location close to home and young Trudy would go out every day at eleven o'clock and distribute about a half a pound of grain per day per bird. For over forty years this project has continued.

If I was away trapping I never had to worry about whether the birds would be fed; Trudy was as faithful at her task as any mother swan ever could be. At first the swans would fly away in alarm at the sight of a human figure approaching but later we could walk among them on the ice, sprinkling the grain there or tossing it into the fringes of the shallow water. When they arrived they would circle above us, their immense white wings flashing in the sun, Down they would plummet, their broad webbed feet stretched out like landing gears. They were a beautiful sight, trumpets tooting, flying in snowy white V formation. On the ground they continued their orchestrations, answered above by others. The voice of one swan carries more than a mile. When they had at last all landed, the mountain-flanked valley reverberated with their triumphant chorus.

First in line for chow were the young, gray cygnets, who were always hungry. Too young to trumpet their demands, they gave out sounds like constipated bassoons. Bolder than their elders, they trooped along behind Trudy or me in a flat-footed trot, gobbling up every grain of barley in sight.

When they rose off the ice, we marvelled at the gradual

change from foot locomotion to winged travel. It usually took about 100 yards for them to get airborne. Their tracks in the snow grew lighter and lighter until only a toe mark was left trailing its tiny farewell. However, the swans, if they were scared or pressed into flight by something, were capable of making a single jump start and could be airborne as quickly as a mallard duck. We grew to love them and never tired of watching their amusing, querulous antics.

In the fall of 1936, November to be exact, there was a flash flood due to warm weather and three days of incredibly heavy rain which melted all the early snow that had fallen. The rivers flowing into the Lonesome Lake chain of the Atnarko system flooded so much that they brought down tons of gravel with them. Goat Creek, which comes down at the southern end of The Stillwater, blocked it off with millions of tons of gravel. The Stillwater, which had once been a quiet shallow lake with meadows, the finest swan feeding ground in the area, was now a lake. The swan's food was submerged, along with many trees along the shore. Local people now refer to it as Snag Lake. It is no longer good haying land and no longer a good swan feeding area.

Another slide raised Lonesome Lake about four feet when Hunlen Creek flooded and blocked it off. Tenas Lake, further up the chain was also blocked off by a flooding river and was raised six feet. The flooding was followed by a sudden freeze-up. The whole valley was altered by the catastrophic flood and torrential downpour. There was no food anywhere for the swans. They had no alternative but to go up into the treeline where there was no food and where they usually were fearful to venture. Over fifty per cent of the flock died; there were thirty two survivors.

Ethel and I were distraught and anguished. "Surely there is something we can do," she said. "We can't just sit by and watch them all die." I agreed. There had to be a better way to feed the swans - something more reliable, adaptable to this changed environment.

163

13

"If The Swans Can Fly - So Can I!"

"If God had meant man to fly, he would have given him wings."
(Anonymous)

As Ethel and I agonized over the cruel way Fate had treated the swans, the swans themselves continued to be an enigma: They came to Lonesome Lake to winter year after year, had done so for a hundred years or more. They were now on the verge of extinction, yet they had the very means to take them up and away to warmer climes where their chances of survival would be far better. Why stay in these frigid, food-less conditions, numbers slowly declining, when they had those powerful wings at their command and could escape anytime they wanted to?

"I sure wouldn't hang around here for long if I could fly," Stanley grumbled. "I'd be out of here like a shot." Stanley, now a strapping teenager, reminded me of myself when I was his age - rebellious. Although his aims were not mine; he wanted a little more civilization, while I had wanted less.

"Maybe the swans are like us, Ralph," Ethel said. "We don't have to stay here and work like dogs to make enough to stay alive. We could all go and live in Vancouver where it's warm, with lots of neighbors and all the trappings of civilization. Why do **we** stay here?"

Ethel had a point. Why did we stay here? Every day was fraught with danger from wild animals, unpredictable weather and lack of social contact for months on end. Deep down, however, we knew why we had to stay. This was our home. We'd decided that after the disastrous fire and the other events that had tested our mettle.

Ethel had said, "maybe the swans are like us." But that was ridiculous. Other species - man himself - had in times past moved to warmer climates and better feeding grounds when the situation demanded. "Stubborn cusses, that's what they are," I said. "It's so easy for them too. They only have to fly out of here. Go south. Find some food."

My mind kept returning to that theme. "Fly out of here." Well . . . damn it, if the birds won't fly out for food, maybe we could fly out and get it for them! It sure would beat making three and four grain hauling trips for them every year.

"Fly an airplane?" Ethel asked, after I had posed the solution to her. "At your age, Ralph?" "What's the matter with that?" I protested. "I'm only forty eight and fit as a fiddle." "I want to learn how to fly too, dad," Trudy said. "Sure you do," I said, putting my arm around my little helpmate. "We can both learn and solve our transportation problems and the swans' feeding problems at the same time."

It certainly sounded like a good idea at the time. I had always been fascinated by airplanes ever since I watched them in aerial combat during the First World War in France. I had attempted to join the U.S. Air Force but didn't have the education. It would take a bit of persuasion, but I knew eventually Ethel would become enthusiastic too.

I reminded her of the long, tough hikes out for mail and supplies. "In the summertime, with the boats on the lake, it takes a day to go down to Atnarko and a day to come back - a good hard two days of hiking twenty miles each way. You have to rest for a day afterward. In the wintertime, with snowshoes, it can take up to four days if the snow is bad. With mail at Atnarko once every two weeks, that means twenty five mails a year and if it takes two days that means nearly two months of our time just going out for the mail.

"And that is in addition to the time spent going out and bringing in supplies. We have to close up the farm and work

165

about a month solid to bring in supplies as well as the barley for the swans." I could see I was making my point about the time we spent on the trail, time that could be spent more usefully at home. "With a plane we could do all that in jigtime with just a couple of flights."

While not exactly jumping up and down with enthusiasm, Ethel at least was interested. "The problem is, where are you going to get the money for a plane?" she asked. "Don't they cost a fortune?" Good point. I thought for a while. Trapping and big game guiding was bringing in the only income, aside from the pittance we earned for feeding and keeping tabs on the swans for the Canadian Wildlife Service.

"I know," I said. "We'll do the same as we've always done when we needed something we couldn't afford or couldn't carry in on our backs. We'll build it." Ethel thought for certain that I had been in the valley so long that my brain had become addled. "Build an airplane? Build a beaver dam, sure. Build a waterwheel, of course. But build an airplane, Ralph? That's a complicated machine."

I refused to listen to any more negative comments so I terminated the conversation on that subject. The children went off to their respective beds and Ethel and I remained in the kitchen for another hour. "Beds" for the boys and Trudy meant sleeping in various locations around the farm. I often slept in the hayloft in a hammock, covered only with a light blanket. I wanted the children to toughen up the same way and they were doing so, albeit, sometimes reluctantly. It was on this subject that I wanted to talk to Ethel.

"What's the matter with Stanley?" I said. "He always seems so sullen and hardly ever looks me in the eye." "You're pretty hard on him, Ralph," Ethel said. "You expect him to work as hard as you do and you give him very little reward when he does. He's not the same as you and you are going to have to face up to it. Stanley doesn't like farming and when he says he's going to fly out of here, he means it." Stanley had never knuckled under, even as much as Johnny had, certainly not the way Trudy had. Maybe I was too tough on him. And on

166

Johnny too. But, what the heck, hard work never hurt anybody. It was a challenge to be met, and what was life without challenges?

"The boys will find their own challenges in their own good time," Ethel said. "You'll just have to be patient." Just be patient. Huh! Being patient was not one of my virtues. I had always bulled things through, regardless of the odds. But . . . not everyone was like me. We'd have to wait and see.

We didn't have to wait and see for long. True to his word, Stanley decided to seek his own destiny at the tender age of seventeen. Two years later, Johnny also departed for "outside", leaving only Trudy who, at thirteen, became our "right hand man". I was upset at their leaving, although I didn't show it to them, and came to accept the fact that they deserved to develop on their own in their own way. Naturally, I was disappointed. I had hoped that one day the boys would take up land nearby and become neighbors. "They'll come home," Ethel said. "They're not gone forever."

But that was in the future, and so was my dream for building an aircraft. I had to wait until 1946, the end of the Second World War, to really put my plans into operation. There was a renewed interest in flying and older aircraft, and parts of all types were selling cheaply. There were also many parts which might be adapted to our specific use. I began to collect literature on the subject. The most interesting models were the amphibians, planes with wheels and pontoons. But they were terribly expensive. A straight float or pontoon plane was considerably cheaper but still far out of our price range.

I subscribed to various aviation magazines and bought several books on aviation design. The trouble was, they were so technical I couldn't figure out half of what they were saying. "I guess I've got to start from scratch," I said. Nothing new about that. "I never was long on maths and science in school, but I never had the incentive to learn like I do now." I mailed away for home study books and courses on mathematics and during inclement weather and in the evenings I studied quadratic equations, algebra, geometry, trigonometry, logarithms and everything connected with aeronautics that I could lay my hands on. Soon I could understand what I was reading.

The next step was to order parts. In one aviation magazine I noticed an advertisement by Leavens Brothers of Toronto. I wrote to them about a seventy five horsepower engine. They replied that the engine had been sold but they had a used eighty horsepower engine which they would sell me for a bit more than the smaller one. The engine was from a Globe Swift that had crashed, but the company assured me it would be airworthy. I asked them to ship the engine, ordered the cowling and engine mounts, and began to plan my plane around the engine.

First, I had to decide on the wing section. Two sections were recommended, the Clark Y and the 23015. The latter, it was reported, had a tendency to cause the plane to drop off suddenly after reaching peak lift force, while the Clark Y had more gradual drop off. Those were the sort of personal choices I was required to make during the next few months as the design for the plane grew in my mind and on paper.

I ordered propeller, bolts, dope, fabric and other fuselage parts from Macdonald Brothers of Winnipeg and when they arrived in Bella Coola by boat I packed them into Lonesome Lake by horse. The engine was the most difficult part to transport. It weighed 180 pounds. An Indian-style travois seemed to be the best way to carry it.

Trudy led her horse Topsy, a mare, while I followed behind, lifting the poles when the trail became too narrow for them to drag their full width along the ground. At one place below The Stillwater we had to cross the river so I took up the poles and Topsy plunged in. "Look out!" I yelled, as I tripped over a big boulder, dropped the poles and took a dip into the swirling water. Luckily only part of the engine went under and no important parts got wet.

Above The Stillwater the trail parallels a very steep hillside and one of my caulked boots hit a loose fir cone which caused me to slip. I dropped the poles again and this time almost fell over the edge. As it was, I was left sitting with my feet over the ledge, the poles in my lap. Topsy held still, which was

168

Ralph Edwards, Crusoe of Lonesome Lake, at his home The Birches.

Looking south up the Atnarko River to Lonesome Lake lying east of Turner Lake with Stillwater Lake in the foreground. The Chilcotin Plateau is to the east and the expanse of the Coast Mountains lies west and south.

Edwards' children Trudy, John and Stanley with wolf and cougar pelts.

Ralph returning from hunt with fine bear hide.

Ralph, Ethel and Trudy.

The Birches, The Edwards' homestead lies in the incredibly rich Atnarko Valley where enormous trees had to be removed before a garden plot and pasture could be worked.

Most of Ralph's tools and implements to subdue the land were handmade, such as this wagon and stone boat. Opposite, the steel plow shear had to be backpacked in and the handles carved.

Hand carved pulley blocks and woven raw-hide ropes transferred power from the waterwheel to the sawmill.

Ralph proudly displaying one of his unique gate hinges. The weight of the gate post sat on a rock or wooden block while a deer antler or specially selected crooked branch acted as a harness around the rotating gate post.

Ethel always had a way with animals and wild deer would eat from her hand.

Usually more deer than cattle sought refuge around the Birches Homestead.

Bountiful garden had to provide full year's supply of vegetables and fruit which were preserved in jars or dried, or stored in root cellars.

Clark's crow or nutcracker feasts on suet offered by the Edwards.

Ruffed, a willow grouse struts on drumming log near homestead.

The log barn at daughter
Trudy Turner's homestead
one-and-a-half miles south
up the Atnarko River.

Barns and cattle yards at the Birches were all of planks cut on Ralph's
waterpower operated mill.

Daughter Trudy Turner now with her own daughter in homemade backpack, 1961.

Ralph on doorstep of Birches displaying "Prevent Forest Fires" poster.

All supplies originally had to come in over the long arduous trail on the back of man or beast. Here Trudy's stove arrives.

Lonesome Lake trumpeter swans.

During the coldest winter month each swan is given one half pound of food daily.

Trumpeter swans congregate on Lonesome Lake during the winter months. It was the grain packed in originally by Ralph that is largely credited with saving this magnificent bird from extinction. Yearly the swans' numbers increase and today they are no longer considered an endangered species—the only North American species to change status from endangered to safe—a fine tribute to the Edwards.

From a low of 14 swans in 1912 the lake now houses more than 500. Many hundreds more winter on other coastal inlets and lakes.

Trudy Turner took over her father's swan responsibilities and today her husband Jack and daughter Susan carry out the daily feeding with equal dedication.

The trumpeter swan is the largest bird in North America weighing between 20-35 pounds. The juveniles wear a gray plumage the first year before attaining the white adult plumage.

In recent years these magnificent birds, which can weigh up to 35 pounds, have so increased in numbers that the population now threatens to overbrowse the natural foods. Almost contrary to the Turner's and of course Ralph's early efforts, the Canadian Wildlife Service provides automatic exploding devices to disperse the birds to surrounding lakes and inlets early in the season. Once the cold weather sets in the noise stops and feeding begins.

Ralph and son John who recently purchased the Birches and is carrying on his father's love of the country. He operates a series of guest lodges and canoes at both Lonesome Lake and the higher Turner Lake claim on Tweedsmuir Park for hikers and camera hunters only.

Ralph and brother Earl
from Bella Coola Valley.

Ralph, Trudy, Ethel and
Ralph's mother in 1956.

Ralph and Ethel just preparing Taylorcraft for takeoff. Ethel's quilted engine cover prevented engine from coating too quickly.

Ralph and his pride and joy. He learned to fly at age 65 — many years later in life than most flyers retire.

The hangar at Lonesome Lake was built from timbers cut on his hand-made, water-powered sawmill.

A take-off on a remote mountain lake.

Ralph gassing up—the little bird's constant demand kept the family busy raising vegetables and beef, their main cash crop.

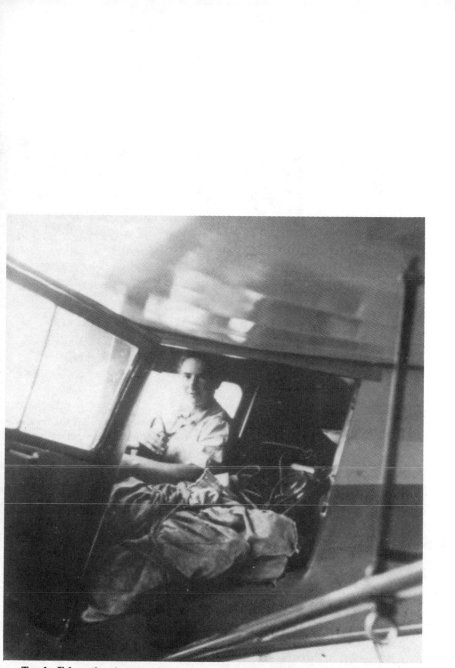

Trudy Edwards, shortly after her flying began, became Mrs. Jack Turner.
Here she flies in a load of carefully wrapped machine parts and spare gas.

Ralph gassing up at Williams Lake 1956.

Regularly Ralph flew his little float plane on and off the frozen and covered surface of Lonesome Lake—pioneering landing technique used by many pilots—though preferably only in an emergency.

Oona River estuary—here the pilot-farmer-rancher became a commercial fisherman at age 70.

The Crusoe was the center of pilots' attention wherever he went. Ralph thoroughly enjoyed the alternate isolation and attention and recognition he received "outside".

Ralph lived simply. With his worldly possessions at Oona River, a cash box, a gift of salmon, he heads off for a flight back to Lonesome Lake to meet Ethel.

Ralph beside his gill-netter. Somehow the twosome weathered over 100mph winds off the mouth of the Skeena River—only sustaining minor damages when grounded on a falling tree.

Ralph in retirement outside his Oona River home.

Ralph giving graduation address to Prince Rupert Senior Secondary School—a great moment for students and Edwards alike. In later years Ralph was honored with the Canadian Governor Generals award for Conservation and met HRH Queen Elizabeth and Prince Phillip in recognition of his pioneering swan work.

Younger fishermen of Oona River enjoy questioning the old bird man about both the mountains and the sea.

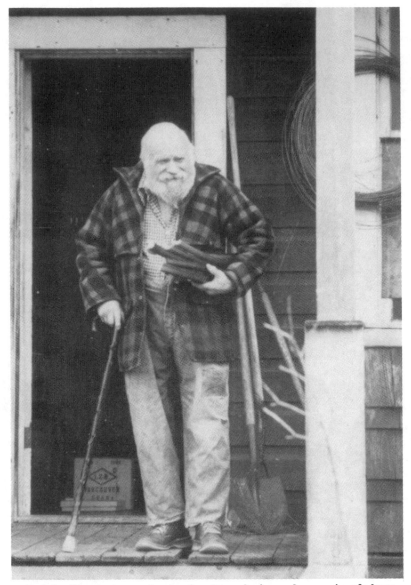

Ralph without wings or boat retires to gardening and memories of a busy life learning about a wilderness he loved.

fortunate, because if she had made a mis-step, she and Trudy and I all would have gone down into the river.

When we got the engine to the ranch we set it on two upright poles, filled the sump with oil, and turned the engine over. It worked like a new watch. Not that it counted for much at the time. It was still sitting on the uprights ten years later because our dream of building and flying our own plane never came to be realized.

And what a blessing it would have been to have had a plane during that period. A series of milder winters and our continual feeding of the swans had been pleasing to us but it had also put an incredible burden on us as well. With more swans to feed and more farm to tend, it was impossible to find time to haul in enough grain. Then the weather changed again and the need for a plane was re-emphasized. Although 1956 was not the coldest on record, it was by my reckoning the longest steady freezeup period during my residency on Lonesome Lake. For months the temperature ranged with very few respites between 20° F. and -20° F.

The swan flock, which we had gradually built up from almost nothing to several hundred, was about to be decimated again. There was little river-bottom feeding from early November until April and the flocks suffered perhaps the heaviest loss since 1936, even though they ate their way through seven thousand pounds of Canadian Wildlife Service barley. At least ten per cent of the flock perished.

I appealed to the CWS to airlift grain into the lake to aid the starving birds. We were practically out of grain, there was no end in sight to the winter, and we couldn't pack in enough to alleviate the situation. The CWS agreed to come to our rescue and one morning there was a strange sound outside. An airplane was circling the Big Lagoon.

"Ethel, come and see this!" I yelled as I ran up to the house from the barn where I had been curry-combing a horse. The plane circled low, dipped its wing at us, and then climbed to a higher altitude. "That's an Air Force plane," I said, craning my neck to read lettering on the wing and fuselage. "It must be

201

the one bringing the swan grain. But why in the world would they send in a big plane like that? And with no skis to land on the ice."

The answer came a moment later. Now that the pilot had attracted our attention, he swung his craft in a big arc and suddenly out of its belly came several parachutes with bags of grain tied to them. The target was the ice and some of the chutes hit dead on, but others drifted into the trees on the hillside. No grain was spilled but the parachutes were torn.

We soon had the grain gathered into our various storage bins and generous amounts of it distributed to the swans who had at first flown away in alarm at the noise of the plane. We also recovered the parachutes and I had to talk Ethel - ever conscientious - out if attempting to mend them. "I don't think a patched parachute would be very popular with someone jumping out of a plane," I said.

The parachuted grain saved the day for the swans. They had by now learned to eat it off the ice and Trudy went down every day and sprinkled about half a pound to each bird and soon, literally, had them eating out of her hand. We discovered that adult swans, like humans, let the offspring have first chance at the food. Also, they seldom fought among themselves and - on more than one occasion that I personally witnessed - waited until the whole flock had landed before beginning to eat. The future looked brighter for our feathered neighbors than it had for years.

The following year looked good for us too. In fact, it was almost too good. Ethel, in her zealous way, had stuffed the root cellar with edibles and even the house now was filled to brimming with the results of our efforts in garden, forest and stream. It was annoying to learn that the government was not going to build any roads close to our site and a railway was just a forgotten pipedream. We certainly could have used it to dispose of some of our abundance of produce.

The swans kept producing more and more offspring and as winter drew on again, we became concerned that we would not have enough grain if the weather turned nasty. Rather than let that happen, we called upon the CWS to bring in extra grain and again the Canadian Air Force came to our aid. This time two sacks of grain fell into the river. We hauled it home and dried it out in the oven so it would not rot. The following year we again required emergency grain and this time a parachute on one flight failed to open and the sacks fairly exploded when they hit the ice.

Grain was thrown high in the air. We swept it up along with the light covering of snow that was on the ice, took it into the house and began the laborious job of drying it out. Ethel was fuming. "We can't go on feeding swans in this haphazard way. Heavens, we've got enough to do without having to fill the house with drying grain."

"I'll write to the Wildlife Service and tell them there are some problems with the airdrop," I said. "Maybe they can work out something more satisfactory." I was saved the trouble. Apparently the Air Force was having second thoughts about bringing in the grain each winter. We never did discover what politics were involved in the maneouver, but a letter from the CWS arrived advising us to order enough grain so it would not be necessary for the Air Force to have to come to the rescue.

This meant we would be required to use a pack train of three or four horses and several trips to just bring in grain. The job of running the farm with its fair-sized herd of cattle, horses and other animals, my big game guiding and occasional trapping, made making that many trips an impossibility. A proper airlift would have solved the whole problem.

"I'm going to ask the CWS to let one plane bring in all the grain once a year and they can also bring in all our supplies," I told Ethel. "Go ahead," she said. "They can only say no." I wrote to the CWS with this request and, to my surprise, they agreed. A few weeks later a plane owned by Queen Charlotte Airlines droned overhead. As we watched, it sideslipped along the mountainside and plopped down the lake. Out stepped pilot Johnny Hatch, a chipper young chap who was to become a valuable, lifelong friend.

With each succeeding flight, the friendship grew and one

night, after unloading the supplies, Johnny decided to stay over. As we sat around the flickering fire, Trudy and I fired questions at him about airplanes. I brought up the question of building my own. The engine was still sitting on the uprights, unused, and the other parts were stored in various sheds.

"The Department of Transport will never let you fly your own home-made plane,"Johnny said. "Even if they do let you fly it, it'll be years before they get around to certifying it. Why don't you buy a good used plane? You can get a good one that doesn't have to cost you an arm and a leg."

We hadn't thought of buying a used plane but now Trudy and I gave it consideration, after figuring out how much we might pay for it. I had hoarded a little cash from guiding hunters and Trudy, who had been feeding the swans for several years and had saved almost all her swan money, had quite a little in her own poke. She had also helped me with the haying so I had given her a heifer calf and after it had delivered two calves which were butchered and sold, she netted more money. In addition, I had given her all the squirrels that got into my traps and she had prepared their skins for market, thus adding to her wealth.

It was decided that we had enough money to buy a small used plane. The immediate problem was that neither of us could fly. Since I was now over sixty years of age, Trudy was elected to go to Vancouver and take flying lessons. When she received her license, and there was never any doubt in our mind that she would, she would then scout around to locate a suitable airplane.

Ethel and I watched, our hearts in our mouths, as our daughter plodded off to the big city to learn to fly. I was envious and all the time she was away I was in a fever of excitement. I kept harkening back to the time in September 1939 when I'd had my first plane ride. I was looking forward to reliving that marvelous experience.

Trudy meantime moved in with the Johnny Hatches at their small farm in the Fraser Valley near Vancouver. Every morning Johnny would drop her off at the International Air-

204

port on Sea Island. In the evening he would pick her up.

Right from the start Johnny had been impressed with Trudy's knowledge about planes and the depth of her queries which sometimes made him scratch his head as he thought up answers about induction coils, magnetic fields and other pertinent information. She finally stumped him - and she learned it all from books!

Such knowledge was of immense value to her because she acquired her private pilot's license in well under the normal time and soon was certified to fly any wheel plane less than 4000 gross weight. That accomplished, she and Johnny Hatch and another pilot, Roy Moulton, went looking for a suitable plane for us. It took longer than expected; it was July before the right plane come on the market: a Taylorcraft float plane which cost 2500 dollars, plus tax. Then Trudy learned she couldn't fly it, not legally anyway. Back she went to the instructor to get checked out on flying a float plane.

While this was all taking place I was in an agony of excitement. I had wanted to fly for so long I couldn't wait for Trudy to bring the plane in to the lake. I'm sure my letters to her during this interval must have amused her. I was worse than a kid waiting for a favorite toy promised for Christmas. Every time a plane flew over, I stopped whatever I was doing to look up at it until it finally disappeared. Nothing new in that of course; I'd always been fascinated by planes. But now I was so near to actually flying myself, my whole body itched for the experience.

In order to keep my mind off the delays of buying the right plane and Trudy's having to acquire the float plane license, I decided to redouble my efforts to complete the hangar Trudy and I had begun to build in the winter of 1952 - 53. It was quite an engineering feat, if I do say so myself. A series of problems were posed. First of all, the structure, thirty feet by forty feet and twenty five feet high, had to be constructed on the ice and on sloping mud sills which would settle on the shelving bottom of the lagoon with spring thaws, yet still leave the above-surface hangar on an even keel once it had settled to the bottom. It had to be built in winter in this fashion in order to provide a deep water approach for the seaplane.

Boring through the ice, I took the differing measurements down to a solid bottom - a sloping variation of two feet or more between where the building's shoreside supports and its lagoon-fronted supports would rest. Trudy and I then laid out the big forty foot cedar logs which would serve as mud sills, putting temporary blocks under what would be the shore-side ends.

In this way the sills slanted forward to their lagoon-front ends, in estimated conformity with the lagoon's bottom. Next, of course, on top of this, we had to contrive a level floor for the hangar itself. This we accomplished by making the shore-side foundation posts, above the slanting sills, only four feet high and those on the front side about six feet high, with other posts in between of an equalizing height. Thus we had a level frame for the floor, set upon what would be a slanted under-pinning once the shore-side blocks were knocked out.

With ten foot posts for its side walls, the building's peak had to be twenty five feet above the floor to supply adequate room. But first we had to connect the ten foot high posts with heavy cross beams called plates; and on top of them, big tie beams for each truss rafter in the roof. These eight truss rafters had to be very heavy and set into the ends of the tie beams so that all the pressures were supported by wood compression or tension.

To protect the hangar's sides from dripping snow, the rafters must project some two feet out from the sides. But how to raise the forty foot tie beams fifteen feet above the ice to swing them into place? How to get the great truss rafters up some thirty five feet from the ice to lower them into place?

With sloping poles up which to slide the 1600 pound logs, and using movable windlasses, and a device called the jin-pole, we got the cross or tie beams into place. A jin-pole is a pole that is easily raised by hand, with a block tied on top. You rope through this block, and then a team of horses can raise objects which would be impossible otherwise. Next came the intractable problem of raising the heavy truss rafters - and here Trudy came up with a highly ingenious invention. These logs were simply too big to be lifted as high as thirty or thirty five feet by a jin-pole alone. Once above the main walls, the truss rafters had to be swung inward, over the main framework.

Trudy suggested we use another pole besides the jin-pole, a kind of cross between a jin-pole and a truss. It worked precisely as she had predicted. She called it a "metagon", meaning a change-of-angle pole. Both jin-pole and metagon required very strong bracing and guying but nothing got loose and there were no accidents. In two months, Trudy and I had completed the hangar's framework. When spring came and the large hangar settled down on its forty foot mud-sill logs, each shorter by some two feet at one end than the other, it came solidly to rest in the oozy bottom, absolutely level. We had many compliments for that particular construction feat. While Trudy was getting her flying license, I roofed over the hangar and built a sloping entrance deck for the plane.

Despite the furious activity to complete the hangar in time for Trudy's arrival, I found it difficult to concentrate. What would the plane look like? Would I be able to get a license at my age? All sorts of questions buzzed constantly in my head. Ethel too was excited and we lived in hope all that spring and summer.

Everytime we heard a plane swoop down into our valley we would drop whatever we were doing and wait, expecting it to land on the lake. Time and time again we were disappointed. Then on July 8, about five in the afternoon, I looked up from my gardening to see a tiny white and blue plane coming straight down the valley alongside Walker's dome. There was no doubt about its purpose. It was going to land on Lonesome Lake. But was it Trudy, or just a visitor?

I felt certain it was Trudy and yelled to Ethel who was already running towards the hangar. We got there just as the little craft taxied up. Out stepped our daughter: The Amelia Earhart of Lonesome Lake.

For the next few days Trudy regaled us with tales of her flying instruction and her first trip to "the big city." In her overalls and work shoes, she cut quite a figure. Her impatience with city life communicated itself to her flying lessons as well. While soloing, she decided to experiment with landing approaches. This upset the instructors who thought something was wrong because each time Trudy whizzed down to within a few feet of the tarmack, she would pull up and wheel around for another run at it. The flying instructor finally sent up another plane to "guide her down". Trudy was so affronted by this that she took evasive action and felt great joy in beating the other pilot to the landing strip. A perfect landing!

She told us about her frustrations at buying the plane. There seemed to be nothing on floats that filled the bill. On her second trip into neighboring Washington State, she and Roy Moulton found and purchased the little blue and white plane. The sixty five horsepower Taylorcraft was at Grand Coulee Dam and Roy, an expert all-weather pilot for Pacific Western Airlines in Vancouver, flew it up to the coastal city for her.

Roy gave her some practical instructions on the trip up and in subsequent trips around the city to augment the book-learning she already had on float plane operation. Roy told me later the maverick in Trudy sometimes went contrary to his own nature and book instructions did not always translate to actual experience. "She was inclined to want to be convinced as well as shown," Roy said.

Trudy soon convinced me that she was an excellent pilot as we flew up out of the valley and began to visit some of the fish camps in the area. In less than forty minutes we were at Charlotte Lake where there were two big camps. We asked the operators if they would like us to fly in fresh vegetables every week or two. Does a duck swim? Of course they would! No luxuries such as fresh produce had been obtainable before.

We began air-freighting fresh milk and cream, butter, lettuce, radishes, tomatoes, corn, beans, carrots, potatoes, strawberries and whatever other fruits were in season. Trudy made two and three flights a day as the camps and lodges would be sold out before she could get back. Another dream had been realized: The long-awaited railroad that would pick up the fruits of our labors for sale had never been built, but the plane was a good alternative.

The following year, in March 1954, I went to Vancouver to try to get my license. That was the only missing link in our goal and I was determined to forge it before I got much older. I was sixty two and had been dreaming about flying a plane for many years.

This was my first visit to Vancouver since 1919 when I returned from the First World War. After spending an interesting evening swapping yarns at the Hatches, I presented myself to the doctor for my pre-flight physical examination. The doctor was not impressed with the specimen standing before him. "Aren't you a little too old to fly?" he asked. I told him that I understood that I could fly if I could pass the physical. He went to the phone and called the Department of Transport, preferring to take their word over mine. He reported back a few minutes later. "Well, I'll be darned," he said. "You're right. I thought they had an age limit . Let's get at it, then. Take off your shirt."

He checked my heart and lungs and then wrapped a pad around my biceps and studied my blood pressure. "Why, you have the blood pressure of a man of twenty eight!" he exclaimed. It surprised even me because during the preliminary discussion I am sure my blood pressure must have gone up a few points. Now I felt much relaxed.

I passed the exam, paid my fee and began flying lessons. Some confusion exists about who taught me to fly. Some say it was Trudy. While it's true that my daughter did give me instruction on how to land and take off the various lakes where she was delivering produce, I still took the required courses in Vancouver. I enjoyed the experience and the Cessna 140 trainer performed well under my direction. It took about a month for me to get the kinks out of my takeoffs and landings but I had no real difficulty and was soon soloing. The instructor sent me down toward a finger of land called Point Roberts, which is part of Washington State, landlocked inside the province of

British Columbia.

I was to practice spins and turns. I did not intend to do any spinning if I could help it but I expected to have to turn a lot so I spent as much time as possible practicing those and forced landings which I thought might come in handy. Since the flying school did not have its own float plane, I had to borrow a Cessna 180 on floats. I appealed to Roy Moulton to check me out on this aircraft so I would be fully licenced when I got back to Lonesome Lake.

Roy directed me to the mouth of the Fraser River which runs into the Pacific Ocean near Vancouver. On a stormy Friday afternoon, with wind and low clouds for company, I practiced takeoffs and landings for three hours. Water had entered the airspeed indicator and the stall-warning device maintained an irritating beeping sound. This, plus my inexpert handling of the plane, must have wreaked havoc on Roy's nerves, but he remained outwardly calm.

Out of Roy's sight, when I gained my license and confidence as a pilot, I developed my own style of taking off and landing. The Taylorcraft we had bought was a perfect aircraft for a short takeoff, if you followed my technique, which few pilots did. What I did was to lift one float, get the aircraft up on one float, build up the speed and then, instead of waiting for the aircraft to fly off at its natural speed, just manually pull it off. Many planes have flaps to get them airborne; the Taylorcraft didn't.

It was just a matter of hauling back on the control yoke, as they say. It would be skipping along and I would just pull the nose up and jump it out of the water and then put the nose back down a bit to build up the air speed - but not down so far that I got back in the water again. Some pilots used to marvel at my technique. I never found anything marvelous about it. I just found it a fast way to get off the water, which is where I wanted to be.

An official of the Department of Transport accepted Roy's report on my flying ability and soon I had the piece of paper that said I was a qualified seaplane pilot. It was March,

1954. I caught the weekly boat for Bella Coola and felt strangely nostalgic as it docked in the coastal fishing community. The previous time I had arrived was when I came home from the First World War. Time had altered many things.

Bella Coola was by now a thriving community. Roads and bridges had been improved. The spotlessly clean homes of the Adventists were like buttons along the ribbon of highway that ran up the valley. My nephew, Glen Ratcliff, met me in his jeep and drove me up as far as the four-wheeled drive vehicle would go. I walked and rowed the rest of the way into Lonesome Lake. My heart was light. Although my arrival at the farm was not as auspicious as Trudy's after she learned to fly, the welcome home was just as warm.

14

Wings Over The Wilds

"Love must have wings to fly away from love, and to fly back again." (Edwin Arlington Robinson)

Trudy insisted I get as much practise flying as possible and with her along as safety pilot, I spent at least an hour a day for weeks trying to perfect my landings and takeoffs. I also accompanied her to several of the fish camps and lodges with loads of produce. Sometimes I went on my own and soon felt confident enough to make a long flight. The opportunity came.

We were advised that our garden seeds were being held at the Custom's warehouse in Vancouver and an order for baby chicks was awaiting pickup at the hatchery down there. I left the next day. "Be careful, Ralph," Ethel said. "I don't want you to fly if the weather is bad. Wait a day or so rather than take any chances." Worry wart. I was facing my first long distance flight and I felt like a bird on the wing. I kissed Ethel and took off.

I guided the plane along the Klinaklini River, past Mount Waddington, a forbidding hulk standing more than 13,000 feet, fifty miles to the east, and along Knight Inlet, emerging into Johnstone Strait which separates Vancouver Island from the Mainland of British Columbia at that point. I felt more relaxed having reached Knight Inlet, remembering what Trudy had told me of her experience flying through that area.

Coming back from a coastal logging camp, the ceiling closed down over the Klinaklini and since there is a long stretch there with no fit place for a plane to land, Trudy flew back to Knight Inlet and landed there. She ran into trouble on the same route a few days later but on that occasion had flown so far through the pass there was no possibility of turning back when a solid wall of gray fog suddenly materialized, completely enveloping the Taylorcraft and cutting off all visibility.

The little plane could fly itself if trimmed properly and the controls not moved. The pass is only about 500 to 1000 feet wide - not much room for error - but it is also short. Twenty five seconds later Trudy came out of the fog still on course with the clear blue Pacific far below. She had been sitting completely still, unable to see a thing. And at eighty miles an hour, top speed in the Taylor craft, you travel a fair distance.

Another time, on a return trip from Bella Coola, the weather was clear but there was a gale blowing down the Talchako River. At about 5000 feet, Trudy ran into extreme turbulence apparently caused by the wind hitting the rock wall on the north side of the valley and mixing with a strong west wind. It was so rough she seriously considered the chance the wings might be ripped off. The plane climbed at a rate of several hundred feet per minute, then suddenly dropped 1000 feet or more, only to jolt to a sudden stop and begin climbing again. She described the sensation as being "like a rat shaken by a savage dog." Because the wind and turbulence were so severe, it seemed to her it took an eternity to fly ten miles. Once past the mouth of the Talchako River, the air was smooth and the remainder of the flight was uneventful.

I was mindful of Trudy's experiences as I flew south, wondering when my turn would come to test my experience. I looked at the gas gauge, decided to refuel at Stewart Island, overnighted there and flew on to Vancouver the next morning.

I felt so confident after my first long flight, I couldn't help expressing my delight to my friend, Gordy Peters, who picked me up at the airport on Sea Island. Gordy drove me to the Custom's warehouse where I picked up the seeds from the United States, then out to Surrey where I took delivery of the thirty, day-old chicks at the hatchery. Everything was well coordinated so I was ready to leave for home in the early afternoon.

My first stop was at Refuge Cove, a little more than one-third of the distance home, where I stayed overnight. Next morning the weatherman reported a forty mile wind was blowing up the coast but I figured on going anyway. I had no plans to turn my plane into a chicken coop; time was of the essence. If the wind got too severe, I would sit down in some sheltered place and wait it out.

Low cloud prevented me from returning the way I'd come, up Knight Inlet, so I flew past Alert Bay on Cormorant Island, a fair-sized community, where I took on gas. The air was very turbulent and overcast as I flew low along the coast, hopping from island to island, until I reached open water between the top of Vancouver Island and past Rivers Inlet to Fitzhugh Sound, well on the way to Bella Coola.

Although it was bumpy most of the way, nothing happened until the plane suddenly began to head straight downward. The airspeed was building up rapidly before I could even reach to pull off the power and gradually ease back on the wheel to put the plane on the straight and level again. It seemed an eternity before the aircraft responded and this was my first real scare.

The excitement wasn't over yet: The wind was blowing so hard I had to maintain a hard right rudder to keep from blowing out to sea. When I reached Fitzhugh Sound I had the wind directly behind me and made good time until I reached Burke Channel where the air became rough again. Just over Bella Coola a snow storm began with large wet flakes swirling around the plane.

I dropped down to within ten feet of the water in case the plane loaded up with snow. That was something we had been warned about in flying school. That bit of misinformation was eventually thrown out completely. In fifteen years of flying, in all kinds of weather, the worst thing that snow ever did was to hamper my visibility.

However, I had no desire to fly over the mountains into Lonesome Lake with snow falling at that rate, so I landed in choppy water near the fisherman's wharf at Bella Coola. After tying up, I wrapped a goat wool quilt around myself and the chickens and feeling quite like a broody hen, went to sleep, lulled by the gently rocking plane on the waves.

About 11 o'clock in the morning the snow stopped so I wound the prop on the Taylorcraft and taxied away from the wharf and boats and took off, landing at Lonesome Lake about an hour later. Ethel and Trudy expressed concern: "What happened? What took you so long? Did you have trouble with the plane? Are the chicks all right?" I told them I had stayed overnight at Bella Coola because of the snow and not to worry about the chicks. I felt like a new mother. Twenty eight out of thirty chicks survived my first flight from Vancouver.

I tried to learn something new with each flight. No flight is exactly the same and as my father told me long ago, experience is the best educator. But: "Learn from others' errors; you can't possibly make them all yourself!" Dealing with the mechanical problems kept flying interesting and overcoming the vagaries of wind and air and waves on the water was a challenge that nothing I had ever experienced could match.

The plane became as much a part of life at Lonesome Lake as the horses had done earlier; we could scarcely do without it. At this time the Post Office Department decided to terminate the fortnightly postal delivery to Atnarko and instead set up little mail compartments with locks on them to serve customers east of Firvale. That meant anyone living at the communities of Atnarko and Stuie had to go to Firvale to pick up their mail. They told all of us that they were improving our service by making us go another twelve miles. The result was that the boxes were now forty miles from us and so small that hardly anyone used them. With the volume of mail that came to Lonesome Lake we needed something the size of a garbage can, not a biscuit box. In still another move to "improve" the service, the Post Office Department finally withdrew its service even from Firvale. We said "to heck with that", and changed our mailing address to Bella Coola and flew out once a week to get it with our supplies.

Trudy continued to make contacts with the logging camps and tourist operators, lining up customers for our various products. She flew me in to meet Bob Stewart, who was establishing a trout fishing camp at Nimpo Lake, about twenty five miles northeast of our place. He was a big, hearty man with a vision of creating a large lodge and tourist resort. At that time, 1954, he had only two tent cabins with the beginnings of the lodge and several other log buildings.

Bob, who had come from Winfield, British Columbia, started his camp in 1951 and two years later moved his wife and two children in. The road that now passes their very successful operation then ended at Anahim Lake, a pleasant Chilcotin community a few miles east of Nimpo. The road now continues on to Bella Coola through some of the most rugged but beautiful terrain in the world. As his development increased in size, he began to order more and more vegetables and meat. He was particularly impressed with Trudy and the fact that she could carry almost as much on her sturdy little shoulders as I could.

We had some amusing incidents concerning landings and takeoffs at Nimpo Lake. One day Trudy landed the plane and was about ready to tie up at the Stewarts' wharf when a big logger named Ernie Quissey put his foot onto the pontoon in a gesture of goodwill. He extended his hand to assist her out of the plane. "Get your big, fat foot offa that float!" Trudy yelled. Ernie was so surprised he almost tripped off the dock.

Undaunted, he was there when Trudy flew in with her next load a week later. He had told Bob Stewart that he was going to "hit her up for a date." This time he helped tie up the plane and carried some of the produce up to the lodge. He was a while getting around to his main object, but finally blurted it out: "Any chance of getting a ride over to Lonesome Lake?" "What for?" Trudy asked, in her blunt way. "I, uh, always wanted to see that place," Ernie said, shyly. "Oh, well," Trudy said, "get in then."

Ernie weighed well over 200 pounds and Trudy still had supplies to be dropped off at two locations on Charlotte Lake.

The load was too much for the Taylorcraft. "You'll have to lose some weight before I can take you to Lonesome Lake," Trudy advised Ernie. The way Bob Stewart recalls it, Ernie actually fasted and lost a considerable amount of weight. He must have been smitten with my daughter to make such a sacrifice, but, as the bard says, the course of true love seldom runs smoothly. Although he got his desired trip to Lonesome Lake, it wasn't a romantic adventure. Trudy put him to work in the potato patch all day!

We got to know the Stewarts well over the years and soon Trudy and I were flying in produce to Nimpo for more than just the resort operators. Bob built a big ice house where we stored vegetables and meat which were sold to other residents who had moved into the area. One day Bob was helping me unload and when I got ready to take off he asked if he could assist me by winding the propeller. The Taylorcraft had no starter. It had to be hand-wound; that is, you had to wind it yourself, then jump in and take over the controls.

"Let 'er rip!" I told Bob, and he gave the prop an elaborate twist from his position on the front of one float. I had forgotten that I had left the throttle on full power for priming and the plane rocketed ahead so fast that Bob was thrown for a belly flop into the water. I had to make another trip to Nimpo Lake that day and Bob asked what happened. I told him. "What happened to you?" I asked. "I got wet," Bob replied. "Well..." I said, "I figured you could swim better than you can fly!"

In point of fact, Bob Stewart became an excellent pilot and with his own plane helped bring cargo into Lonesome Lake. We purchased a tractor which was delivered by truck to Nimpo and Bob helped me transfer it in pieces in his Cessna 206.

The Stewarts and the Edwards became good friends and I looked forward to my visits there, although one landing was not as successful as some others. I flew in too fast and instead of coasting slowly up to the dock, the plane kept skimming along until it went right up on the beach, across a strip of grass, and came to full halt in a clump of trees. The Stewarts came running down to see if the crazy fool from Lonesome Lake had killed himself but all that was damaged was my pride and a bit of fabric on each wing.

Not all my misadventures were as slight as that. One quiet Sunday I was bringing Ethel back from a short visit with her sister in Bella Coola. As we passed the farm where my brother Earle and his wife were living, I dipped the wings and they waved. Within minutes the engine began to run rough. Earle told me afterwards that a trail of what looked like black smoke billowed out behind the plane. We were at the 5000 foot level and the plane began to lose altitude. I switched off the engine and turned back down the valley.

"Hold tight, Ethel," I said, patting her on the knee. "This might be a bit rough." I had long ago ear-marked spots throughout the valley as emergency landing places and I had passed one about seven miles down, by the Bob Ratcliff farm. The propeller kept turning, so I switched the engine on, but it only ran smooth for a few seconds before it acted up again. I switched it off and glided about seven miles, constantly losing altitude but maintaining sufficient height to allow me to bank and land in the Bella Coola River by the farm.

My airspeed was about fifty miles an hour as I came down softly on the water. Ethel heaved a big sigh of relief. "I suddenly became a religious woman again," she said. I've seen a lot of people, even experienced pilots, feel nearer to God when they are flying and even more so when they are crashing.

While descending we had passed the school house where Sunday church services were being held. The whole congregation came pouring out, trampling across a wheat field to see the accident. I was sorry to disappoint them; another emergency landing had been safely accomplished. However, we were far from safe yet. I somehow had to beach the plane without wrecking it on rocks or floating debris. The north shore of the river was shelved and a landing there would be most desirable. The south side was a cut bank and the wind kept steering the plane in that direction no matter how hard I worked at the current with my paddle from my position on the pontoons. I

218

stuck the paddle down into the milk-white, glacier-fed water and discovered it to be only about two feet deep at that point.

I leaped off the pontoon with a tie-up rope and waded to the south shore, towing the plane behind me. Ethel had been sitting still all the time. I marveled at her composure. As I got to the shore, Bob Ratcliff appeared with a rope over his shoulder. He helped me pull the plane down the river to a backwater where it wouldn't drift.

By this time Earle arrived and he helped Ethel out of the plane and up onto the bank where she was taken to a phone to call her sister and make arrangements to spend a couple more days with her. "We were sure you'd crashed," Earle said. "Isabel has been on the phone calling people all the way to Bella Coola to be on the look-out for you." I went up to Earle's place to think things out.

That afternoon Earle and I returned to the plane and inspected the engine. A rod connecting the crankshaft to a piston had broken off and punched a hole through the oil pan. It was oil and not smoke that Earle and Isabel had spotted pouring from the plane. This would mean I would have to remove the engine, crate it, and ship it to Vancouver for repair. Earle helped me take it out and after crating it on the spot, he and I and Bob Ratcliff dragged it over to the road where it could be carted into Bella Coola.

With a block and tackle the plane was pulled up as high as possible on a sandbar among young willows and I drove stout pegs into the ground beneath the ring on the struts so the wing could be tied down with rope to the peg, stabilizing the plane should a wind come up. Earle promised to check on the water level so there would be no danger of its rising, lifting the plane, and tearing off the wing. Ethel and I then left for home, walking from the end of the road into Lonesome Lake.

The adventure wasn't over yet. Following a few days of very hot weather, Trudy became concerned about the safety of the plane. I told her that everything had been done to secure it, but she wasn't satisfied. It was partly hers and she had a right to check to make sure it was safe. She rode out to Atnarko and phoned Earle. When he told her he had been having to make frequent adjustments to the ropes holding the plane to the pegs, she decided to go down and look over the situation herself.

She caught a ride with some friends and after assessing the situation, decided to build a raft and put the plane on it. That way it would not be affected by any raising or lowering of the water level. She had most of the logs for the raft cut and dragged into place when a storm struck. Residents of the Bella Coola Valley said no one could remember a thunder storm of such intensity in the area. The sky turned an eerie yellow and a great black cloud came rolling down from the east with a wind of up to eighty miles an hour from the west.

The wind and lightning kept up for hours, followed by torrential rain. Trees were being blown down everywhere. Trudy remained with the plane all night, adjusting ropes and securing it against the wind. She finally fell asleep in the cockpit when the storm abated toward morning. The plane was safe but if her intuition hadn't been right, and she hadn't attended to the plane despite my assurances, no doubt it would have been wrecked.

Cramped and cold, Trudy climbed out of the plane at daybreak and cut some more logs. Just as she was finishing the job, the axe slipped and cut her foot quite severely. Bleeding, she limped over to the Ratcliff house and woke up Bob who took her to Bella Coola hospital where her foot was stitched up. She said she was more embarrassed than hurt by the accident.

One morning in January, after the engine had come back from Vancouver and had been reinstalled by a local mechanic and myself, I took off for home again. The engine seemed to operate well enough, but I soon wished I'd had it completely overhauled instead of just having the piston rod and oil pan repaired. Problems with the engine continued. For example, I was warming up the engine intending to fly to Bella Coola for the mail one morning when it began making strange noises. I shut it off, started it again, tested the magneto, and, satisfied, taxied out on to the ice and took off. About 200 feet up, the engine quit dead!

Straight ahead was the river with big willows on the banks and beyond that was the head of the lake. I knew that the ice was too thin to land there so I made a forty five degree turn. The controls went "soft", so I turned the nose down and made a rather hard landing crossways on the lagoon. I was shaken up a bit but not hurt and the plane was not damaged - aside from the fact that it wouldn't fly. I hauled it back to the hangar with the tractor and took a look at the engine. The fuel line was jammed with ice crystals next to the fuel strainer on the carburetor. During the pre-takeoff runup, the pressure had not been sufficient to compact the ice crystals enough to halt the flow of fuel. But it was a different matter when full take-off power was required.

No one at the flying school had told me how to avoid ice in the fuel lines. When I arrived in Vancouver after one particularly hair-raising flight, some other pilots told me to use methyl hydrate in my fuel. I promptly got some and used it from then on and never had any more problems with ice in the fuel system.

Other irritations continued, however. Many times I had difficulty getting the little sixty five horsepower engine to start and sometimes it hadn't the power to lift the plane off the water when it had a load on. One day I had about 175 pounds of vegetables aboard - not a heavy cargo - and got ready to leave for Bella Coola. I couldn't get airborne so I unloaded two crates of vegetables in the water and went looking for a breath of wind. There was none, so I headed back to the hangar, first picking up the two floating crates of vegetables. Just then I noticed ripples on the lake at one point, indicating some wind action, so I taxied over and was able to get aloft.

The engine continued to be a source of concern all that summer. One evening when it got dark early I decided not to return to Lonesome Lake from the Smith's place on Charlotte Lake. I pulled the plane up on the beach and stayed overnight. To pass the evening hours I threw sticks for the Smiths' friendly retriever.

In the morning I started the engine and taxied out to make my takeoff run when suddenly I heard a dog howling. I looked back behind the seat, thinking perhaps the silly hound had got into the plane when I wasn't looking. No sign of her. The howling increased, so I cut the engine and drifted to shore. I took a good look all through the plane but couldn't find the source of the howling, which had now ceased. Then I saw one of the Smiths gesturing to me from the shore. I opened the door, and there was their boxer dog, sitting on the pontoon! She had come close to having a short but exciting ride off the lake.

All through the summer, problems developed with the engine. It became easier and easier to push it through compression; sometimes one flip of the prop would take the engine through two compressions. It became very unreliable and after standing a few days it refused to start at all. Roy Moulton and a mechanic came to the lake and although they tried their best to start the engine, it wouldn't fire.

Roy suggested I change engines, switch the sixty five horse power for the eighty five which was still sitting in the mill where Trudy and I had placed it many years before. It only weighed an additional ten pounds and used the same size propeller and engine mounts. Roy and the mechanic had to go about their business so Trudy and I undertook to make the changeover. We had to get at it soon: 1200 pounds of washed and sacked vegetables were sitting in the hangar awaiting delivery to our lakeside customers.

In making the change we found there would not be room between the engine and the fire wall for a starter, which this engine had, and the larger magnetos required a half inch more room so I had to use washers on the mount fastenings. We also found that the tachometer ran in the opposite direction so I had to install a different instrument to indicate the speed of rotation.

When everything was hooked up Trudy took charge of the controls and I flipped the prop. The engine started on the first pull through and so surprised Trudy that she immediately switched the ignition off. I pulled it through again and it performed perfectly. After a runup and a mag test, we took the plane down to the lake to try it out. I did not necessarily intend to fly it right then.

Without much effort, I **was** flying - to the foot of the lake and back to the Big Lagoon. The only sign of trouble was the smear of oil on the windscreen. After checking the engine I discovered the oil was coming from under the cover over the hole for the generator. This cover consisted of a piece of gasket material and a thin metal plate. I replaced the thin metal with a thicker piece and bolted it down tight.

The final test would be the flight to Vancouver to have the Department of Transport approve the engine replacement. I headed there via Bella Coola and as I flew over Queen Charlotte Strait, I noticed the oil pressure had dropped so drastically that I looked for a place to land. I found a little bay where the waves were quiet and tried to tighten the oil cover some more. I added a quart of oil and then taxied out into the Strait in search of a boat that might have another quart of oil to spare.

A large white steamer was coming up the Strait. I taxied over to intercept him, turning around in a tight circle. He kept right on course and I had to hustle out of his way to avoid being run down. I gave up that idea and drew in behind an island where the water was calm and took off, flying close to the water, using only 1800 r.p.m. Although low on oil, I landed safely at Alert Bay which has a seaplane base. An airline mechanic located the leak and fixed it. It seems there was an oil hole in the flange of the generator which was covered by a gasket but not by the metal cover. This oil was under pressure. The local machine shop cut a new metal cover with a lug over the oil hole. It worked fine.

I took off for Vancouver again but as I neared Powell River, it grew dark and all the elements were right for a storm. I couldn't see any lakes because of low cloud so I sat the plane down on the saltchuck below a breakwater where some boats were anchored. I tied the plane up to a boat and during the night a furious storm came up. Wind and rain blew against the plane and rocked all the boats. Many fishermen and owners of pleasure craft came during the night to check their moorings. I didn't sleep well but in the morning the storm had abated and I flew on to Vancouver.

The Department of Transport inspector bawled me out for switching the engine in my plane. "You have no business installing an engine unless you have an engineer's papers," he said. He insisted I install the old cowling for the sixty five horse power engine which was too small for the new eighty five horse power engine. The smaller cowling did not permit enough air to circulate past the engine for proper cooling and it over-heated. But there was no arguing with him.

Other alterations had to be made: Heavier metal parts on the spars, different fuel lines from the wing tanks to the nose tank, different fuel gauge on the nose tank. I was fairly fuming by the time I got back to Lonesome Lake. Red tape and offi-cialdom sometimes add up to stupidity. The replacement of the cowling is a classic example. To heck with that, I decided; it was time to innovate.

I made alterations in the cowling to permit proper cooling of the engine with the small cowling. I made "egg cup" projec-tions over each cylinder that gave cooling air access to the cy-linder heads. The upshot of my innovation on the engine was that when the government re-inspected the newly-installed cowling with the aluminum egg cup extensions, they were im-pressed. The inspector who had originally bawled me out, com-plimented me on the careful workmanship and my improvisa-tions.

I didn't tell him my innovation was completed in the back of the barn with no power tools or modern equipment. Now, I have been told, the Department of Transport is demanding that all engine conversions to eighty five horsepower have egg cup extensions over the cylinders for better cooling. So much for the advancement of technology!

Curiosity made me remove the pistons from the old sixty five horsepower engine. I found one-quarter of an inch of car-bon on the piston faces and caked carbon on the cylinder heads so as to nearly cover the spark plugs. The piston rings were frozen in their grooves and the valve stems riveted so tight I had to use a file to remove them. This engine was guaranteed to have had only fifty hours' service since a major overhaul. That is, according to the papers that came with it when Trudy bought the plane in Grand Coulee, Washington. Grand Coulee be damned.

15

Further Flights
& Fancies

"Flying in grain and taking out produce became pretty routine, compared with freighting hog-tied calves or a German Shepherd in a gunny sack." (Ralph Edwards)

Early in my flying days I received a letter from a couple living on Vancouver Island saying they wished to come visit us at Lonesome Lake. They would fly to the lake with me, after driving to Anahim Lake. They were only two of many visitors or hunters who came in to see us - for one reason or another - but they were the first to request me to fly them in.

When I got to Helmer Christensen's little float on Anahim Lake I tied up and shook hands with the waiting couple. I did not shake hands with their companion. They did not mention him in the letter. "This is Bruno," they said. "How do you do, Bruno?" I said. Bruno did not reply, nor did I expect him to. St. Bernards seldom do.

"My plane only carries about 200 pounds plus the pilot, so I'll have to make three trips if I take the dog," I informed the couple. I did not like the look of the sky. Three trips. It was going to be dicey.

The first two trips with the man and his wife were fairly routine. It was July, very hot, and thunderclouds were building up over the valley. The first lightning struck just as I landed to pick up Bruno. He whimpered as I shoved him aboard, then stowed the couple's baggage in the compartment behind the passenger seat. The dog started to howl as I climbed in after winding the prop. He was not happy being bound to the passenger seat with a chunk of rope. He looked at me appealingly with large, brown sad eyes.

Animals, like humans, do strange things when they're scared. Some humans tend to talk a lot; others grow silent, almost afraid to say anything lest they disturb whatever it is that is scaring them. Over the years I flew many passengers, humans and animals, and gradually got used to expecting the unexpected. A calf hog-tied and in a sack was no problem. An overweight Collie and a huge, slobbering Labrador seemed to find the flight about as exciting as a car ride. Bruno was something different.

He looked fearfully at me as lightning flashed outside. A few big rain drops hit the windscreen as we took off. The valley was full of small thunderclouds, which I had to fly among. The air in the cockpit was hot and stuffy and smelled of dog and human perspiration. I rolled up my sleeves as the dog worked some slack loose in his bonds. I had once had a heifer break its bonds and try to get in the front seat with me, so there was no telling what a loose animal would do. I could only keep one eye on him; I was too busy flying the plane. He slowly moved toward me, his big brown eyes never leaving my face. I didn't know whether to try to push him back and perhaps end up getting bitten, or just let him crawl all over me. Suddenly, he settled back on the passenger seat and extended his head so that it rested on my bare arm. He closed his eyes, sighed loudly, and stayed that way until we landed!

The first animals I ever transported were calves off the range. We never knew the exact date a cow would calve so sometimes we would find a stranger standing by its mother's side when we went to inspect the herd. The cow could be driven or led home around the rocky trail to the ranch, but sharp rocks were hard on a calf's tender feet so the calf would come along as co-pilot, hog-tied, wall-eyed and bawling.

Unexpected weather changes are always the most dangerous aspect of flying in the Bella Coola area. If I thought rough weather was ahead, I did not start out and if I ran into fog or heavy snow, I never hesitated to turn around and head for

227

home or sit down until conditions improved. Nevertheless, I gained a reputation among other pilots for taking off in weather that only a fool would venture out in.

Another point that concerned and amused my fellow pilots was that I seldom flew by map or chart. I have always had an uncanny insinct for directions. I was known for "flying by the seat of his pants." But this wasn't so. Some people have an inborn compass; others can't find their way to the bathroom. I can't ever remember becoming lost, although I have been in fog so thick I couldn't see where I was, but I soon got back on course once I got clear of the mist.

I was frequently kidded about my carefree landings on the Bella Coola River or on Bentinck Arm. My old friend Cliff Kopas, general store owner and author of an excellent book about Bella Coola, swore I would crash someday. I had a habit of cutting the engine and gliding down onto the river. Residents became accustomed to this practise. At first they would rush out in panic but realizing it was me they would shrug and say: "Oh, it's just Ralph Edwards. I wonder if he'll make it this time?" My motto was like that of an old pilot friend: "A good landing is any landing you walk away from."

On one memorable trip from Vancouver Roy Moulton asked me to take 200 pounds of swan grain. He could then bring the balance of the grain in one trip in his Beaver. When I got to Powell Lake, about 100 miles northeast of Vancouver, the whole waterway complex was under low fog. I landed on the lake and spent the night in the plane, sleeping across the seats with the one door open.

The weather report the next morning warned of strong winds off Alert Bay. I decided if nothing else, this would mean the fog would lift and as I took off all I could see were the tops of mountains, indicating some lay of the land, and channels under the gradually dissipating fog. I was gratified to see blue water beneath me at Loughborough Inlet, still only about half way to Alert Bay. I decided I had enough gas to get me home so abruptly swung the plane up Knight Inlet and into the Klinaklini Valley.

My right hand was resting lightly on the throttle knob when the plane hit a severe bump which caused two sacks of barley to come flying forward to the front of the aircraft. As I wrestled them back to where they came from I got a terrific shock. I couldn't hear the engine and thought it had quit! When I looked down at the controls I saw the throttle was pulled back to the off position, but the engine was still idling. When I thrust the throttle ahead, the engine took up its sweet song again.

Worst come to worst I probably could have made a safe landing on one of several bodies of shallow water below me. I was thankful I didn't encounter any more bumps during the next moments when I had to leave the controls to manhandle the two sacks of grain into a good ballast position again.

Updrafts and downdrafts are common in northern British Columbia; the country is dotted with small and large lakes and hundreds of rivers and streams, to say nothing of the Pacific Ocean with its upthrust rocky islets, huge and tiny islands, and fingers of land that jut outward making its coast one of the most forbidding in the world. One downdraft I encountered caused some ropes to fly out of the baggage area behind the seat right over my head onto the control panel.

I was forced to relinquish control of the plane for a few moments in order to disengage the ropes which had snaked over me as well. While I was coiling them up, the plane began to glide downward from the 4000 foot level with the airspeed indicator registering 100 miles an hour. I was more fascinated than frightened by the next occurrence. Suddenly the plane was standing perfectly still and in the next moment rising rapidly until the altimeter read 6000 feet, a lift of 2000 feet in a few seconds. Just as mysteriously, the plane descended again. I put on power and continued up the channel I was following until I reached the Big Lagoon on Lonesome Lake. The air was calm and the landing was perfect.

Another condition float pilots run into frequently on the British Columbia coast occurs when the water is so calm it is impossible to tell where air and water meet. The water simply reflects back the sky. Only the vague presence of mountain ridges or shoreline indicate what height you are flying at and the pilot must keep a close watch on the altimeter to keep from flying into the water. Landings are treacherous under these conditions. The plane is trimmed to a nose high shallow glide so that you hit the water with no danger of the float tips catching.

One January I was flying beef into Bella Coola and returning with loads of swan grain. On the fourth trip out from the lake that day I noted that the wind had increased but there appeared to be a calm spot near the south shore of the North Bentinck Arm near the government dock. I came down, putting on and taking off power to maintain a smooth glide and land in a lane between a log boom and some pilings. The plane touched down softly into the choppy water.

I have never been a master of the art of sailing an aircraft in water, and most of my experience was limited to windless conditions. I began a downwind turn, the elevator in the up position as I had been taught to do at flying school. Halfway around, a gust of wind got under the right wing and elevator and before I knew what was happening, the plane rolled over, slow and easy, and I was left hanging upside down in the cockpit.

I unfastened my safety belt and fell with a crash to the roof of the overturned craft. A door flew open by itself and I scrambled out onto the bottom of the portside pontoon. The plane, which would stay afloat in this position for some time, was drifting with the current. It came to an abrupt halt against a piling. Some men aboard a big Indian fishing boat called the **Bentinck Chief** observed my distress and quickly came alongside. Smiling broadly, one man passed me a rope which I tied around the spreader bar and a strut on the wing of the plane. My rescuers then pulled the Taylorcraft close to the **Bentinck Chief** which was equipped with a powerful winch and boom. It lifted the plane out of the water and set it down rightside up.

The boat was unloading boom chains when I had my mishap and a man aboard informed me that they had to get clear or become grounded as the tide was rapidly receding. I asked if

230

he could lift the plane onto the dock where I could tie it down. I knew that if I had to remove the engine the plane would not be heavy enough to remain stable in the water. They performed this task. I thanked the crew of the **Bentinck Chief** and hiked up to the village to get Frank Gildersleeve who had army experience with airplanes.

We worked for several hours in the subzero weather but even with magnetos and carburetor dried out the engine would not start. I crated it for shipment to Vancouver for another overhaul. It was becoming a costly business, to say nothing of a downright nuisance, with delays and inconveniences when some mishap took the plane out of service for months at a time.

I had many more mishaps and adventures aboard the little Taylorcraft, some of them alone, others with Ethel or Trudy aboard. Trudy was slightly resentful toward me for commandeering the plane as much as I did and for only letting her fly when conditions were ideal. Suddenly she had become a twenty one year old woman. She had inherited Ethel's and my independence and wasn't content to stay working for us for the rest of her life. She looked around for a piece of land of her own to "civilize". She found it about a mile and one-half south of The Birches, up the Atnarko River. Here she set out to create Fogswamp, the name she called her farm.

Trudy has written her own account of the establishment of her little kingdom in her book, **Fogswamp: Living With Swans In The Wilderness,** so I will not dwell on it at length here. Suffice to say she worked at clearing land, building a house, barn and outbuildings with the energy of two men. She did most of it alone, unless you include the horse. I aided her in building a bridge across the Atnarko so she could keep in contact with us at The Birches. We also later installed a telephone network between the two farmhouses.

To complete the route to our place necessitated her hacking a road through the rocks and trees, all of which she completed in winter while putting in a half day's work feeding the swans, a job which she now took over completely. During her solitary trips to her new-found haven, Trudy chased off a moose and several grizzlies who refused to move over and allow another resident to establish a home on the upper Atnarko.

She had a formidable manner which deterred most wild beasts and also timid male humans. She literally roared at wolves and bears and managed to convince them that she was there to stay. If there was any argument, it would be ended clean and fast. By February 1956 Trudy had cleared a half mile strip of land, about ten acres, and had somehow found time to furnish her cabin with homemade chairs, table, benches, and a built-in bed. All the place lacked was a man and that seemed the most difficult item on the list to find. As already indicated, Trudy is a most independent woman and since she seldom ventured outside and marriageable men did not often come in to the lake, it looked as though she would remain the Maiden of Lonesome Lake.

Nevertheless, a young man named Jack Turner walked into the area one day and after a fair amount of judging on both sides the two decided to see more of each other. They courted seriously, became engaged and planned to be married the following winter. Jack went away and Trudy decided his capabilities for withstanding the rigors of wilderness living were pretty fair, if not downright excellent. In January Jack came back and took Trudy down to Bella Coola to be married.

The temperature had dropped to below zero with a strong north wind but my brother Earle met them at the end of the road with his car and took them to the church in Bella Coola for the ceremony which took place on January 9, 1957. Trudy's Aunt Laura provided the wedding supper and Earle took them back to the end of the road the next day where they hiked into a honeymoon at Fogswamp.

On January 1, 1959, Jack arrived at The Birches with an urgent request. Trudy was starting labor; a baby was on the way early. Ethel and I were to become grandparents! I secretly wished that babies would be born in the summer when flying conditions were more suitable but nature and babies have time-tables contrary to mine. I removed the plane from the hangar

232

and prepared to fly to Bella Coola to bring in Dr. Rose, the local physician.

Stanley Levelton met me at the seaplane dock with his car. He came down thinking it must be an emergency that would bring me to Bella Coola on New Year's Day. We tied up the plane and drove the two miles to the hospital in town. Dr. Rose did not care much for flying. "Listen, Ralph, tell you what, I'll go up the valley as far as possible by car and then walk the rest of the way in."

I entertained Dr. Rose with several stories about my contacts with various denizens of the wild and with a description of the trail in winter. This was when he suddenly remembered he had a game leg. "On second thought," he said, reluctantly, "I'll take a chance and fly in with you." If Dr. Rose hated flying before, he loathed it after that trip.

While I was at the hospital, a sudden gust of wind had tipped the plane's left wing over across the narrow float and into the water. A coating of ice had formed on the tip. Some men had seen what had happened and had righted the plane, tied it down with rope and it had remained upright, but the rudder and one elevator had been torn when they hit a railing on the ramp. I added to the damage by tearing the fabric of the left aileron while beating off the ice.

A cold east wind was freezing ice onto the fuselage and control wires. "We better fly out of here fast before it sinks," I told Dr. Rose, which did not add much to his confidence as he stood shivering on the float. "I don't wish to commit suicide, Ralph. Do you think we should go at all?" I told him I didn't wish to commit suicide either. "Everything will be fine once we get into the air." He got aboard then and after some men at the dock slashed the frozen ropes, we headed due east into the wind and took off with a very short run.

My assurance that "everything will be fine", didn't inspire the good doctor to sing or tell amusing stories as we bucked our way up the valley. The plane hit a down draft that dropped us 1000 feet. I had to put on full power to regain my flying altitude of 4000 feet. We then hit a severe bump and the doctor

233

looked ill. I smiled at him to let him know that all was well; he smiled wanly back.

A cruel north wind whipped the lake so I made my approach from the south. What looked like a perfect touchdown on bare ice nearly ended in disaster. I ran out of room on that end of the lake and had to pull up sharply. I made another approach and this time I pulled the control wheel back to slow us down and a gust of wind caused us to take off again. The third landing was hard. The doctor was not smiling.

Landing on clear ice is no problem; you can easily tell how far above the surface you are. In making turns on bare ice you have to be sure to select an area without cracks in which the rub irons on the bottom of the floats might get caught. When making turns on smooth, bare ice the plane will slide sideways but will straighten out if power is applied. One hazard to beware of is sliding after touching down. I have glided as far as three-quarters of a mile after switching off the engine.

Landing on snow is a different proposition. If the snow is deep, it is necessary to land nose up. I tried landing in a level attitude one day, as I would in landing on bare ice, and the plane began to "porpoise", getting more and more violent with each leap. I put on more power until the plane smoothed out and a normal landing was completed.

In taxiing in deep snow it is necessary to look out the side window constantly to gauge progress. Lots of power must be maintained. If the plane slows to a halt it will become mired like an automobile without chains or snow tires. I have been stuck like that and have had to get someone to wiggle the plane from behind or get out myself and shovel the ice clear for a considerable distance ahead.

After the hard landing with Dr. Rose, my problem was to get the plane into the hangar. The wind was so strong and unpredictably gusty it slid the plane backwards. Luckily, it was in the direction I wanted to go. We soon had the plane inside but when we came to slam the doors shut, a gust of wind blew the doors right off the hinges.

Dr. Rose was too busy thanking his lucky stars to be alive

to make any compliments about my hangar construction and while he hustled up to attend to Trudy, I faced the task of patching up the plane. The "dope" used in mending aircraft fabric requires a temperature of 70^0 F, so it "cures" properly. I rigged baffles to carry the heat from a coal oil lantern to the patches. In the meantime, nature redoubled her fury outside. The river level rose, dumping about a foot of water on the frozen surface of the lagoon. This new surface immediately froze but not solid enough to bear the weight of a taxiing plane.

The doctor was forced to stay overnight and there was no sign of Trudy's baby, despite the labor pains she thought she was experiencing. The good doctor's own wife was expecting and became worried when her husband failed to return that night. Somehow a rumor got started that we had crash-landed on the way into the lake. We heard the news over the radio and the Canadian Airforce Search and Rescue squad sent in a DC-3 which flew over the lake at 5000 feet to scout the territory the next day. Seeing the hangar door open they assumed the plane was out - down in the mountains somewhere.

We had no transmitter but could hear all this speculation on our battery-operated receiver. I knew they would come back so I put a big marker on the Big Lagoon indicating the ice there was unsafe to land on. I tested the thickness of the ice on the lake with an axe and put a marker at one point indicating where it was safe to land. Later that day a Search and Rescue ski plane landed on the lake and when it took off it carried the Turners and Dr. Rose with it.

Doctor Rose had enough adventures to last him for life and Trudy, who went to the hospital in Williams Lake and then to Vancouver, didn't deliver her daughter Susan for another two months!

The hard landing on the ice had bent a cross member on the bottom of the fuselage of the Taylorcraft. I put a splint on it and wired it up as best I could until I could get it to Vancouver. I didn't want to attempt a flight, however, until the ice had melted on Lonesome Lake. It wasn't taking off that bothered me, it was returning to unknown landing conditions that caused

235

me to delay my departure.

When spring arrived I flew to Vancouver where mechanic Gordy Peters checked the fuselage. "Bad news, Ralph," he said. "Look at this." He took a pocket knife and poked it through the steel tubing which was corroded badly in many places. The Department of Transport took one look at it and condemned the plane. It would cost about 1800 dollars for a new fuselage, an expense we could not afford. With a heavy heart, I boarded the boat for Bella Coola and home.

Ethel and I talked over the situation and decided we just could not do without an airplane. We had been spoiled by the access it gave us to civilization - but more important - to markets for our produce. After talking it over with her, trying to work out finances, I made arrangements for a loan from the credit union in Bella Coola, then left for Vancouver to give orders for the repairs.

After a careful search of newspaper and magazine advertisements, I located a man who was selling parts of a Taylorcraft he had brought into British Columbia from Vernon, Washington. I went to see him and after making some cuts into the tubing found the inside of the fuselage frame as bright as a new penny. I had it transported to the Vancouver Flying Club hangar where a Dutchman named Gruenberg, a master craftsman, went to work on it.

However, I had to get back to Lonesome Lake to supervise farm operations; it looked like the repairs were going to take considerably longer than I had anticipated. Finally, after nineteen days, I was informed that the plane was ready. Gordie Peters, who had overseen the operation, and Roy Moulton, my pilot friend, told me the aircraft checked out and flew beautifully. I was anxious to see it.

"Before you do, Johnny Hatch wants to see you," Roy said. "He wants you to stay at his place tonight and bring you down in the morning." I was reluctant to spend another day in the city and wanted to see my plane, but the pilots, mechanic and DOT officials had all been so kind I didn't feel right complaining. Besides, it was a good opportunity to renew the acquaintance with my friend Johnny Hatch.

We sat around talking about various adventures we both had experienced and finally Johnny inquired about my financial position. I told him how I had mortgaged the cattle through the credit union and hoped I had enough for the repairs. "It's going to come to quite a lot," Johnny said. "Especially with that radio and the new upholstering and windscreen and all." "Radio? New upholstering?" I spluttered. "I didn't order any of that done. What the heck is going on?"

I was in a proper funk by next morning when Johnny drove me back to the West Coast Air Services hangar at the airfield. Roy and Gordie were waiting there, along with a lot of other men I had met during my various trips into the city. They were all looking curiously smug. If it was because of the crackerjack job they had done on the plane, they had a right to look pleased. But how was I to pay for all that extra, unrequested work?

I walked around the plane where it sat on the ramp, full of fuel and ready to fly. It never looked better. I would not have recognized it with the new windscreen and a new door which replaced the old one which had been scraped and bent and was difficult to close. I hadn't asked for that to be replaced either. I was starting to feel slightly annoyed and all those smug looks weren't doing much to alter my souring mood.

"Ralph," Roy Moulton called to me from the group of men. "Here are your bills for the labor and materials." I was almost afraid to look at them. I tallied them up mentally as he handed me each slip of paper. They totaled almost 5000 dollars! I had no idea how we would ever pay it. Ethel was already upset with me for mortgaging her beloved cattle to get 1800 dollars for the repairs. What would she say when I came home 5000 dollars in debt?

"Ralph," Roy said again. "Give me back those bills for a minute." I was still in a state of shock as I handed back the slips of paper. Then he did a curious thing: He tore them all up and threw them into the wind! "Yay!" the other men shouted. "What the . . ." I gasped. "They're all taken care of," Roy said, clapping

237

me on the back. "The guys here all donated their services and Grant McConachie and another airline brass threw in a few hundred bucks or so to pay for the new radio and the seat and the door and the other stuff."

I couldn't believe it. The plane was in better condition than when we bought it. No wonder all those guys were standing around looking like cats in a saucer of cream. I didn't know how to thank them, my throat was all choked up. I had to turn my head away as tears filled my eyes.

I wiped them with my hand and mumbled something inadequate. I noticed there were tears in some other eyes too. It was the nicest thing that ever happened to me in my life. Instead of being in debt with no steady income to reduce it, Ethel and I could face the future with a smile.

16

Nature Has Her Way

"Come forth into the light of things, let Nature be your teacher." (William Wordsworth)

Ethel was astounded when I returned with the plane to Lonesome Lake. I must admit I couldn't help kidding her, the way I had been kidded by the mechanics and airline and DOT officials in Vancouver. "This must have cost a fortune, Ralph," she said. "We'll never be able to pay that debt off. And what about my precious cows? We'll lose them if we don't."

I couldn't keep up the pretense for long. She was taking it too seriously. Besides, she caught the mischievous look in my eye. "You old fraud," she said, slapping me on the arm. "What's going on?" I told her the whole story. Her eyes brimmed over as I related the good news. I found myself becoming emotional again too. "I guess I better go do some chores," I said, clearing my throat. "The place has probably fallen apart since I've been away."

If flying the old Taylorcraft had been a joy, it was redoubled now. With a radio installed, I felt we had truly joined the modern age, but still held on to our wilderness enjoyment. The best of both worlds. In the meantime, my son Johnny, had become an excellent photographer and cinematographer.

"What I'd like to do, dad," Johnny said, "is to film a normal day's work on the farm and then a flight out and back. Have you got anything planned this week?" As a matter of fact I had. I was to fly down to Fraser Valley to bring back a bull calf to add to our growing herd. "Great," Johnny said. "I'll take shots of you leaving and some more when you return. In the meantime, just act natural and I'll take some of you as you go about your duties."

It wasn't easy for me to "act natural" with a movie camera buzzing around me while I did my chores, but anything to keep peace in the family! I was almost relieved to be on my own as I took off to pick up the bull calf. No camera to bother me until I got back, at least.

I collected the calf, got him boarded and properly secured in the passenger seat, and headed for home. With a tail wind all the way, it was a record flight. I landed at the lake in brilliant sunshine, perfect not only for flying, but for the taking of movies. And there was Johnny cranking away, when I taxied up the hangar.

There was one thing he hadn't counted on, and neither had I. I thought I'd let him find out on his own. I stepped down from the plane and Johnny moved in for closeups. I skipped around the pontoons to the passenger door and he followed, recording every move. I wrenched open the door and he zoomed in beside me for an interior shot, with the calf as the focal point. Suddenly the camera stopped buzzing.

"Uhhhhh . . . what the heck?" I heard him say. "What's that awful stench?" I couldn't help laughing. The poor bull calf. To say nothing of the poor old pilot. It seems the little beast had developed a bad case of the scours, a type of dysentery common to cattle. Flying him to Lonesome Lake in that condition was not the most pleasant experience of my life. I looked at Johnny, who was now standing well back of the door as I struggled to get the bull out of the cockpit. "Come on, Johnny," I shouted. "Get that camera going if you want your dad and life on the farm in living color." "Oh, please dad," Johnny said, gazing at the unappealing interior of the airplane, "this is a family film - not a horror movie!"

I became quite adept at flying cattle off the range and the experience with the bull calf taught me a lesson. I built a little platform to wedge between the passenger seat and the instrument panel. The calves would thrash about at first, trying to get loose of the ropes, a sack and the safety belt, but when they found it impossible to escape they relaxed.

Trudy was also adding to her herd at Fogswamp and one specimen, an Ayrshire yearling named Spicey, lived up to his name. One incident with him reminded me of the earlier experience I'd had with the renegade bull who'd nearly killed me. When he grew old enough to be dangerous, I decided to dehorn him. Some cattle undergo this operation with nary a problem but Spicey was born to be difficult and the removal of one horn led to copious bleeding. I was afraid to cut the other one off in case he bled to death so after the first stump healed I bolted a block of hawthorn wood across his head to prevent his hooking the cattle he ranged with. He looked a bit odd, to say the least.

It was time to put salt blocks out on the range and I flew the plane up to the head of the river and began to place salt licks in the places where the cattle have come to expect them. Several of the cows had bells on so I was able to hear them. I didn't particularly want them to see me; there was no point in attracting them if I could avoid it. One spot where the lick had been was boggy so I wanted to find a new place for it.

I crawled up on an enormous dead spruce tree that was lying on the river bank and called "come bossy, come bossy." a few times and the cows all came running and bawling. I lowered the salt block onto the ground in front of the cows without getting down. Now they knew where it was and while they were quietly milling around awaiting turns to get a chance to lick at it, I jumped the back off the log and headed for the plane.

Spicey spotted me and whipped around the top of the fallen spruce and came after me at full gallop. I knew it was useless to run so I turned to face him. Side stepping matador fashion, I managed to reach a clump of small alder trees. I climbed up one, my rifle in my free hand. The branches ended abruptly still within reach of Spicey's hawthorn headpiece so I whipped my belt off and wrapped it around the tree, enabling me to stay aloft and still keep my rifle hand available.

241

The mosquitoes were almost as fierce as the bull. They dived and bit and swarmed around my face, flying up my nostrils and into my mouth and eyes. My attempts to fend them off agitated the bull more and as he stormed around below me he got a small dead pole stuck in his "horns" and waved it around, nearly hitting me with it. Removing a small trail axe I had attached to my packsack, I cut off a branch and dropped it on his head. This bounced harmlessly to the ground. Recalling the loss of the ornery killer of years before, I carefully weighed the next action.

I levered a shell into the rifle and, intending to frighten him away, aimed a shot right under his nose. He never even moved. I tried firing even closer to his head. The spurt of dirt and leaves only made him angrier. By this time the cattle were lying down witnessing the spectacle, chewing their cud and enjoying the antics of the bull, the mosquitoes and me. There was nothing to do but wait.

Finally, the cattle became bored and wandered back to the salt. Spicey trailed along shortly afterwards, stopping every now and then to look back at me. He hustled back several times, snorting and switching his tail, to make sure I was still on my perch. Then, with an arrogant, victorious air, he stalked off. I bounded down from the tree and beat a retreat to the plane.

Bulls are always dangerous animals because they are so unpredictable. Domesticating them is sometimes impossible. On the other hand, even horses can make problems, particularly if you try to educate them to a different way of life than they intend for themselves. I have already mentioned Ginty who had a mind all his own, yet who was flexible. Sometimes he figured I was too stupid to be believed and argued with me, but he always came around in the end. For example, trying to get him to leave a well worn trail sometimes led to the pitting of human will against horse sense. Eventually Ginty would plunge off the trail at my insistent urging, but he would glare back at me, wondering why anyone would choose a more difficult way to get some place when an easier way was available.

242

The wonderful thing about Ginty was he was as useful as a riding horse as a pack animal; it made no difference to him. Not so with a big Percheron stallion that ended up at the farm. He was big, but he was dumb. Maybe I should say he was the smart animal and I was the dumb one because often he was the one who won out. He had to be led at all times when he was carrying anything or he would forget all about being a beast of burden. His principal interest and appointed role in life - according to his actions - was to get at the mares. He had a loving nature.

I saddled and tethered him by the corner of the house. I had not yet tied the latigo, a long strap fastened to the saddle-tree which tightens the cinch, but had laid it over the saddle and he had shaken it off. I was half-hidden by the corner of the house when I bent over to pick it up. If the Percheron had known it was me he probably wouldn't have kicked, but he lashed out, catching me in the thigh. The pain was so intense I had to lie down to keep from fainting. The packing had to go on so I slowly got to my feet and by manipulating my body without flexing my thigh muscles, I finished packing the horse.

Trudy and I were moving supplies up to the lake, then we had to move the horses around to The Birches on a very rough trail. Trudy was in front leading Topsy, followed by two geldings. I brought up the rear with the Percheron stud. At the narrowest point of the trail he got past me and I had to use all my ebbing strength to keep him from pushing the geldings off the trail in his excitement to get at the mare Topsy. After receiving a smack from a rope across his nose, he desisted.

Most of my misadventures with domestic animals resulted from stupidity or carelessness. Cattle and horses - with the exception of bulls and the occasional stallion - may be ornery at times but can be kept under control. Bears and wolves are never to be completely trusted. I say this knowing that certain eastern writers who have spent a few months in the woods and claim to be experts will disagree. I spent more than sixty years watching the activities of bears and wolves and the gentle nature of the wolf cannot be substantiated by fact. They treat their own kind with love, but they are designed to be killers.

The wolves of Tweedsmuir Park area in which I spent most of my life were always fat. I never skinned a thin one. I got to know their habits very well because as a trapper and bounty hunter it was necessary for me to watch their tracks and often followed them for miles. This was not difficult. Timber wolves are large animals, some weighing as much as 150 pounds. Active beasts, they spend a great deal of time running and playing.

A hunter can determine whether wolves have been in a given area simply by studying the activity of the deer as displayed by their tracks. One of the myths about wolves is that they only take the unfit and the aged. I contend it is the unlucky who ends up as wolf dinner. After satisfying themselves over a meal, the wolves will climb up a ridge and howl, an eerie sound that can be heard for miles. Afterwards, they move off to another part of their territory, returning about two weeks later to the same spot.

As the lakes and rivers freeze over they extend their territories by traveling on ice. I was walking along a bench of land 100 feet above the river one afternoon in the fall. Little gulches led steeply to the valley floor. The signs in the snow indicated that a small deer had been bedded down in a gully just off the trail and that six wolves had jumped her and dragged her down to the valley bottom where she was partly consumed. While I marvel at the strength and skill of the wolf as a hunter, I was always revolted at the thought of wolves disembowling a deer.

Perhaps that is how nature provides. The eagles, ravens and foxes would feast. Nothing goes to waste in the end. This I am willing to concede, but I will not subscribe to the madcap notion that wolves are kindly souls and they never, never attack humans. I would prefer to believe Baron Manchausen and his tall tale about the wolf that attacked his sled horse, devouring him as he ran. The Baron kept drawing on the reins and the harness until the wolf was in harness and pulling the sleigh home!

You have already read my account of being attacked by

four wolves who surely would have done me harm had I not had my trigger finger bare, having lost my mitt earlier in the day. There were other such experiences. One January morning when the lakes and rivers were frozen solid I started out for Atnarko with a big bundle of furs, an axe to test the ice for thickness, snowshoes for the deep snow I expected to find down the valley, and enough food for four days on the trail. I hadn't seen any wolf tracks that winter so I decided to leave my big rifle at home. However, I did take a .22 which could be dismantled and carried in my pack. Thus laden, I headed down the middle of the lake.

There was a light snowstorm coming from the north. About a mile down the lake I saw what I thought was a pack of dogs streaming out from a point of land jutting into the lake. I counted five of them while trying to determine what they were doing there. As they drew closer I realized they weren't a pack of dogs and they weren't coyotes. They were timber wolves. I started for shore immediately. Instantly a big, long black wolf worked around me to cut off my approach to the shore and the timber. A big gray fellow came close up on the other side while the rest ran in a loop in front of me, about 100 yards away. Seven in all, they began to circle nearer. I struggled to get my pack off my back. With cold and trembling fingers I assembled the little popgun which I knew was only effective against squirrels.

The big gray moved in to have a closer look. He exhibited that Oriental cast to his yellow eyes, the appearance that separates him from his cousin the German Shepherd. I didn't wait to see if he would attack me so the argument could be settled for some eastern journalist about whether wolves attack humans or not: I shot at him.

I doubt that I hit him; there was no evidence of blood, but he lit out. The others all turned back down the lake and disappeared around the point of land from where they had come. Upon reflection, I decided it was the noise of the shot, amplified in the crisp cold air over the silent lake, that scared them off. I wondered too if the furs in my pack had carried a scent that prevented them from identifying me as a human. Or did they just want to investigate what looked like a potential meal, regardless of species?

I cut off these ruminations and returned home to fetch my .35 Remington. I saw no more wolves nor even any tracks that day but I never made a trip of any distance again without taking along a rifle that would mean business against an attacking wolf. I never went out of my way to senselessly shoot any of these animals, but there have been times when I felt like taking vengeance on wolves for their behavior.

An example of this was when I was walking my trapline one winter when the lake was partly frozen over; a warm wind had blown the snow into little drifts with bare ice in between. On one drift I saw a spot of blood but there were no tracks that I could see. Presently, I found signs of two large wolves, obviously after a deer. All tracks entered an area where a jog in the land had prevented the wind from forming drifts. The wolves were there, crossing back and forth behind a frightened buck. On the glasslike surface of the ice, covered with a dusting of snow, the deer circled, his legs splaying out like a crazy fourlegged novice skater. As I slowly approached, the wolves were moving in.

I quickened my stumbling gait through the rutted snow and on to the ice, my snowshoes then making cracking noises with each step. The wolves saw me and drew back a distance and waited as I approached the buck. He was alive, holding his head high. Wolf hair was caught in his antlers like wool on a bush, indicating the wolves weren't going to get him without a price. He was breathing heavily, his eyes glassy. In the short time he had been there, an impression had been worn into the ice from his body and the pool of steaming blood. A great hunk of flesh, big as two fists, was torn from his right ham and he was bleeding profusely. He looked me straight in the eye as I shot him.

The wolves, scared by the sound of the reverberating gunshot, headed for a rockslide several hundred yards away. I threw a couple of shots after them but missed. It was anger more than bad conditions that accounted for my poor marks-manship. I was still angry as I returned to the deer, butchered it, hung half of it high in a tree to be safe from scavengers, and packed the rest home to Ethel.

Frequently we found signs of wolf attacks on our stock. When slaughtering a big steer at the ranch we found a place on its ham where wolves had attempted to bring him down. The wound had healed and the steer lived to fight again. The advantage that cattle have over deer is that when attacked by predators, they do not turn tail and run but will rally and give battle. Facing a herd of angry cattle is a serious matter, even to a pack of wolves. To further protect our herd, we hung bells around their necks. Bells spell "man" to a wolf or a bear. Through the years we discovered that the best fighters among the various strains of cattle we raised were Ayrshires, animals of a hardy breed that originated in Ayr, a county in Scotland. They were a match for bears, cougars and wolves and as time passed we learned to let their horns grow, rather than cut them off, so they'd have an even better chance against attackers.

I used to leave my cattle on the range on the wild meadows of the head of the river as long as the snow wasn't too deep for them to scrape it off to get to the grass. The big slough grass stays green all year round and the cattle learned to do as horses do, pull it gently out of the ground rather than nip it off. The big white root comes out of the soil for several inches and, believe it or not, those stems are nutritious enough for a starving human to exist on.

I had three cattle at the head of the river this particular winter. The area consists of flat bottom land between steep rocky hills. Shallow ponds lie below; the driest land is a narrow band of alluvial soil along the river sides covered with willow and alder. The cattle wintered there, feeding in meadows on either side of the river as it meanders down to the head of Elbow Lake.

The river had frozen over and the wolves were able to approach my herd without being seen, the water level being several feet below that of the hummock where the cattle were sheltering among the willows. Wolf tracks were everywhere as I approached and I expected to find the bloodied remains of my three cattle. Judging from the depths of the tracks, two of the wolves must have weighed at least 150 pounds each.

Anger rising in my chest, I plodded across to the spot where the cattle should have been. All three cows looked at me and bawled. They hadn't a scratch on them. I studied the tracks again and surmised that the wolves had indeed attacked the cows but the bovines had backed up into the trees, then made sorties at the wolves as they circled on the meadows. After some feinting and thrusting by both parties, the wolves had decided perhaps deer would be easier to kill for dinner, and left.

Another winter day I was coming home on the frozen lake. As I approached The Narrows, a dark object coming quickly towards me could have been a wolf or a coyote. Whatever it was, it was unaware of me as a human. I unshouldered my rifle just as a huge gray timber wolf became aware of my presence. I levered a shell into the chamber, then remembered that I had knocked the rifle sight out of position earlier that day. A long distance shot was not likely to hit home. I waited; the wolf hesitated. I fired and missed. He ran off the trail.

A few days later I returned and found that the wolf had been engaged in herding a big buck around the lake shore. Even after my shot at him he continued the relentless pursuit of his quarry. I found the deer where the wolf hauled him down on the ice and gorged.

No normal person enjoys seeing an animal suffer. But we have to respect the intricate balance of nature, grimacing perhaps at the pain of the mouse caught in the talons of the owl; the rabbit dying, squealing in the claws of the lynx; the deer being cut down by a pack of wolves. Detached by distance from these death scenes, we marvel at nature's way: Witnessing them in person, we feel repelled.

17

Good Shots, Bad Shots, Guides And Other Fools

"To the hunters who hunt for the gunless game, the streams and the woods belong." (Sam Walter Foss)

In addition to being a means to transport our produce to market and to bring in the swan grain, the Taylorcraft began to play another large role in our life. Since there was no shortage of moose, bear and mountain goats in the area, and since I had given up trapping and fur farming because of low fur prices, increasing my big game guiding activities seemed a natural step to take.

The plane could be used to bring in hunters to a territory where trophy animals roamed at will. It also permitted us to enter remote places where practically no one ever went. However, even with the plane at their disposal, there was never any danger of over-harvesting any species.

These hunters came in a variety of sizes, shapes and temperaments. Some could actually shoot a rifle; others shouldn't have been trusted in the backyard with a slingshot. A number of times my own life was in danger because of a hunter. A wild animal is easier to deal with than a bad shot with a quick trigger finger.

A San Francisco detective came up for grizzly one autumn and the grizzly almost got both of us. He and I started our hunt by walking up the valley from The Birches along the road that connects our place with Trudy's Fogswamp. The river comes down the valley, running slow and quiet, making a right angle just before getting to "Trudy's Bridge", a truly marvelous structure, considering my daughter built it almost single-handedly, with only a small amount of help from me.

As we came onto the bridge we saw two bears on a flat about 100 yards ahead of us. They looked up and began to run into the woods. An old trail that had been cleared out with a chain saw years before was lined with fallen lodge pole pine, some of which had been killed by pinebark beetles. The bears could be seen hustling up the trail and one of them climbed up on a log, making him appear to be larger than he actually was. The detective immediately raised his 350 Magnum and fired.

"It's only a cub," I told him. "You shouldn't have shot without getting a closer look." We came up to where the bear was lying gasping on the ground. "He's not dead," I warned the detective. "You better shoot him again." The detective expressed regret at his hasty action and pumped another shot into the dying cub. He then sat down and propping his rifle against a log, lit a cigarette.

This movement caught the eye of the little "dead" bear who rolled over on all fours and whirled toward me. I had no time to shoot but tried to fend him off with my rifle butt. The bear got his head past the rifle and clamped his teeth on to the little finger of my left hand. The teeth went straight through to the bone as he began to shake his head back and forth with my finger in his mouth. I drew back, stumbled over a hummock, and fell down. The bear swarmed over me.

The detective reached for his rifle but before he got his hands on it, the bear climbed off me and buried his teeth in the hunter's thigh. With no other defense, he swung at the bear's head with his fist. The bear then directed his energy at the detective's wrist. In the meantime, I got to my feet. Not daring to shoot at the struggling pair, I got around them and brought my rifle barrel down on the bear's head as hard as I could.

The bear then lost all interest in the detective's wrist and headed for the woods over a pile of logs. I snapped a shell into the barrel and shot him dead. "Don't sit down for another smoke," I told the detective. "That other bear was probably the cub's mother and she might not care for Lucky Strikes."

The detective didn't appreciate my humor but I didn't appreciate him shooting at an animal before finding out first what the animal was. Too many hunters are prone to investigate after they've fired their shot, sometimes wounding or killing other hunters, game wardens or out of season game.

As it turned out, the mother bear didn't show up, so we skinned out the cub and took the meat home to be cooked with mash for the chickens. Mr. Detective was somewhat mollified by the time we'd had our wounds tended to and Ethel had cooked a fine dinner of canned salmon, our own preserved vegetables and fruit and lots of strong, hot coffee.

Next morning he was in a mood to try for a moose. We left at ten o'clock in the Taylorcraft. I landed on what we called Widgeon Lake, a series of lakes to the west of our place in a bay where it would be out of the wind and we went back through the woods to a meadow to look for tracks. After finding only old signs of moose, we returned to the plane, had something to eat, and walked east, upwind. Within a few minutes three moose could be seen working their way toward us: A cow and calf in the lead and a bull with a fair-sized rack of antlers following. They waded across the shallow bays and climbed over timbered points and soon were within range of a bullet.

The San Francisco detective fired at the big bull but the bullet went between the moose's legs into the water. The next shot brought him down. The cow and calf swam across the lake and soon disappeared from the scene. The next problem was to figure out how to get a waterlogged half ton of moose butchered and back to the ranch. You can't cut up a moose in the water, so we built a raft and floated the big fellow to shore where I bled him, quartered him and hung most of the meat in a tree out of the reach of bears.

The detective weighed about 200 pounds so there was only room in the Taylorcraft for him, myself and the trophy antlers, which he proudly strapped into the passenger seat with him. Like most trophy hunters he wasn't interested in the meat but

I seldom let any go to waste. It took three trips next day to get all the moose meat home.

The next hunter to come to Lonesome Lake to pay me the handsome sum of five dollars a day (American hunters later had to pay 500 dollars a day for a guide in British Columbia) was a Greek-German who was a physicist at the University of California at Los Angeles. His name was Theo and he was jinxed from the beginning. We hunted the river near home but found nothing so we got into the plane and I flew him to The Stillwater and hunted down the valley through fir and cotton-wood bottoms crossed by old river channels and rounded boulders. It was good bear country and it wasn't long before I heard one old bruin talking to himself. We climbed across a gully and found him.

"Shoot, Theo, shoot," I urged him. "You'll never get a better shot than that." Theo stumbled over a boulder and pitched forward into some low bushes. By the time he got up and shouldered the rifle the bear had ambled out of the gully. Almost immediately another bear appeared, about 100 yards away. It stood looking at us. "Shoot, Theo," I shouted. Theo fired at it three times. The bear got bored and left. "He may be wounded," I told Theo and he limped after it. "Be careful." Theo ignored my warning and continued to hobble in the direction the bear had taken.

I didn't really think the bear had been hit but a warning against hasty action can pay off, as already noted. There was no blood on the rocks or in the leaves or the tracks we followed into the bush. We decided to call it a day and try again the next morning. The following day Theo and I walked up the valley to a spawning ground at Elbow Lake near the head of the river. Here there are long reaches of shallow gravel pools, some a-bout fifty yards wide, favorite spawning and bear-feeding country. We sat down to watch and wait at an elbow in the river and after a short time a bear stepped into the river and began to fish for salmon about 200 yards from us. Theo's first shot hit the water short of the bear. The bear ran to the other side of the river and Theo fired again. The bear ran back to the

252

other side. Theo fired and missed.

Admittedly, the river banks were similar in color to the bear which made it difficult to see once it got to the bank. "It's probably gone out of the area by now," I told Theo, who was looking pretty dejected. We crossed a tumbled clump of willows and headed up river. On the way we saw a bear on the opposite bank no more than sixty yards from us. Theo shot twice at him. The first shot hit a log on the ground and the second bullet flew into a cedar tree and richocheted. I hoped for Theo's sake it might have glanced off and hit the bear.

Theo hadn't come close to anything. He had used up ten bullets and all he had to show for it were a few bruises from falling over logs and rocks. I suppose I could have killed a bear for him but I never suggested it and he never asked. A guide can kill an animal and let the hunter tell everyone he got it himself. I've been asked to "assist" in this way; all big game guides get such requests. It would be interesting to know how many trophy animals have actually been killed by a bullet fired from a guide's gun.

I was glad when Theo decided to call it a day and I wasn't called upon to perform further support. We went back to the farm and played chess for the rest of his stay.

My next hunter was more expert in the use of a rifle than the two just mentioned. In addition, he had lots of determination. A Swedish-German from Seattle by the name of Mollander, he was a big railroad engineer who had been hunting since he was a kid. We set out to get him a large animal and I had no trouble finding grizzlies but none was big enough. He wanted a world beater.

I flew him to the head of the river where we used a fifteen foot skiff to navigate on Elbow Lake. The valley widens above Elbow to about a mile, bordered on the west by slough grass and shallow ponds and on the east by alder and devil's club and more shallow ponds. Devil's club (**Oplopanax horridus**) is a spiny shrub which can grow higher then a man and is as wicked as its name; a veritable cactus on a thorny stem. The spikes are sharp enough to go right into your flesh and may cause festering.

A creek feeds west down a valley from a snowfield about 8000 or 9000 feet high and flows over a delta of huge boulders. Another creek from the east comes out of a lake at about the 4000 foot level and flows over a much more restricted delta with fir timber on it. The hillsides, as elsewhere, are covered with Douglas fir and lodgepole pine. Where the two rivers meet there are extensive gravel beds suitable for salmon spawning and here the sockeye, coho and spring make their annual pilgrimage to lay their eggs, fertilize them and die. Bears congregate in large numbers in spawning season.

As Mollander and I poked carefully through the devil's club and edged around the ponds, we found tracks of several huge grizzlies paralleling and walking over cattle hoof prints. I had thought to bring along some salt because I knew if we passed near my herd the cows would follow and might get in the way of any bear shoot. Sure enough, the cattle heard us and came bawling, so we laid down some salt licks and that kept them occupied for the time being.

The wind was blowing from the north as we reached the south end of the bear's fishing grounds. A large log jam in the river became our vantage point. Mollander established himself on one end; I went to the other end and waited. Soon a large grizzly working upriver came into view and I called Mollander's attention to it. He shot at it; it fell but got up and disappeared into the bush. I sighed. Another wounded bear to contend with.

We moved down the bank opposite where the bear had entered the bush, hoping to spot it while at a safe distance. We couldn't see anything so returned to our log jam, crossed on it to the bear's side of the river and walked very slowly toward where we'd last seen him. We found some blood spots and then I heard a stick snap near the foot of a hill which was covered with young cedar and hemlock.

"He's probably over there," I told Mollander. "The fact that he hasn't gotten farther probably means he's badly wounded. Let's finish him off." It was getting dark. Looking for a dying bear in thick brush at night is not wise. I changed my mind. "Let's wait until morning and come back for him. I don't like the feel of this."

It took some convincing but Mollander finally agreed and my description of the warm, cozy little cabin a short way down the trail gave him something to look forward to. We would spend the night there visualizing the record trophy and how it would look hanging in his den. Off we went. On the way to the cabin, the trail runs alongside the river. The brush is shoulder high and spiked with devil's club and vined underbrush.

"Hey!" Mollander said suddenly. "What's that noise?" He drew my attention to a clump of small alders. Could it be our wounded bear? It wasn't the wounded bear. This one was extremely healthy. I wasn't in the mood for shooting any more bears that day so I told Mollander to back up slowly and see if this bruin would go away peacefully. We had retreated about thirty feet when the bear started for us.

"Shall I shoot?" Mollander queried. "I guess you better or we'll end up for supper," I advised, which is about all I had time to say before the bear was upon us. Mollander fired and the bear fell but it got right back up and came roaring at us again. Mollander fired and once more the bear collapsed.

It was now nearly dark, but it was light enough to see the bear waving his paws from his prone position in the path in front of us. Mollander shot him twice more and we crowded carefully around the inert form and continued on up the trail to the cabin. We had brought some food with us and there was a supply of dry kindling and wood so we spent a comfortable night except for an occasional nervous moment spent listening to the bears padding by outside.

In the morning we found the bear that had been shot near the cabin. We skinned him out and went to look for the wounded grizzly. Fresh bear tracks were on the trail. Traces of blood were mixed with mud so if the bear was mortally wounded he had come a long way in our direction. If we were cautious before, we were doubly so now.

The trail ran right along the foot of a hill which was a

jumble of downed logs, big firs and thick young cedars which formed an almost inpenetrable wall. The tracks led into an old river channel and, thinking the bear might have gone for a drink, I crossed over and through a mass of devil's club. Mollander followed. Then we saw the bear. Incredible as it sounds, the bear was still very much alive. He was coming at us with huge strides; blood was on his hide and in his eyes. I immediately fired three shots into his chest with my .35 Remington Autoload and Mollander added two more. The bear turned around before he collapsed. I had never encountered such a tenacious brute in my life.

When we came to skin him out we found all the bullets had hit inside of a two inch circle in the chest. Mollander was happy. He had acquired his big grizzly. The hide alone weighed more than eighty pounds stripped of all excess fat. We carried it and the head back to where the first bear's body was lying. Another eighty pounds and head had to be carried to the skiff on Elbow Lake.

It's one thing to find a trophy animal, another to shoot it, another still to skin it out. Then all that remains is to pack it for several miles on your back to where you can get easier transportation for home. In this case, Mollander - who was half again as big as me - was not in as good physical shape as I was. He huffed and puffed along behind, wondering aloud if hunting bears was such a great hobby after all.

Some guides provide a bearer service so that all the hunter has to do is shoot his animal and go wait in the truck, plane or boat and drink beer until the operation is completed. For my paltry fee, hunters worked for their kill.

We were a long time getting back to the plane, in fact it was completely dark again as we edged along a narrow trail and across the river on a forty foot log. I decided we'd better camp out, built a fire and cooked some food. Mollander helped me strip off some more fat from the bear hides to make them lighter to carry. "There must be a better way to make a living than this," he moaned.

"There is," I replied. "Taking pictures of these creatures

instead of killing them for sport. And a whole lot safer in most cases." I told him how my son Johnnie had made a good living filming wildlife, in addition to the two-hour feature movie on my life on Lonesome Lake. He was so successful he saved enough money to establish a fish camp and small resort up on Turner Lake, close to where Hunlen Falls drops over a precipice nearly 1300 feet into a basin which flows into the outlet of Lonesome Lake.

(More recently Johnny had built additional cabins at Lonesome Lake near our original homestead, offering good accommodations and canoes for rent at both Turner and Lonesome Lakes, a pleasant day's hike apart.)

Mollander was not interested in becoming a wildlife photographer but another client came to see me one day whose hobby was the photographing of wild animals. The provincial government had appointed agricultural agents in each locality to help farmers with their problems and to aid them in raising more produce. The Bella Coola agent and his wife, native Australians, were avid photographers and both had an adventurous streak. They asked to visit Lonesome Lake so I met them at Atnarko and guided them up to The Birches.

On the way, near The Stillwater, we had to cross a river channel on a very long, slim springy cottonwood log. I went first, holding the agent's wife's hand to steady her. The agent waited until we were across and then confidently strode across. In the middle of the channel he stopped to allow the swinging log to steady for a moment. Looking at the swirling water mesmerized him. "Whoops!" he yelled, and fell in.

He was in water up to his shoulders but came up laughing. After getting his arms around the log, he swung his long legs up and straddled it, looking sheepish. "Darn it," his wife said, "I wish I'd had the camera ready for that." "Easy enough done." the Aussie said. And like a gallant young husband, obliged his wife's ready lens by toppling back off the log and assuming the same pose!

18

Fame But No Fortune Comes To Lonesome Lake

"We had many distinguished guests visit Lonesome Lake but no one affected our lives so much as Leland Stowe." (Ralph Edwards)

In February 1956 I received a letter from **Reader's Digest** asking if we would be willing to let a reporter visit and interview us about the swans and our way of life. We could see nothing objectionable so I wrote back consenting to this request. It was a decision that was to alter our lives forever.

The weather was -22⁰F in late February when the ski plane carrying Leland Stowe landed on the Big Lagoon. He was a jolly white-haired man who strode confidently across the ice toward us carrying a suitcase and an armful of cameras and recording equipment. He introduced himself as the reporter from the **Reader's Digest.**

He was a most agreeable chap and we liked him at once. At the time I had no idea just how famous or well-qualified a writer he was. I found out later he had written six books, had won a Pulitzer Prize for foreign reporting and had many honorary degrees as well as decorations from the French and Greek governments. During the next twelve days and nights we learned a little more about him, although he was a modest man, more interested in hearing about us than talking about himself. Lee had met and written about dignitaries such as Marshal Ferdinand Foch, Winston Churchill, Franklin D. Roosevelt, Dwight Eisenhower, Prime Minister Nehru and the American folk hero, Will Rogers.

"After interviewing all those famous folks, what would you want to write about us for?" I asked. "You've got a story here that will appeal to millions and interest them more than the latest news about any world leader," Lee said. "What you have done to save the trumpeter swans from extinction alone is a story of worldwide significance. To say nothing of carving your little kingdom out of this wilderness."

Flattering words, but said with such genuine sincerity, we were immediately taken with this engaging fellow with all his impressive credentials and fancy equipment. Where to accommodate him was our only problem. We had no spare rooms in the house so I set up a tent inside the barn. He was quite cozy in there and could tap away at his typewriter and smoke his pipe and take his occasional cheering nip without anyone bothering him. We didn't drink or smoke so he confined his puffs and snorts to the barn but came up to the house for meals.

Lee would get up early and look and talk and walk around asking questions. He followed Trudy at eleven o'clock when she fed the swans. The swans would fly up, circle high above the lagoon, caught by the rays of the evening sun, great golden birds soaring up into the sky. Their clear trumpet calls would echo back from the mountains, then dwindle into the distance. The hush of night would lie over the valley and Lee would begin to talk and listen.

We had never been subjected to such a thorough questioning about our past, present and future as we were by Leland Stowe. He asked the most intimate questions, taking copious notes and tape-recording constantly. No detail was too small. What did we read? What happened when the house burned down? What did I think about when the bull gored me? Why had Trudy developed into such a pioneer, more like her father than his two sons?

He was impressed with Trudy's devotion to the swans and noted in his book **Crusoe of Lonesome Lake**: "In the course of her long and intimate association with the swans, Trudy Edwards has undoubtedly become North America's outstanding female authority on the **Cygnus buccinator,** although it is unlikely that this has ever occurred to her."

He noted that we had made some interesting observations about the birds and that many outside conservationists credited us with saving this rare and beautiful species from extinction. His book was a bestseller and undoubtedly focused attention on the plight of the swans, especially by the Canadian federal government which, up to that time, had taken only a token interest.

One morning an aircraft came in to take Lee Stowe back to civilization. Ethel and Trudy waved goodbye from the lake; I traveled with him on the plane to Bella Coola and bid farewell there. It was not the last we were to see or hear from Lee Stowe but there was to be a time lapse. Meanwhile we began to get letters asking questions and double-checking facts, requesting sketches and corroborating details. Considering the mammoth job of detailed reporting necessary to tell our story to that point, Lee's book was on the bookshelves in an incredibly short time, something just over a year. As soon as it was published, letters began to pour into Lonesome Lake from all around the world.

At first it added a bit of excitement to a bleak winter, but soon it became a burden. We didn't always have time to spend answering letters when there was so much to do around the farm and the cost of postage alone was a factor to consider. Jack and Trudy, who were married just after Leland was here, also received hundreds of letters asking for advice on how to pioneer in the wilderness. Others requested permission to come and visit. Some did not ask but just arrived, expecting to be welcomed with open arms.

Many people were envious or bored with their city lives and thought a stint in the great outdoors might restore their vigor. We did little to encourage dreamers, stressing the loneliness and hardships which could be expected. Some would not be put off and asked to come and work on the farms. Others gave advice to us about how we should conduct our lives and chided us about trapping or killing animals for food.

When an excerpt from the Stowe book appeared in Canadian and American school textbooks the mail flowed anew. Some children would have cheerfully left home to rush to Lonesome Lake to live out their dreams. Not many youngsters, or adults, would find much time to dream working an eighteen hour day, every day of the year.

Gradually the mail subsided - although Trudy and Jack still get letters from young people wanting to know where they can get free land. Certainly life was never "normal" again, not as we knew it when the children were small and the only planes that landed on our lake were government-owned or contained people we knew and expected. Nowadays a plane that lands on Lonesome Lake may bring hunters, fishermen or sightseers.

Our fame was to spread further. In 1957, the same year the book was published, I received a letter from Lee Stowe indicating that a producer in Hollywood wanted to make a movie based on his book. He said a certain amount of fiction would be introduced and our consent would be required. The promoters of the movie would be willing to pay my expenses to Hollywood and back. Since the meeting with the producer coincided with my plans to take the plane to Vancouver in November for its annual inspection, I agreed to go.

I wanted to stop at Bella Coola for fuel but when I arrived there I found the inlet was a mass of white caps so I continued to Rivers Inlet, further down the B.C. mainland coast, where I landed and gassed up. Strong head winds blew up when I got to Campbell River, a large logging community on Vancouver Island, so I landed and taxied up to the seaplane dock. Every flier in the country must have had the same idea because the dock was full. I tied the Taylorcraft to a log boom and slept in it overnight.

Next morning I filled the plane with gas and got permission to land at Vancouver's International Airport on Sea Island. Gordie Peters, my mechanic friend, met me with his car and a "dolly" to move my plane to West Coast Air Service's hangar where it was to be serviced and inspected for a new certificate of airworthiness. I went with Roy Moulton to his house for the night, but he soon left. He said he had to fly to the west coast of Vancouver Island. It was all very mysterious.

He didn't return that night and his wife became anxious. The weather had turned stormy. I assured her that he was an excellent pilot and not to worry. "If it gets too bad, he'll stay overnight some place. If an old fogey like me can fly in bad weather and make it all right, Roy will come through in great form." Little did I know that Roy was off to Lonesome Lake on a far different assignment than I was led to believe.

Just before I took a commercial flight to Los Angeles next day, I walked around the Vancouver department stores, looking and buying a few items. It was crowded with shoppers. When I met Lee Stowe at the airport in Los Angeles I was feeling distinctly queasy. He thought it might just be the plane ride and the excitement of meeting a movie producer. "You'll feel better after we get settled," he said.

We booked into a hotel where our adjoining suites each had a sittingroom, air-conditioning and bathroom. It seemed an unnecessary extravagance, although the air-conditioning was a Godsend because I was not accustomed to smog and eighty degree heat. Since it was still fairly early in the day, Lee took me on a tour of several movie studios but not the one where I was to meet the producer of the movie. Later on, a friend of his, P.C. Phillips, invited us to dinner and on the way to his home in his car I began to feel poorly again. I did not feel like eating dinner.

Mrs. Phillips had been a nurse and she got a thermometer out and thrust it into my mouth. It registered 104 degrees and rising. She hustled me into bed and called her doctor who soon arrived and ordered an ambulance to take me to St. John's Hospital. I was given a private room and bath and my condition was diagnosed as pneumonia.

Lee came in to see me as soon as I was made comfortable and informed me that I would probably be in hospital for two weeks. "I'm going back to my journalism teaching job at Ann Arbor," he said. "How much is this going to cost me?" I asked. I had heard about the exorbitant fees American hospitals and doctors charged, especially in California. "Don't worry about a thing, Ralph," Lee said. "It's all being looked after by the studio. Just relax and get well. I'll come back and see you just as soon as you are up and around."

I'd never had such care in my life, although I hadn't been in a hospital since the First World War. They wheeled in a television set so I could see commercials and a lot of bad western movies if I wished to do so. Several doctors came in to look me over and feel here and there. One put a tube down my windpipe and inspected inside. He pumped some fluid out and recommended a lot of penicillin, which seemed to help. A long, slim nurse came around every few hours with a tray of needles and seemed to take particular delight in puncturing my rump until it felt like a pincushion. After I broke out in hives the doctor ordered me off the needle. The hives cleared up but I don't think the nurse forgave me for interfering with her needlework.

Aside from her, the staff was very courteous and attentive. St. John's is a Catholic Hospital with pictures of Jesus hanging everywhere. Some had pictures of him with holes in His chest so you could look right into His heart, a most unusual sight. I had been brought up to believe that Jesus looked into our hearts.

It is the law in California that all hospital beds be fenced in at night so patients won't fall out. I did not like this little fence nor the receptacle left behind for nature's call. I climbed over the fence and went to the bathroom down the hall. It was a darned nuisance. And quite a strain on my lungs which were still very painful. Finally I recovered enough to qualify for different accommodation. What this cost I had no idea but it was fit for a king: A housekeeping unit with electric heat, private bath, kitchen with refrigerator, garbage disposal unit and electric stove. All this equipment to heat up and serve what amounted to a TV dinner. I wished Ethel was there to serve me a real meal.

I had been in the hospital for two weeks and now was ordered to spend two more weeks recuperating in a motel on what they call The Esplanade. I could wander about at will, indoors and outdoors. Los Angeles, I discovered, is a terrible city. In fact it is not a city at all, but a lot of stores and houses held together by smog. It got in my eyes and throat and I could hardly wait to get away from it. We were close to Sunset Boulevard, a main street that runs forever and the roar of traffic begins at four o'clock in the morning and ends at three o'clock in the morning.

At last Lee Stowe returned from Michigan and we moved into the Miramar Hotel and spent many enjoyable afternoons walking about the city of Santa Monica. One day Lee said: "You're looking much better, Ralph, I think it's time we went to see this movie producer." I did feel better. I hated being sick and was proud of the fact that I had most of my hair and that my tonsils and appendix were still on the job; I couldn't remember if I'd ever seen a dentist; my teeth could do damage to a bear steak.

I told Lee I figured I was well enough to go and thanked him for taking the walks with me; they had obviously helped restore my health. We joined some other people in a restaurant and while sipping wine or tomato juice, depending on individual choice, someone mentioned a movie was being made in a studio across the street.

I said I was not supposed to go out into crowds yet in case I suffered a relapse. "You look fine," one of the wine sippers said to me. "Don't be an old killjoy. Let's go see them make a movie." Lee said I looked "in the pink", so I finished my tomato juice and off to the studio we went.

The studio was gained by a stairway which led to a gallery in front of a stage. An usher greeted us and took us to seats near the front. A lot of people had already gathered there to watch the making of the "movie". The gallery itself was connected to the stage by another stairway and on the stage were several large machines which I thought must be motion picture cameras. Behind them were curtains. Men kept emerging to fiddle with the cameras. At a signal from someone down on the floor of the studio, a good-looking young man climbed down from the stage and walked up the aisle to where I was sitting with Lee and the others. "I am looking for a man who was ill in October," he said. I had been sick mostly in November so I said nothing. "I was sick in October," a man in the gallery said. "You're not the one," the man from the stage replied.

Then Lee Stowe got up and said: "Ralph Edwards, I would like you to meet Ralph Edwards." I was astounded. I had heard the famous Ralph Edwards radio show a few times and knew it was now on television. Called "This Is Your Life", it brought unsuspecting guests onto the stage and reintroduced them to people from out of their past. I had often thought about our two names being the same and about how different our lives were. Different is right: He was tall, dark and handsome; I was short, bearded and twice his age.

"Pleased to meet you, Ralph Edwards," the other Ralph Edwards said. I said I was pleased to meet him too. I reckoned then that Lee knew the host of this show and wanted the two Ralph Edwards to meet and that would be the end of it. "Please come down to the stage," Ralph Edwards said. "I have a couple of things I'd like to talk to you about." As we walked down the aisle, a curtain went up revealing a scene that looked vaguely familiar. When we got there the emcee asked me what I thought of the "set" and the "props". Then I recognized it! Someone had recreated a scene of Lonesome Lake. Lee Stowe must have given them some photographs to work from.

I told Ralph Edwards we were "standing behind the wood shed." He invited me to sit down on one of the benches and then he withdrew a short distance. "Do and say as you please," he said, just as a sepulchral voice asked from somewhere backstage: "Ralph, do you remember the earthquake in India?" I couldn't believe my ears. As I looked around for the source of this question, I saw my ninety five year old mother coming toward me from behind the curtain. She was supposed to be in Canton, Ohio.

I was so surprised and pleased that I cried as I embraced her. After that I almost lost total control of my emotions as relative after relative, friend after friend, made little comments from behind the curtain and Ralph Edwards asked me to try to identify them. Then they trooped onto the stage to hug me, and the master of ceremonies, the other Ralph, continued to stitch together the threads of my life, interspersing it with the guests' appearances.

After my mother came Ethel, whom I thought was back at Lonesome Lake looking after her cows and chickens. Then came my brother Bruce who was living in Canton, Ohio, where he ran a successful business. Frank Ratcliff was there from Bella Coola and Osmond Pate from Greensboro, North Carolina, with another special friend of mine from World War I. And of course, my flying buddy, Roy Moulton from Vancouver, B.C.

After all the guests had been presented and my life story brought up to the present, Ralph Edwards came out and told us about the presents This Is Your Life was giving us. They were many and impressive but the special prize was a log cabin they were going to fly into Lonesome Lake. "What do you think of that, Ralph?" the television host asked me. "Well . . . " I replied, "it's a lot like carrying coals to Newcastle." He laughed a little nervously. I didn't bother to explain I could build a log cabin in less time than it would take to ship this one to Lonesome Lake. Also, I didn't want to seem ungrateful.

The next day all the guests and myself were hosted to a giant banquet at the Roosevelt Hotel and afterwards, as we all dispersed to our various destinations, everyone was in tears. I knew there were some I would never see again. One of them was my mother.

I found out later that my brother Earle had been in cahoots with the show's producer and Lee Stowe almost from the start. Under some pretext he had come to Lonesome Lake and after getting Ethel aside, told her the true story and swore her to secrecy. She was also to make a list of all the things her heart desired and the TV producers would supply them.

Ethel, ever the practical one, stayed up half of one night composing a list that included such items as material to upholster a chair, chicken wire to keep the fowl out of her flower beds, special thread for a number of sewing projects. It was a useless gesture. She never received any of them. My son

266

in law, Jack Turner, was also brought into the picture and was against it from the start. He feared the publicity would bring more unwanted visitors to Lonesome Lake. I might have agreed with him but I was at all times completely unaware of the true nature of the project. Trudy also refused to come for the same reason given by Jack. She'd rather converse with a swan than a tourist.

"What happened to all these people when I got sick?" I asked Lee as we said goodbye at the airport. "We all went back to our respective places," he said. "You know I went back to my teaching job at Ann Arbor. Ethel and Bruce and your mother and your army buddies and Roy and Earle were all down here the day you got sick. They all had to fly back. Earle couldn't make it the second time. Too bad."

The day we flew from Hollywood to Vancouver was American Thanksgiving Day and there were few other passengers on the plane. The captain came back and invited Roy and me to visit the cockpit, which made the trip very pleasant. As we soared over the "Evergreen Empire" of Oregon, Washington and British Columbia, I was especially happy. I did not care for the land of palms and eucalyptus and the brown countryside of southern California.

Arriving at Vancouver, I picked up my own plane and flew home to Lonesome Lake. The farm never looked better. Trudy had been looking after our stock. Shortly afterwards we began to total our rewards for being on "This Is Your Life." There were a lot of electrical gadgets like a coffee pot, fry pan, mixer, motion picture camera and projector and a Land camera for still photos. The motion picture camera and projector came with a complete film of the show.

About the only thing we needed was cheap electrical power to run all those gadgets with, so I hit upon an idea. It was ridiculous to fly a log cabin into Lonesome Lake. The material included five inch diameter poles from a company in northern Michigan. In order to complete it, I would have to supply the sub-flooring, rafters and other parts too long to transport by air. I wrote to Ralph Edwards with my proposal and the suppliers of the gift to the show were most cooperative. The Pioneer Log Cabin Company allowed me 1000 dollars in lieu of the cabin and the producers of "This Is Your Life" gave me another 1000 dollars in place of the cost of freighting the materials into the lake. They told me to make my own arrangements for buying and bringing in what I really needed, a hydro-electric power plant.

As Trudy and Jack feared, there was another spate of unwanted visitors and the mailman's sack was loaded each week with queries about the wonders of pioneer life. But there were positive effects as well. The story of the saving of the swans was seen by millions of viewers and people were made aware of how rare these birds are and how close they came to disappearing from the face of the earth. Perhaps it helped make them consider how other species are similarly endangered.

19

New Horizons

"Increased leisure and increased means are the two civilizers of man." (Benjamin Disraeli)

The next years were the most fruitful and happiest of my life. I continued to fly out our surplus produce to isolated fish camps and logging operations. The demand for our products far outstripped the supply and in some cases, as with potatoes, the cargo barely paid for the gas for the plane. But I loved to fly.

Soaring over the mountains, winding along the beautiful green, rock-studded valleys, enjoying the lush land from the vantage point of a bird - it was my only leisure and I treasured every moment of it. I even enjoyed the challenge of the elements: Sudden storms, quirky winds and clouds in this enchanting wilderness land of British Columbia.

I was grateful too when Trudy received at least token recognition for her devoted service to the swans. The Queen of England asked for some trumpeter swans through Peter Scott, head of Britain's Severn Wildfowl Trust. Scott consulted with the Canadian government about obtaining a number of rare trumpeters as a gift. Trudy and two Canadian Wildlife Service ornithologists undertook the capturing of the beautiful birds. Trudy said later she felt like a "traitor" for betraying the swan's trust but she was rewarded with their eventual return to that treasured position and the birds flourished in Britain.

Trudy herself was queen for a day when she received a

personal letter from Buckingham Palace thanking her on behalf of the Commonwealth. More publicity about the gift of the swans arose through newspaper and magazine articles and radio and television newscasts. A TV program was taped and shown on CBC's "The Nature Of Things." Tweedsmuir Park, a provincial domain in which The Birches and Fogswamp are embraced, was enlarged and made more accessible to tourists and campers.

More and more resorts and private cottages popped open on the large and small lakes around us. Our magnificent isolation was ending. Hardly a day went by without planes circling overhead. I was beginning to feel hemmed in.

Here I was, old age creeping up on me. I began to wonder how long it would be before the Department of Transport would ground my plane and the infirmities of old age would ground me in other ways. I approached Ethel with the idea of selling out and moving on to a place where we could begin again. I didn't feel old. Hell, I was only sixty nine!

However, Ethel was adamant about remaining at Lonesome Lake. If I wanted to go find a new place to live, that was my business. I felt stunned and hurt. She wouldn't leave her cows or Lonesome Lake until I had found a new place for them. But I was so certain I could find a suitable place that I went ahead with plans for the sale of The Birches.

A Reverend Taylor of the Seventh Day Adventist Church notified me that his California flock was interested in acquiring a communal environment where they could live a spartan existence away from the crush and bustle of the big centers. Our location seemed ideal. A few weeks later I flew him into Lonesome Lake to look over the property.

The day he decided to return to California to tell his parishoners about Lonesome Lake, a terrific storm came up. Along with the Reverend was his wife and their huge Dalmatian. At Nimpo Lake they had a vehicle waiting to transport them back to Williams Lake and south to Vancouver and home. The minister seemed the most nervous of the three would-be passengers so I decided to take him out first.

The Taylorcraft bucked and bounced and dropped into

270

chasms of air as we flew over the mountains between our place and Nimpo Lake. The lake was choppy and the landing was rough. Bob Stewart assisted me in tying up the plane. A very shaky Reverend Taylor stepped out. He looked at the sky and shook his head. "For heaven's sake, Mr. Edwards, don't take any chances bringing my wife out. If it gets worse, leave her there for the time being."

It got worse and when I landed at Nimpo with the second passenger the Reverend was almost on his knees in thankfulness. "Thank God you made it safely," he said. His prayers were answered. You should have seen his face when I unstrapped the passenger. It was the dog. "Where's my wife?" he screamed. "Why didn't you bring her out before you brought out the dog?" I explained to him that there was no real danger and besides, it was his wife's decision that the dog go first. I thought he was going to have apoplexy. "Don't worry," I said, revving up the engine again. "You've got God and the dog on your side now." A few minutes later I landed at Lonesome Lake, picked up his wife, and we flew safely over to Nimpo Lake to rendezvous with the rest of the Taylor "family".

In July I loaded the Taylorcraft with some provisions and extra gas and headed north to look at land. There had been no word from Reverend Taylor and his California flock and Ethel still was stubborn as ever about staying at The Birches. However, I felt if I found a perfect new spot, maybe she'd change her mind.

My first stop was at McClure Lake in the Bulkley Valley north of us, then into the Kispiox Valley, across to the Nass and Bell-Irving Rivers to Bowser Lake, not far from Alaska. From nearby Kinaskan Lake I headed north but ran into low clouds between Dease Lake and the Stikene River, going south again in a line roughly paralleling the Alaskan border,

Low clouds the next day forced me back as I tried crossing the Stikine Plateau in the Tuva River area heading for Teslin Lake on the Alaska Highway. I flew east to the head of Dease Lake, landed and loaded up with gasoline and supplies at a seaplane dock and marina. The owners invited me to stay for dinner.

Whenever I met inhabitants on these remote lakes I asked if there was available land; each time I was told the same story: There was nothing available and that which was didn't have enough arable land to make living on it possible. It reminded me of the time when I first arrived in the Bella Coola Valley.

I took off one blustery morning and flew the length of Dease Lake then followed the road that leads to the community of Watson Lake on the Alaska Highway. With a fillup of gas, I flew northward. The Alaska Highway is a gravel road built during the Second World War from Dawson Creek, British Columbia, to Fairbanks, Alaska, a distance of about 1500 miles. It was a remarkable achievement of cooperation between Canadian and American governments whose armies combined with civilian contractors to construct a good all-weather road across sinking muskeg, trackless mountains and forests.

Leaving Watson Lake I encountered a heavy rain storm, so heavy I was forced to drop down to tree level so I could see the highway and keep my bearings. When I got to some hills east of Teslin Lake, low clouds forced me to turn back and I set the plane down on a small lake south of the highway and waited until I could see the hills. I took off when the fog lifted and almost made a fatal error. In the thin air of the higher altitude I failed to allow myself enough running room to clear the hills and had to execute an emergency turn to land at the foot of the lake again. If I had continued trying to climb straight ahead I would have ended up in a cloud-shrouded hillside.

Although I hadn't had any encouraging remarks from anyone who lived in that wilderness I had been flying over, I liked what I saw and decided to seek out someone who would know for sure whether there was any land available. Next morning I flew to Whitehorse, the capital of the Yukon Territory, and landed on the Yukon River above a dam. I walked into the city.

Whitehorse is a modern community, with wide-open taverns, hotels, motels, paved streets and suburbs. Not the sort of place that appeals to me but important as a supply point

272

for the north and home of the Territorial land agent. A man in that office told me the Territorial Government was discouraging land settlement such as I proposed for myself. "There has been a land rush up here of late," he said. "A lot of Americans have come trying to escape their own rat race but they haven't really got a clue about what it's like to live in this climate and in wilderness conditions. They think if they get a bit of moose pasture, a stream and a few logs to build a house they can live off the land."

I told the agent I'd had some experience in living off the land. He looked me over carefully and shook his head. "Look, mister," he said. "There are only two viable farms in the whole Yukon Territory. These were established years ago and although there have been dozens of attempts to start more, they've all failed. I suggest you try farther south if you want good farm land."

I could see there was no convincing him that maybe a third "viable" farm might just turn out to be mine in a few years. I stayed around Whitehorse a couple more days and then flew to Mayo, a mining town connected by road to Whitehorse. I found that the taking up of land was entirely at the discretion of the local land agent, an officious redheaded chap who would not even allow me to see the maps showing which land was available.

"Go look around and if you see something you like come back and I'll tell you whether you can have it or not." he said. Seemed a strange way to operate a land business. I persisted and after further queries he sent me over to another local yokel who was supposed to know of places for sale - a sort of real estate operator. This man told me of a place at the head of Mayo Lake. I followed his directions and landed on the lake to look at the house which was supposed to be close by.

The "house" was an old log cabin with doors and windows missing. A good wind would have collapsed it. It was situated on a ridge about 100 yards from the lake which meant it would not be handy for water. It was totally desolate; a person living there would be cut off from other people from fall to spring.

I flew the Taylorcraft back to Mayo in the morning and inquired about a place where I could leave the plane during the winter in case I decided to stay on. While I was making my inquiry, someone tried to pull the inspection plate off the underside of the wing, tearing the fabric in the process. I liked Mayo and the people but didn't see much control given to the younger generation.

On the other hand, the residents demonstrated ingenuity. Experiments to grow tomatoes and other vegetables under glass seemed to be successful. And they were industrious. A sewer had been placed six feet under frozen ground. Prices in town were surprisingly low, with a ham and eggs breakfast costing one dollar and forty cents, the same as at Prince Rupert, on the B.C. coast. Heavy trucks brought in everything on the road from Whitehorse, making the road really a continuation of the White Pass and Yukon Railway freight route.

The most expensive item was gasoline and transferring it from pump to plane, depending on the distance the serviceman had to haul it, made it even costlier. However, I decided to take a last look at some more land before returning home to tell Ethel what I had seen and heard. I had received word from Lonesome Lake that the sale of the property to the Taylor group was proceeding so I would have some money to spend on a new place, if I ever found one. However, it quickly became evident that pre-emption of cheap, suitable land wasn't going to be found in the Yukon and I returned southward.

Flying south of Teslin toward the Stikine Canyon, the plane suddenly dropped about 1000 feet and I had to put on full throttle to climb back up to safe flying altitude. It was easy to get distracted because of the beauty of the land and sky and the spectacular atmospherics which often accompany storms. As I approached the pass leading to Eddontenajon Lake there was a black thunderstorm looming up with a strange light shining out of the center. It hadn't so much the iridescence of a rainbow as that of a sort of sunburst - the like of which I had never seen before.

The sun was at my back as I flew straight toward this eerie

brilliance. I was almost mesmerized by its attraction. I didn't want to fly into a storm cloud so dropped to a lower altitude and continued following a road several thousand feet below.

I stayed over at Kinaskan Lake and in the morning prodeded to Stewart, B.C., via Meziadan Lake and Bear River canyon. The latter was a beautiful sight with a glacier that reaches from the top of the mountain down to the bottom of a canyon, creating a lake with small icebergs. I tied up at a float and went ashore where I struck up a conversation with some residents of this little community which, at that time, was not accessible by road to the rest of the province of British Columbia.

They were appreciative of the conversation of a stranger and more than a little curious. "What's a man your age looking for a homestead for?" one asked. "Seems to me you'd be more interested in a nice little community to retire in. Why'd you want to work your guts out clearing land and building roads when you can be rocking in a chair and watching the TV?" I hadn't thought about it till then but it was my seventieth bithday that day and when the townsfolks learned that the crazy old coot who'd flown into town looking for a homestead was having a birthday, they gave me a party and staked me to free room and board for two more days.

I enjoyed the town and people at Stewart but there was no place for me to settle there. I decided to wing home to Lonesome Lake to cut hay for the winter ahead. It was October before I flew out again, this time to the Estevan Islands between Princess Channel and Hecate Strait on the way to the Queen Charlotte Islands. The employees of the Department of Transport station invited me to stay for a visit, putting me up in a dormitory that was built for the armed forces during the Second World War and the Japanese invasion threat.

"So, you're the Crusoe of Lonesome Lake," one official said. "I read that book about you. It sure was interesting what you did in that place. But, tell me, why would a man your age want to leave now? Seems to me you must be near retirement." I was getting fedup being told I was too old to do anything but sit in a rocker. Hell, I learned to fly at sixty two. And I was still flying. Next morning I flew across Hecate Strait where it was so cloudy I had to use my compass. The air cleared over Sandspit and it was sunny when I landed at Queen Charlotte City. This community is hardly a city, but a largely Indian and logging town but the people there greeted me enthusiastically. I located several old friends who had taken up homes there but it didn't appeal to me. I flew back across Hecate Strait to Prince Rupert, the principal city of the northern British Columbia coast.

After tying up the plane at a marina, I asked a chap with a beard who was watching me from aboard a Fisheries Department vessel if there was a cheap hotel around. He directed me to a place that was cut above what I could afford. I found another less classy place. Later on, the Fisheries official, a man named Fred Gates, came up to see me at the hotel. He wouldn't believe I could fly a plane until I showed him my valid license. "So you want to buy a piece of property?" he asked. "That's what I'm here for, " I replied.

Gates, Ed Walper, the marina owner, and a Dane I met in the lobby of the hotel, encouraged me to take a look at Oona River on Porcher Island. The name sounded familiar to me. Then I remembered. It was more than fifty years ago that I'd heard of the lush grasslands of Oona River. Now I was going to see them. (The grass was marshland and unsuitable for hay for cattle.)

Gates said land was being offered at a low price so I flew to Porcher Island, about thirty miles southwest of Prince Rupert, the next day and landed near what they call the "outer float". I taxied up the Oona River estuary to a large, long dock where many fishing boats were moored. A jolly chap named Chrissie Fossum helped me secure the plane.

I told him I was looking for a place to buy and that I had come from Bella Coola. He said, "We're mostly fishermen here but there are lots of empty houses belonging to people who've moved away. You might be able to rent a house or buy some acreage right close to the center of things." "The center of things" was the dock! Houses, some of them quite substantial, stood along both sides of the estuary which becomes a muddy flat marked by log booms and derelict wharves and old boat hulls at low tide. A sawmill belonging to a Johnny Bergman seemed to be the center of the "center" and a well-constructed bridge connected both sides of the settlement.

Chrissie directed me to a boathouse beyond the bridge where Johnny Bergman and Norman Iverson were working on a boat. They finished nailing down a plank and then took me on a tour around the community. Oona River, Johnny Bergman explained, was a sizeable place at one time but because of its isolation and the fact that the general move on the part of the provincial government seems to be to centralize essential services such as schools, hospitals and post offices at larger centers, the residents had been moving out.

So far it had held on to its post office and school. It had its own sawmill and some logging was being done. Well-maintained fishboats indicated that fishing was the main source of income. Above all, Oona River had some of the friendliest people I had ever met.

One site Johnny and Norm showed me had an old house, completely furnished, in good condition, with running water, an inside bathroom and a large garden. The price was right so I decided to buy it. I hoped Ethel would like it too. "Where are you planning to stay tonight?" Johnny asked. "On the plane, I guess," I replied, "To heck with that," he said. "You're coming up to our place for supper and stay the night." That was the beginning of a lasting friendship.

"Nice little place you have here," I told them after eating a delicious meal. "Yes," Johnny said. "We're mostly simple folks. There's an occasional feud, but in a place like this you've got to get along or get out. Sooner or later you're going to have to help somebody out or have him help you. We've got to stick together to keep a teacher and a post office. If they go, the place will fall apart. You've got to have mail and you've got to have your kids with you, especially when they're young. So far we've done it."

I looked down at the plane berthed among the bobbing

fish boats at the dock. I could see across to the big wooden bridge to the old house I was to buy. Somebody said it was about 100 years old, the floors leaned and the roof needed replacing. But it was still solid and could be made cozy. Then I heard something familiar. It was the sound that was as much a part of my life as the beating of my own heart. A small flock of swans trumpeted past the bridge, heading north to the salt marsh at the end of the island. I was home again.

20

High And Low Tides

"A whole new life began for me: New adventures, new friends, new disasters." (Ralph Edwards)

I soon settled into the community life at Oona River. I had never had such social life before. The Crusoe of Lonesome Lake, a veritable hermit all his life, was the life of the party. I got invited everywhere. The community sponsored crib tournaments, sports days, Hallowe'en, Christmas and birthday parties, Easter parades and basket socials. I was chosen judge at contests because I had no kin at Oona River and was expected to be above prejudice or purchase.

I had never felt so much a part of a "family". This was a new experience for me. The hospitality was so new and strange, I almost had to fight it off with a stick. I had always done everything for myself before. The men of the community helped install a power plant in my house so I could have electricity at the push of a button. Several young fellows helped me put a new aluminum roof on to keep the rain out and later tried to replace the roof on my woodshed. I knew it needed replacing but I figured I'd get around to it in my own good time.

Winter was coming on and the wood would get wet, they said. Wood that some of the men had come over to help me cut and stack. I told them I didn't need their assistance but Fred Gates worked it so it looked like I was helping them. They must have thought I was a pretty cantankerous old man. It was really just my stubborn independence. I had spent all my life doing things my own way and on my own. In my own way I tried to repay them for their help.

I assisted in removing stumps from the field next to the school house. Everybody pitched in, volunteers from the community, the teacher and the children. The school board paid for the cost of a stump puller and the result was a sports field. There were other community involvements that were just as gratifying. Wire was strung and phones installed in most of the inhabited homes. We all shared the cost of the old World War II telephones and my experience as a telegrapher in the First World War was of some value.

Another of the diversions the isolated "River People" proposed was a crib tournament. About sixteen people - experts all - turned out and the school house, which doubled then as community hall, was packed as usual. Any event was well attended and the prize this night was a brand new Cadillac. I had whetted my appetite for the game and had sharpened my skill by inveigling the contestants to play a game or two at my house in evenings prior to the tournament. Still, I was surprised I won. The "Cadillac" was a tiny toy car, which I gave to a child.

The teachers were almost as much an object of amusement and entertainment to the community as the funny old fellow with the whiskers and sou'wester hat. I met quite a few of them because every year there was a different one. They were mostly English, newly-landed, and full of quirks. One young woman was so English she hardly could speak at all. I told her she spoke "broken English", a remark that would have made her angry, I expect, but an old man with a sparkle in his eyes can get away with a lot.

Another English chap, like the others, planned to put in his penal servitude at the River and then escape to a civilized city post. He was a fair cribbage player and an even better chess man, particularly after he'd had a beer or two. The favorite teacher with the children and the adults was the Hawaiian woman of Japanese extraction who taught a couple of seasons.

Games and sports made life pleasant at Oona River and until my legs gave out I even joined in at a few of the dances where the music was supplied by a couple of old Swedes who got louder and more musical as the evening and beering wore on and the dancers wore out.

There was cultural life at Oona River as well. Janet Lemon accumulated a large number of books, some educational, some classics, some paperback fiction. All were read and the Lemon library was well-utilized by the residents who had the pioneer thirst for knowledge that I knew and admired. I had brought a large number of books from Lonesome Lake with me and could see no reason to hoard them so I passed on the word that they too were available for borrowing. After several years we combined our collections and today they fill a room off Mike and Janet's livingroom. That's how the Oona River Library came into being.

The River kids seemed to like me too. No one at first knew I was the so-called "Crusoe of Lonesome Lake." Those who did know never let on. Simple down to earth people don't judge a person by what's been written about him in a book but by what he does. What I did for the kids was only suspected by them: For five years I was Santa Claus. "With your white beard Ralph, you're a natural for the part," the parents told me. Being Santa and being Ralph Edwards involved a combination of role-playing and outright trickery. The youngsters, like kids everywhere, wanted to believe in Santa, but they also knew that Santa in Oona River looked a great deal like Ralph Edwards. It became quite a game at the Christmas concert in the school house for me to be in two places at once. The program directors accomplished it by keeping the kid's attention riveted to the stage so I could leave my chair at the back of the room and sneak around to the woodshed to dress up as Santa.

A lot of the older ones put two and two together and came up with Ralph Claus but the deceit was harmless. I was only sorry I had to give it up because my old legs got so stiff and sore I couldn't lift them fast enough to make a believable disappearance-reappearance.

Not all the activities at Oona River were fun. One day Johnny Bergman's planer mill caught fire. The flames could be seen for miles and since it was located in the center of the community everybody turned out to form a bucket brigade to put it out. Luckily, the mill is right next to the estuary and the fire was confined to the mill and did not sweep right through the village. It was a severe economic blow, employing as it did up to five men in good times. With another burst of community spirit and lots of available lumber, the mill was shortly back in operation.

During the time all this community interaction was taking place I continued to pilot my plane. Flying still was my first love, next to Ethel. And here I encountered a snag. I had not been able to convince her to leave Lonesome Lake and join me at Oona River. She had worked out an agreement with the new owners of The Birches whereby she could remain on the farm and look after her beloved cattle.

My son Stanley moved onto the farm too and gave her a hand with the operation and she seemed content with that arrangement. I was lonely and missed her more than I cared to admit. The flights I made from Oona River to Lonesome Lake became the highlight of my life. Taking in the mail and supplies once a month or so was a good excuse to see Ethel and satisfied a deep longing.

As with the residents of the Bella Coola Valley, there were members of the Oona River community who were concerned about my age and flying. "Honest to God, Ralph," Fred Letts told me one day after I had landed in the river while the tide was going out, "you'd land that thing in a handful of spit if nothing else was available." Fred, a fisherman, and his wife Thelma, who runs the post office, were like parents to me. And I'm old enough to be father to both of them. But they weren't bossy like some parents and didn't try to dissuade me when I told them of my plans to buy a fishboat and apply for a commercial license.

I expected they might give me the same runaround I got when I wanted to learn to fly. Why . . . I was over seventy, didn't

I know? For anybody who did ask, I had an answer. I had to do something for a living and knowing how determined I am, they soon accepted the fact. So I purchased a thirty two foot plywood gillnetter from a Japanese fellow in Prince Rupert and with my ten dollar license, got set to join the fleet from Oona River.

Judging from the performance of that boat I would say that the man who sold it to me was neither a fisherman nor a boat builder. Right from the first day I began to have trouble. On the way home from Prince Rupert, a distance of twenty six miles, through some of the most unpredictable weather and water conditions on the northern coast, the steering cable came off and got lodged between the pulley housing and the pulley so I lost control of the boat. The boat builder had failed to align the pulley with the line of pull.

Freddie Letts and Mike Lemon were with me for the maiden voyage and Johnny Bergman and Axel Hanson were alongside in the fishboat **Jan Michelle**. They threw us a line while we effected some repairs and then turned us loose when we came out of Kelp Pass, a treacherous stretch of water where the wind was blowing between thirty and forty miles an hour, whipping up the waves like cream. But the boat floated like a duck.

Like most novice fishermen, my biggest handicap was the lack of experience in handling nets. I could always manage to cast off and dock the boat but I got into some terrible tangles with nets. Fred and some of the others showed me how to mend them and I spent many days at the dock in mock patience getting rid of snags and holes in the snarled mess and ready for the next day's outing. Everyone was very helpful but when you are out in the saltchuck all alone with nobody around you to help cut loose all the commercially - worthless dogfish and the knotted logs that have become your only bounty for your hard-earned efforts, you begin to realize how much work goes into the meagre rewards of a commerical fisherman.

One stormy November morning I wanted to go to Prince Rupert but the River People said it wasn't wise. "You'll run into rough weather off the mouth of the Skeena," they advised me. The Skeena is a large river near Prince Rupert which has three channels and is world famous for its salmon run. I couldn't see any weather disturbance off the mouth of the Oona River so decided to take a chance anyway.

"Keep hugging towards Kennedy Island," one of the fellows on the dock told me as I cast off. This would make as short as possible the crossing between the mouth of the Skeena and Smith Island where the weather disturbance was centered. I followed instructions and encountered rough weather but nothing exceptional until I was within viewing distance of the Skeena. There I could see a solid mass of whitecaps.

Off the west coast of Smith Island a mist was rising a couple of hundred feet into the air. I had never seen anything like it in my life. The sky above was clear. Where was the mist coming from? As I approached, the wind howled and I found myself penetrating a solid sheet of water. Gusts of wind laid the boat over on its beam ends so that the propeller came out of the water and the engine raced. The dinghy I was towing acted like a sea anchor but it filled up with water and the tow line broke. I was helpless and blinded by the mist.

When I got to the west end of Smith Island I found that the "mist" was actually water picked up by the tremendous wind. I encountered a new wave formation: Five or six foot waves all in steep cones. It was almost impossible to judge which way to steer to avoid coming broadside of one or another of them. I didn't have time to feel scared; I was too busy wheeling and turning.

When I got around Smith Island I headed up Inverness Channel toward an old cannery where I hoped to tie up and wait out the storm. As I circled I found there were no floats left and the huge waves threatened to smash the boat against the remaining pilings. I re-crossed the channel to seek shelter in the lea of a point off Smith Island when the boat struck something and stopped abruptly. The engine quit as I plunged forward and thumped my head against a bulkhead.

When the constellation in my head stopped exploding, I peeked outside to try to locate my position. Obviously the boat was stuck on a big rock. It began to tip until it came to rest with one side flat against a shoulder of rock. I couldn't walk on the deck without slipping and it was so dark I did the only thing I could safely do: I waited to see what would happen next.

I could tell that the tide was running out fast and before long I could see by shining a flashlight into the inky blackness exactly where I was: Stuck high and dry on top of a fifteen foot pinnacle in the middle of a big mud flat! The next high tide wasn't due until two in the morning, several hours away, so I made myself as comfortable as I could in my faithful old goat wool quilt and tried to sleep.

Suddenly a light began to blink at me from somewhere. Someone in a boat had seen my predicament. I turned on my flashlight and Morse-coded to whoever it was that I was all right. A short time later I heard the sound of a boat engine. I could make out the shape in the darkness and from the lights it appeared to be a fair sized craft. It couldn't draw very close to me because of the broad expanse of mud flats between us. Meanwhile, the wind had begun to abate but it was still strong enough to blow me off the slippery, sloping deck if I were fool-ish enough to try to move around outside. I stayed as still as possible to await the incoming tide.

As the winter moon fought its way across the sky, the tide rose enough that the rescuers could bring their boat within shouting distance. "Do you want a tow?" one man hollered, his voice just audible above the wind. "You bet!" I called back. He threw me a rope which I fastened to a cleat on the transom. The rescue boat chugged away until the line became taut - and pulled the cleat off my boat.

I rigged another line between two cleats on the stern and when the boat heaved, they soon had my craft free of the rock and afloat. I had no charts of that area and in the early light would not have been able to find my way, except maybe onto another rock. Realizing this, the captain of the other boat, Ed Wampler, the marina owner from Prince Rupert, towed me up the Skeena to Port Edward where I tied up at a cannery float. I thanked my friends in the other boat and they sped off to Prince

Rupert.

The wind dropped and when daylight finally came I started the engine and cast off. Something was very wrong. I had no control over the steering! I hastily spun the boat around and tied up at the float again. After a quick investigation I discovered my friend the boat builder had nearly scuttled me again. The rudder chains running down the sides of the boat to the pulleys at the tiller end were fastened to two small pieces of plank attached to the bottom of the boat by a couple of two inch nails. One of them had pulled loose.

If that had happened while I was pitching and tossing out in the open water during that high wind I would have been shaking hands with Davey Jones in his famous locker. I finally got the boat fixed so I could limp back to Oona River where I could beach it and give it a complete stem to stern checkover. Most of the villagers turned out to welcome my return. I felt a little sheepish about the whole affair and certainly wasn't going to advertise the fact about my floundering up onto the rock.

Then someone came into the River, obviously fresh from a trip to Prince Rupert. Hardly tied up, he jumped onto the dock waving a newspaper. The **Prince Rupert Daily News** reported that the wind that night had reached more than 100 miles an hour, which accounted for the strange "mist" that was lifted off the water. But it was the headline on another story that really attracted attention to my escapade: "Crusoe Spends Night On Mount Ararat!"

21

Lessons In Survival

"I laid down certain laws to follow in my life that I expected my family to follow as well. The goal was survival." (Ralph Edwards)

Ethel was neither impressed nor amused by the account of my latest escapade. She remained unresponsive to my entreaties to come to Oona River or even to visit and meet some of the good friends I had made there. Oona River might have been on the moon for all she cared. Although she welcomed my frequent visits to bring in the mail and supplies, she was quite content to remain at Lonesome Lake.

I never dreamed I would be happy anywhere but there. Nevertheless, I had achieved a certain amount of contentment in my new home. As well as the new friends, I was glad to escape the much colder climate of Lonesome Lake that was slowly crippling my body. The independence I sought was largely illusory; the peace I found was the discovery of that illusion: We are forever part of nature and dependent upon her. Of course, moving to Oona River was a compromise, but I had compromised before.

After the loss of my beloved airplane described in the first chapter of this book, and then the almost forced retirement as a fisherman, I fell into a period of depression. What else was there for me in life? Although I continued to make visits to the lake, often I could not afford the cost of the commercial flights.

The kind folks of Oona River were over one night for a visit to cheer me up, reminiscing, when someone suggested I write all my stories down for a book. "You've compiled twenty two years of further adventures since Leland Stowe's book about you," one said. "You should bring it up to date."

Separated from fifty years of living at Lonesome Lake, where so much had happened, so many memorable events, I now began to see things differently. Reliving the past also brought the present into focus.

It would be a story of survival. The separation from my parents; striking out on my own while still a very young man. Survival of those first few lonely years at Lonesome Lake and during the First World War as a telegrapher in the front lines. Survival with Ethel through those terrible winters and during the Depression when fur prices fell and for a whole year our cash income from all sources was 150 dollars. But our family of five did not miss any meals. We adapted because we used what was available.

I smiled when I thought about my first efforts at making shoes. We couldn't afford to buy but learned to make mocassins from animal skins. The woods also provided us with tanning agents. In the spring, when the sap was running, we collected hemlock bark, ground it up with a bone grinder and boiled it in water. The "tea" that resulted was placed with the hides in a hollowed-out log "tank" and after a period of soaking the leather was soft and easy to work with.

Since we all had different sizes, I built wooden forms, shaped to the foot of the wearer, made soles and tops and sewed them together with deer sinew, the tough fibrous tissue that grows on the outside of the back muscles of the deer. After drying and scraping it can be split into threads that are strong and wear-resistant.

We had no sheep but we had ingenuity and we survived that hurdle. We bought a sack of wool and Ethel and Trudy spun it into a yarn to knit socks, mitts and toques that were better than anything in the stores. We had a bountiful supply of garden vegetables, milk, cream, eggs, home-grown fruit, wild and domestic meat and fish. We did not have to go "on relief" as so many others did during those dreadful days.

As I cogitated on these small events, I thought back even further to the time of disappointment when my childhood sweetheart Helen Cathie would not come to be my bride and live at Lonesome Lake. How would I ever find a replacement for my first love? And then came Ethel. Poor Ethel. How she suffered during the delivery of our children, particularly Stanley, the first-born. He survived that awful ordeal and near-suffocation coming to live at Lonesome Lake.

His brother Johnny survived the kick in the face from Ginty the horse. We had nothing to kill the terrible pain he suffered, just Ethel and me and an abiding faith in God. And Trudy. Good, reliable Trudy. Never did she feel duty-bound to help me, whether pulling stumps or digging ditches. I couldn't keep her away, until Jack Turner came along and Lonesome Lake took on another dimension.

The boys went their own ways early in life and both did well, Johnny with his movies and later with his fish camp up on Turner Lake. He never agreed with me about the sale of The Birches and since the American owners decided against settling there he is buying it back. It will survive in the Edwards' name. Stanley became a master electrician and earned good money at the pulp mill for many years at Ocean Falls. I know the children regarded me as a strict father, and they were right. I laid down certain laws for them to follow and survival was the goal.

One of the laws, formulated when they were young, was that they never go out of sight or sound of Ethel or myself. One day all three went exploring and did not hear Ethel calling. When they returned, Ethel took Trudy into the bedroom and walloped her with a willow branch. I took the boys by the scruff of the necks out to the woodshed to mete out similar punishment to them.

However, while I was stern, I had to admit I admired them for their curiosity which I did not want to curb. I chose a wide cedar shake which made a lot of noise as it landed on their rumps, but it was fairly painless. The cries that accompanied the smacks were impressive nevertheless. Through it all I hoped the boys knew what I was telling them: "You know you weren't supposed to wander off, but darn it, I want you to get out and explore life, test it, see how far you can expand your horizons without getting killed or hurting anyone else."

I recalled the first real Christmas we celebrated at Lonesome Lake. My brother Earle came to stay. He carved toy guns and made sleds for the boys. I tanned leather for a variety of handmade gifts, including a leather bag for him. Ethel embroidered flower sacks for dresses for Trudy and for doll's clothes, although Trudy did not care for dolls. She'd as soon have had a new axe.

Together we made decorations for the tree, Ethel taking the initiative in that endeavor. She removed the meat from walnuts, glued them back together and attached strings. Painted, bobbing from the yule tree branches, they were prettier and sturdier than any decorations you can buy today.

The children, of course, were unaware of any such preparations. We had worked mostly late evenings when they were in bed and the tree, with its pile of home-crafted presents and glittering with hand-made trinkets, was hidden behind a curtain in a corner of the livingroom. After breakfast and chores were completed, everyone was invited in. Ethel slowly pulled the curtain aside. The children were speechless. After what seemed an interminable pause, Ethel suggested that Stanley, since he was oldest, go forth and take the first present off the tree. He was so fascinated he couldn't move. Finally he did and then began the best Christmas we ever had.

Those readers who have followed us throughout this narrative will know of our major and minor accomplishments and tragedies. There was the disastrous fire that destroyed our home and possessions. A tree fell on the barn and demolished it. A crazy bull nearly gored me to death. I survived several encounters with grizzlies and wolves.

Flying had been my greatest joy and - as recounted in the first chapter - my greatest loss. Nothing in my life could ever replace the wonderful pleasure of soaring like a bird. However, there were some pretty close scrapes on the way. Fishing from the tiny gillnetter had given me some bad turns as well.

Most important, from the overall view, was the survival of the swans. Not only did they come through, they prospered and will continue to do so now that they are off the endangered species list. The population has grown so that in the 1960's there were between 400 and 500 trumpeter swans wintering at Lonesome and its chain of lakes. Too many swans, in fact, for the feeding area to support.

The Canadian Wildlife Service had a solution to the problem: Scare some of them away and hope they would scatter to the coastal inlets and rivers to propagate in their former, long-forgotten habitats. The method of scaring them was simple and effective: Trudy and her husband Jack would place automatic propane guns at strategic points during the early part of the feeding season. These guns, supplied by the CWS, made a loud noise, but were otherwise harmless. Trudy felt guilty about terrifying her swan friends but something had to be done. The scheme worked: In 1977, a record mild year, the swans had migrated so there were only 185 at Lonesome Lake.

Where had the others gone? In the last three or four years re-population had taken place in the Peace River area of northeastern British Columbia where a host of small lakes has become a major breeding place for the great swans. They were moving back to sites their winged ancestors had chosen 100 years ago before man and his greed decimated trumpeter swans everywhere. They were moving back to many parts of the northern United States as well.

The wintering birds were now spreading up and down the coast from Lonesome Lake. Over 200 trumpeters were seen at Salmon River on Vancouver Island.

Swans lay an average of six to eight eggs and therefore, if the young survive, the species has a high potential for recovering their numbers. I have been told by wildlife biologists that our timely feeding of the Lonesome Lake flock largely contributed to the species' remarkable recovery.

The trumpeter swans are now one of the few endangered species on this globe to make such a dramatic comeback. Gone forever is the passenger pigeon and Carolina parakeet. The California condor clings tenuously to survival and species like the whooping crane and peregrine falcons are largely with us due to captive propagation.

The re-emergence of the trumpeter swan, the world's largest waterfowl, was a triumph in the eyes of the world. Trudy had been honored by a letter of personal thanks from the Queen of England for donating cygnets to the Severn Wildfowl Trust. All but one survived and many descendants have been moved to other localities to continue to increase.

I too received some recognition. The Queen on a trip across Canada, talked to me for several minutes at a gathering in Prince Rupert on May 10, 1971. She told me how pleased she was with the results of the swan feeding that had begun so many years earlier.

I was to get further honors but first, students at a high school in Prince Rupert asked me to speak to them at their graduation ceremonies. Rather than dwell on my life, I encouraged them to go north rather than south to open up the magnificent country that is crying out for brave, independent spirits. They could be the new pioneers in what is the last real frontier on this planet. They presented me with a complete set of the Churchill memoirs in a hand-made case.

I suppose the signal honor of my life came with an announcement that arrived at the Oona River post office bearing the seal of Roland Michener, then Governor-General of Canada. I was requested to go to Ottawa, the nation's capital, to receive the Medal of Service of the Order of Canada.

A high award indeed, but the River People were more excited than I was about going to Ottawa for the investure. I have never been much impressed by ritual and protocol. However, it was a chance to get a glimpse of what people in the world of pomp and politics lived like and I agreed to go, with one stipulation: Ethel had to come with me.

After some persuasion she agreed. Expenses were paid to and from Ottawa for both of us. After a series of airplane flights and cab rides we arrived at the Governor-General's mansion.

We lined up with others who had come to receive these annual awards. During the brief ceremony, I was congratulated by His Excellency for my work with the swans, presented with the Medal of Service, and had my picture taken. We were then presented to Prime Minister Pierre Trudeau who chatted with us about the swans. The Canadian Prime Minister knew the story about how Trudy and I had been keeping them alive and we mentioned the great assistance given by the Canadian Wildlife Service and the Royal Canadian Airforce in the early years.

We then enjoyed a buffet supper, served on long tables with sterling silver dishes and implements. "It's too beautiful to eat," Ethel said. Her eyes were bright with excitement. But eat it we did and it seemed no time at all before we were back outside in the cold, wet rain, waiting for a cab to take us for a tour of the Parliament Buildings. It seemed a long way to come for such short formality, although I was gratified that my a-dopted country had chosen to honor me.

It began to rain harder and we declined the tour of the Parliament Buildings. Ethel felt it was "all very nice" but she wanted to go back to her cows. I looked fondly at her as we drove back to the airport for the return flight to Vancouver. I was wearing a rented tuxedo and white tie which I had been told was the necessary garb for such a State Occasion. Ethel had made her own floor-length dress. She never looked more beautiful.

Yes, reliving my life would be good for an old man.

293

Epilogue

Shakespeare said, "There is a tide in the affairs of men which taken at the flood, leads on to fortune; omitted, all the voyage of their life is bound in shallows and miseries."

In the closing chapters of my life I'm inclined to believe that many times I was swimming against the tide, or had missed it entirely. I doubt if I took it at the flood more than once but my life was never completely bound in shallows and miseries, although there were plenty of both throughout.

More important to me than catching the tide at its flood and garnering whatever fortune was available was the hope that I might find peace and independence. Most of my efforts in the wilderness were of a selfish bent. I had to wrest a livelihood from the wilderness and to provide sustenance for my family, utilizing what Nature had put there.

As the reader will have noted, I did not always give as much as I received. If I learned anything, I learned to live with Nature rather than trying to compete with her or, worse, trying to defeat her. Nature will not be defeated; she will abide long after puny man has gone the way of the dinosaur. In the meantime, we can accept her bounty with respect and give back what we can. Is that not conservation - the wise use of our resources?

Because of man's technological progress, his ability to alter and render unserviceable to wild creatures great tracts of land, conservation becomes an obligation and a safeguard that all plants and animals will be around for future generations to use. Nothing can return the passenger pigeon. That is why I am donating half of the royalties earned from the sale of this book to set up a non-profit wildlife fund. These funds are to be utilized by private citizens or scholars to research topics that will foster a wiser use and appreciation of our natural resources.

It is a small effort. In the beginning, so was the feeding of the swans. There is no telling how far a first step will go.

Ralph Edwards
Oona River, British Columbia
Canada

ACKNOWLEDGEMENT

First, I am particularly grateful to Isabel Edwards of Hagensborg, B.C., who read all of the manuscript and made many valuable comments. Her husband Earle, Ralph's younger brother, indicated to me adventures that he and Ralph had shared in the early days at Lonesome Lake and in the United States.

Janet Lemon read parts of the manuscript and supplied facts related to Ralph's experience at Oona River and in Prince Rupert. Mrs. Lemon, her husband Mike, Fred Gates, Mr. and Mrs. Fred Letts, and many other "River People" extended great courtesy to me during my stay in their friendly community.

I would also like to thank Bob and Ginny Stewart of Nimpo Lake, pilots Roy Moulton of Cassidy, Sandy Hatley of Cougar Air, veterinarian John Roberts of Williams Lake and author Cliff Kopas of Bella Coola. A special thanks to Bob Fortune, CBC Vancouver's "Weatherman," who did as much as anyone to supply me with anecdotes and insights into the psyche of this warm and wonderful human being—Ralph Edwards.

I appreciated the friendly interest shown by author Leland Stowe, with whom I correspond regularly and who continues to have an abiding interest in the Edwards family. I wish to thank publisher David Hancock who flew into the lake with me to introduce me to Jack and Trudy Turner at their Fogswamp farm, and interviewed John Edwards at Turner Lake.

Most of all, I would like to thank Ralph Edwards, the man who made it all possible. My only regret was that I did not meet him sooner. He died in Prince Rupert Hospital in the fall of 1977 while I was still writing the book.

He was a most remarkable individual and I was glad to have had the opportunity to meet him, and to hear his story from his own lips. He was looking forward to seeing the results in book form. I hope he would have been pleased.

—Ed Gould

Editor's Note:

Shortly after Ralph's death, Mrs. Edwards also passed away. Their son, John, now operates THE BIRCHES homestead as a tourist lodge on Lonesome Lake in Tweedsmuir Provincial Park. His address is:
John Edwards
The Birches
G.D., Bella Coola, B.C.

THE WOLF

Timber Wolf howling on the hill
Celebrating another kill,
Telling the world he's big and strong
As he yodels in another song;
Telling the wilds he's just been fed
And that another deer is dead.
But he only kills that he may feed
And seldom kills unless there's need.
The one who kills and calls it sport
Is a wolf on another sort
Who buys himself a highpowered gun
And goes and kills and calls it fun.
Innocent blood he spatters about
And calls it sport, without a doubt!
Big and brave he likes to boast
And gluts himself on venison roast.
He shot the thing from half a mile
In perfect safety all the while
And yet he has the gall to brag
"The mighty hunter slew the stag"
As though this made him more a man
Doing what a schoolboy can.
Just because he pulled the trigger
Doesn't make him any bigger.

Killing it with strength of jaw
Risking bruise and broken bone
Accepting same without a groan
For when they try a moose too big
It is their own rough grave they dig
For he strikes and breaks a back
Or punctures with a swinging rack.

To the man who has a brood
And finds he hasn't any food
And has to go and kill a deer
Because he cannot buy a steer
I say, "Good luck old man,
Go and get what e're you can,"
For this the law throughout the wilds
Where Nature rules and sets the styles
Some must die that others live
The strong must take, the weak must give
But Nature doesn't call it fun
It's just the way that Nature's run.
And Wolf doesn't kill and call it play
He kills because he's made that way.
So if I must do one or other
I'd rather call the Wolf my brother.

By John E. Edwards